THE BATTLE OF THE LOUVRE

THE BATTLE OF THE LOUVRE

THE STRUGGLE TO SAVE FRENCH ART IN WORLD WAR II

by

Matila Simon

HAWTHORN BOOKS, INC.
Publishers
New York

THE BATTLE OF THE LOUVRE

 This book was manufactured in the United States of America and published simultaneously in Canada by Prentice-Hall of Canada, Limited, 1870 Birchmount Road, Scarborough, Ontario. Library of Congress Catalog Card Number: 79-130709.

DESIGN BY MARTIN J. BAUMANN

1 2 3 4 5 6 7 8 9 10

FOREWORD

ALL OF US WHO were involved in any way with the work of the Monuments, Fine Arts and Archives Division of the Office of Military Government have always been painfully aware that there was much more to the story of that confused, immediate postwar period in history than has been told so far.

The fact that many who had so recently been our enemies were as dedicated to preserving the endangered works of art as we were was often ignored, precisely because they had so recently been our enemies, whereas those we believed to be our friends have, in some cases, been proved by the passage of time to have been at best opportunists, and at worst liars.

The recent declassification of a considerable body of previously unavailable documents now provides an opportunity to take one giant step toward setting the record straight. There will undoubtedly be more such steps as the motivations of some of the actors in this drama become apparent and the historical sequence of events is restudied from the vantage point of twenty-five years.

JOSEPH ANTHONY HORNE

ACKNOWLEDGMENTS

A GREAT MANY people contributed in a great many ways to the writing of this book. Although by far the majority have wished to remain anonymous, I cannot neglect to thank a relatively few for invaluable assistance and encouragement. I am particularly grateful to Dr. Gordon W. Gilkey, professor of art and dean of the School of Humanities and Social Sciences, Oregon State University, and during World War II, head of the War Department Special Staff Art Projects in Europe, for his suggestions and unflagging interest in and aid to the manuscript from its inception to its conclusion. I am no less indebted to Joseph Anthony Horne, a former Foreign Service officer and Monuments, Fine Arts and Archives officer from 1946 to 1948, for his wise counsel, for his evaluations, and for his impeccable translations of German documents. I must thank Dr. Edgar Breitenbach, also a former M.F.A. and A. officer and now head of the Print Division, Library of Congress. I wish to express my appreciation to Thomas Hohmann, John Taylor, and John F. Simmons, of the National Archives, Washington, D.C., for their enthusiastic assistance in locating documents and making them available, a task they describe as part of their jobs. Joe Avery and Mrs. Sally Orton at the Washington National Records Center in Suitland, Maryland, the War College aides at Fort McNair, Washington, D.C., and the Photographic Section of the Department of Defense at the Pentagon were all extremely helpful. So too were those with whom I spoke or corresponded in the Cultural Sections of the American embassies in Paris and Bonn. Mme. Jacqueline Bouchot-Saupique, honorary curator of the Department of Drawings of the Louvre Museum, was most gracious in offering advice and assistance. A group of deliberately anonymous guards at the Jeu de Paume and the Orangerie museums in Paris made their wartime experiences as protectors of art and as Resistants come vividly to life, as did wartime Paris while I spoke with

Camille Renault, lifelong friend and benefactor to dozens of artists. I cannot overlook the photographs and documents provided by weapons expert Hans Schedelmann, of Salzburg, Austria, nor the assistance of art historian Dr. Bruno Lohse, of Munich, Germany. To all of these and to all others who have talked with or written to me, again, my gratitude.

M. S.

CONTENTS

Part III

COUNTERACTION: 1944–1969

Photographs appear on pages 133–152.

PART I

PREPARATION: 1933-1939

CHAPTER 1

THEORIES AND INSTITUTIONS

IN JANUARY, 1933, Adolf Hitler became Chancellor of Germany. He began at once to implement his dream of a thousand-year Reich, a greater Germany that would finally encompass a purified, "Aryanized," Europe. Twelve years later, when the Third Reich had vanished in a cloud of smoke, millions of men, women, and children, hundreds of cities and towns, and countless books and works of art had been reduced to ashes.

Associated with Hitler during his years of power was a group of men whose careers were as infamous as his. They were Hermann Göring, the fat man who had been a World War I aviation ace and became Hitler's first heir-apparent and head of the Reich's Air Force, the Luftwaffe; a crippled neurotic, Joseph Paul Goebbels, the Propaganda Minister; the Russian-born "party philosopher," Alfred Rosenberg, assigned the task of supervising art plunder in all occupied countries; the sadistic Heinrich Himmler, head of the Schutzstaffel, or S.S., and the Gestapo; and a champagne salesman elevated to diplomacy, Joachim von Ribbentrop, who became Foreign Minister. They had in common: vanity, greed, bigotry, and arrogant ambition for personal power. Their bible was *Mein Kampf*, written in 1924 inside Landsberg Prison. By 1940, inside Germany alone, six million other readers had purchased the book. Perhaps if more buyers had carefully studied the text, fewer fires and less smoke would have polluted European air between 1933 and 1945.

The theories upon which the "Aryan" dream was based were not manufactured to order during the years when Hitler and his followers struggled for power. A bevy of writers had already provided ample material to help shape the ideas of the Third Reich. Three of these men, none of German birth, wrote influential works on themes of racial differences.

The first was a French diplomat, Count Arthur Joseph de Gobineau, who dedicated his four-volume 1853–1855 work, *Essay on the Inequality of the Human Races*, to William I, King of Hanover. Gobineau acknowledged three races: white, yellow, and black. Among the "superior" whites, necessary for the development of civilization, the "Aryans" were supreme. Since the term "Aryan" applies to language and refers to a dialect of Sanskrit and the people speaking it, this myth should have been immediately exploded by philologists if by nobody else.

The second important influence came from the writings of an Englishman, Houston Stewart Chamberlain. He had been trained for diplomacy but could not pursue a career because his health was poor. A strange man, subject to overpowering visions under whose spell he wrote rapidly, as if possessed by demons, he published *Foundations of the Nineteenth Century* in 1899. The work was foggy and confused. He first found the Semitic and the "Aryan" the two finest races, then descended into anti-Semitism in a discussion of Jewish traits. He did not provide a specific definition of race, hinting that in the last analysis each individual should let his instincts decide the matter. Chamberlain found Christ not a Jew because he had been born in "Aryan" Galilee. His examples of inferior anti-"Aryan" groups were people following the ideas of the Church of Rome, the French Revolution, socialism, and Judaism.

It remained for an American, Lothrop Stoddard, to link racial and cultural theories in works in which he railed against "Bolshevism," a term the author applied broadly to cover anything new in the fields of art and literature. His first book, *The Rising Tide of Color against White-World Supremacy*, published in 1920, exalted the white man as superior to Negroes, Chinese, Japanese, and Indians. Two years later, his second book was published in Germany. Its long title may be roughly translated as *The Cultural Upheaval, the Subhuman Peril*, and in it the author tried to prove innate differences between people as to human talents and qualities. Stoddard did not believe that all men were created equal and suggested the segregation and sterilization of inferior beings. In the cultural area he spoke of "latent pathological traits" in men of genius and found such "decadence" in Jean Jacques Rousseau and Leo Tolstoy that he suggested banning their works. The Nazis were to apply his critical standards with gusto. Stoddard's knowledge of art was minimal, and he considered all forms of modern art and literature "an angry revolt against things as they are and a dissolute, degenerate return to primeval chaos."

An attack on the influence of "Jewishness" on the art world had appeared earlier in *A Handbook of the Jewish Question* by Theodore Fritsch, published in 1887. Impressionism, for Fritsch, was the result of Jewish propaganda upon the Latin temperament. The author also disliked Impressionist art because artists worked outdoors, directly from nature. The best artist, he wrote, worked in his studio and was a German who put his whole heart and soul into his work. The German Expressionist movement, the most important manifestation of German talent since the late sixteenth century, was, according to Fritsch, led by Jews and unacceptable. He ignored the fact that one of its leaders, Emil Nolde, was a pure Nordic. He also noted that Cubism, Dadaism, and Constructivism—nonrealistic art movements initiated by North German, Dutch, Scandinavian, Russian, Italian, and French artists—had as their primary objective the destruction of "German ethnic consciousness."

Immediately after the end of World War I, racist theories propounded by Germans strongly influenced Nazi thinking. Anthropologists contradicted each other to point out that the Germans were alternately gifted in organization and statecraft or moody and individualistic, musically talented or without musical talent. One stressed German artistic ability, denying this quality to the French, Italians, and Spanish. One found Impressionism anti-Nordic because it made "ugliness the only reality." The same man insisted that only Nordic models were classically beautiful and considered El Greco "Near Eastern" and an artist presenting only evil in his works. *The Nordic Soul* by Ludwig Clauss offered a single and singular thesis: that racial traits are not determined by physical measurements but by an inborn attitude toward nature and culture. Thus he denied the factors of education and environment entirely and provided a happy springboard for Nazi decisions on race.

A purified Europe could only be achieved by the elimination of the Jews, automatically "enemies of the Reich" because they were not "Aryans," and Nazism made good use of the existing, already popular anti-Semitic material, refining it, adding to it, selecting from it. But Hitler was not content merely to create an all-"Aryan" state; he intended to mold the people in that state into blind obedience and into adoration of everything Germanic. To do this, he had to apply rigid principles, for "it is the business of the state—in other words, of its leaders—to prevent a people from being driven into the arms of spiritual madness." Spiritual madness was induced by anything written or painted, drawn, or sculpted that might question, contradict, or stray from his bellicose, racist program.

The principal Nazis were intensely interested in art for a variety of reasons. Although twice refused admission as a student at the Vienna Academy of Fine Art, Hitler firmly believed, as he said himself, that "if he had not decided to be a politician, he would have become an artist of the stature of Michelangelo," and he thought highly of the pathetic little daubs that he sold for pennies to keep from starving in his Viennese days. By 1938 he had conceived and even drawn the plans for a great museum to be dedicated to his mother and situated in the town where he had passed a comparatively happy adolescence, Linz. To fill that museum, which was to be called the Führermuseum, and make it the finest in Europe, he needed money with which to buy art as well as whatever he could confiscate during his conquests of European territories.

Himmler, father of the S.S., was also the spirit behind the Ahnenerbe, or Institute for Research into Heredity, and needed books, art, and art objects to prove racial theories. Göring, although erratic as to taste and undiscerning as to values, fancied himself a collector and had eight residences to decorate with appropriate symbols of wealth and power. When questioned before the Nuremberg trials, he talked also of a vaguely planned public museum to be built at Karinhall, his favorite home. Rosenberg, the party's confused intellectual, author of *The Myth of the Twentieth Century*, a book so long and dull that even Hitler joked about its being unreadable, dreamed of a special educational institution, the Höhe Schule, in which young men could be instructed in Nazi theories. For this he needed books, art, and money. Ribbentrop and Goebbels were not at all averse to beautifying their homes with valuable art works, especially at no cost to themselves. Lesser fry followed the lead of the masters. In the midst of plans for total war, conquest, and occupation, of building concentration camps and imprisoning Jews, Freemasons, and enemies of the state, and of confiscating books, the Nazis turned their attention to art, for some of it, too, was an enemy.

It was a Jew, Max Nordau, who inadvertently gave the Nazis the term used to label any art that did not fit Hitler's notions as to what was Nordic, Aryan, or national. In 1893 Nordau published *Entartung* (*Degeneration*), a discussion of his rationalistic views on literature and art. A cofounder with Theodore Herzl of the Zionist movement and a brilliant physician, Nordau was also a cultural reactionary with no understanding of modern art. He disapproved of the earliest attempts at abstraction, and, as a doctor, he tried to account for it in terms of physiological malformation, explaining modern color as the result of a malfunction of the artists' retinas. Curiously enough, he did not suggest any specific medical treatments for the ailing artists, although he indicated that psychiatrists would find them all suffering from worn-out central nervous systems.

Other books on aesthetics provided more material. One discussed the devaluation of German art through partisans of Impressionism and found Manet a painter of whim, possibly motivated by lack of ability, and said that Cézanne, Van Gogh, and Gauguin were mentally unbalanced and that Monet represented the death of artistic development because his dissolution of form "could not be improved on." In 1911 the artists of Worpswede, near Bremen, published a protest against modern art signed by 120 German artists, of whom scarcely one is remembered today. The victims were Cézanne, Van Gogh, Matisse, Picasso, Braque, and Kandinsky. They were described as "exaggerators," "straining," "impossible spooks," and "senseless." One critic complained that German museums had spent too much money on foreign paintings and should have purchased national art in sturdy, realistic styles. Another denied the analogy of nonobjective art with music and considered Cubism "a dead end," Expressionism merely an exploration of the subconscious, and found the beginnings of the "decline of art" in Rembrandt and Goya. Another critic argued that Italian Renaissance art was the result of German influence, citing as proof the blond hair and blue eyes in many Italian paintings. He did not seem to know that there are many naturally blond Italians or that bleaching hair was fashionable in the Renaissance. His research led him to state that 85 to 90 percent of what the world accepted as Italian genius was to be credited to the Germanic race and to conclude that Italy's decline as a nation resulted from the gradual disappearance of these blond people.

Hitler's own views on art were a conglomerate of the ideas promulgated before his advent to power. Since "a nation that in time of racial pollution devotes itself to nurturing the best racial elements is bound . . . to become master of the earth," he found mixed blood an abomination, and "Jewish" paintings anathema. Of course some

Jewish artists painted exactly the kind of realistic works he liked, whereas some "Aryans" painted just what he despised. He complained that nonobjective artists could not draw, but did not know that one of them drew animals in such correct detail that the Munich School of Veterinarians used the sketches for anatomy lessons.

Two months after Hitler became Chancellor, in March, 1933, he set up a Ministry of Public Enlightenment and Propaganda. By summer, an official from the cultural division of the Black Shirts—the Schutzstaffel Race and Settlement Office—was charged with the coordination of all artists' associations to prepare for their inclusion in a nationwide fine-arts program. By late September, Goebbels had brought all artists under state control. Anybody who wished to paint, draw, sculpt, compose, or write for the public had to register with the Reich Board of Arts and Culture. The board was divided into seven departments, none presided over by a man distinguished in his field. To insure tighter controls, there were thirty-one regional offices, one for each party district, which issued permits for all public exhibitions and performances; those who forgot this requirement found the police quick to interfere. Directives on art came from everybody, but party members with liberal ideas soon changed their attitude toward artistic freedom. Albert Speer noted that Goebbels was pleased with some Nolde watercolors that the architect borrowed from the Berlin National Gallery to decorate the minister's renovated house, but that Goebbels found the works "impossible" after Hitler paid him a visit and "expressed . . . disapproval." And the more sophisticated Speer, who felt quite comfortable with modern art, "tacitly accepted" the Führer's taste. Another early liberal, Baldur von Schirach, the country's youth leader, quite soon decided that the Führer's edifices "categorically demand a revival of fresco painting and the art of tapestry"—a remark that may explain the later Nazi zeal for collecting French tapestries.

Two official decrees—the *Malverbot*, or ban on painting by blacklisted artists, and the *Ausstellungsverbot*, or ban on exhibiting—put hundreds of artists in the position of having no way to sell their works. They were forced to accept menial jobs or to choose exile inside or outside Germany, and if they were Jews, they faced prison or concentration camps. By 1935 Eugen Hönig, head of the board's Fine Arts Department, could announce that "order" now existed everywhere in the visual arts.

For the next ten years contemporary German art glorified war, "Aryanism," domestic virtue, and the Nazi party. Seven thousand pieces of this sentimental, prettily colored art created to order were collected by the United States Army in 1945 and now lie almost forgotten in a Virginia warehouse. In these works the war is bloodless; bombs explode in fireworks of violets, pinks, and blues; German women placidly pick their way through the rubble of bombed cities, as if looking for wild flowers and not prized possessions; German soldiers, all splendid "Aryan" types, admire Norway, Greece, France, and Italy as if they were tourists posing for travel brochures; and the propagators of the war are noble, thoughtful men, although the artists have not concealed their nervous hands and icy eyes.

Hönig's "order" created a vacuum in what had been in 1931 an art world called second only to Paris in the field of painting and equal to that of any country in sculpture. Up until the advent of Hitler, one of the most famous art schools in Europe was the Bauhaus, established in 1919 by the architect Walter Gropius for the coordinated teaching of all the plastic arts, based on a new idea in structure. A window in a Gropius building is not a hole in the wall, for a wall is merely a curtain against the elements and may even be all glass when maximum light is desired. Hitler considered this idea "un-German" and closed the Bauhaus. Its distinguished professors of architecture, painting, and sculpture scattered in various directions. Gropius went to Harvard as chairman of the Department of Architecture. His Dutch colleague, Mies van der Rohe, went to Chicago and practiced as an architect. One country's loss is often another's gain; the face of America changed radically in the years that followed as glass-and-steel buildings rose to the skies.

Among the teachers of art, Paul Klee returned to his native Switzerland, carrying with him his notebooks and his highly original concepts of drawing and painting. Kandinsky, the first man to paint pure abstractions, went to Paris. The sculptor Oskar Schlemmer remained in internal exile in southern Germany, working as a plasterer. His marvelous, humanistic bas-reliefs on the walls of the Weimar Art School were removed with sledgehammers. Lyonel Feininger, an American of German ancestry, tried to remain in Germany as a journalist. He found this equally impossible and returned home to set up a school in New York. Kurt Schwitters, founder of the collage movement, went to Sweden until the Nazi armies took over Norway. He then fled to England, where he suffered extreme hardship and intermittent blindness.

Germany's greatest sculptor was Ernst Barlach. Although 381 of his works were confiscated and he wrote that pimps and murderers were better off than creative artists, Barlach remained in Germany. His "War Memorial," a wood carving commissioned for Magdeburg Cathedral, was dismantled in 1933 and stored in Berlin's National Gallery until an enterprising Nazi commissioner bought it for a thousand dollars. The United States Army returned the sculpture to its owners, the Saxe-Anhalt Government, in 1945. Alfred Rosenberg had called its figures "little half-idiots under Russian helmets." When somebody had tried to sell Barlach's work to Hitler by showing him some sketches, the Führer had shouted, "Take them away!"

The first woman ever elected to the Berlin Academy, the humanitarian Käthe Kollwitz, had her name stricken from the roster and lost her teaching post in 1933. Although she was urged to leave the country, she was fearful of reprisals to her family if her name were used in anti-Nazi publicity. She remained in seclusion in southern Germany until the year she died, just before the fall of the Reich. She had done no work for twelve years, but her international reputation was so great that in 1945 American GI's who knew very little about art knew enough to buy every Kollwitz print they could lay hands on.

"Cultural Bolshevik Number 1" was George Grosz, painter and cartoonist. Arrested for anti-Nazi cartoons several times before 1933, Grosz would have been killed outright if he had not managed to escape to New York with his family. The painter Karl Hofer protested in 1933 that the Jewish art trade had never influenced German artists and added that Nazism encouraged mediocrity and stale art. He remained in prison until the Allies arrived in Germany. Christian Rohlfs was asked to resign from the Academy of Arts in 1937. He wrote a letter "leaving the judgment of this matter to posterity" and refused to change his style of painting.

The list of banned and exiled artists is long. Hundreds of men and women in the arts, German and non-German, were killed by the Nazis. Most of the Jews were condemned to death no matter what they thought or how they painted. Non-Jewish artists painted secretly in back rooms. To continue to live, some artists submitted outdated or inferior works to dealers or public exhibitions. Distinguished professors deprived of their posts worked at any sort of menial task to eat and buy paints. A kind of passive, dogged resistance never quite died during the long, dark years, despite heartbreak and hunger.

The year 1935 was a banner one for the Nazis. On July 1 Himmler created his S.S. research foundation, the Ahnenerbe, to furnish scientific proof of the validity of Nazi ideas on racial superiority. Its slogan was: "A people lives happily in its present and future so long as it is conscious of its past and the greatness of its ancestors." Its aim was to present to the German people, in a lively and attractive manner, the accomplishments of the northern Indo-Germanic race, and every true German was expected to cooperate.

About forty-five research projects were either begun or imagined on such subjects as linguistics, botany, fairy tales, nuclear physics, prehistory, and popular medicine. The main library and archives were in Dahlem, and subsidiaries in Munich and Salzburg included a photo laboratory, a sculptor's studio, and a model-making and museum workshop. The enterprise was so huge that about a hundred men did research on the forest and tree in Germanic culture and history. Twenty thousand contributed to an atlas of German folklore.

Himmler's interest was both personal and political. He gave the Ahnenerbe practically unlimited funds and combined a pet hobby with an aggressive political and ideological aim: the propagation of the theory of Germanic superiority and the practical application of the theory of world conquest. He wanted cold facts, scientific thoroughness, and fine scholarship. To this end, he organized a staff of trained scholars. Both he and Wolfram Sievers, Minister of Culture and business manager of the Ahnenerbe, were masterly propagandists who used half-truths, each itself unattackable, to propagate a stupendous lie. They wanted no amateurism, slipshod work, or forgeries and set up a special police section for the detection and prosecution of forgers. The Ahnenerbe was not a crackpot undertaking but a deadly weapon to rewrite the past to influence the future.

Prior to the war the Ahnenerbe sponsored scientific expeditions outside of Germany, with fifth-column activity a secondary business. The war changed this, and the Ahnenerbe was activated for assignments in important areas. In France in 1940 its object was the wholesale looting of cultural objects from public and private sources. The looting was euphemistically described in Nazi documents as "securing," "searching," "packing," "cleaning," "buying," "bartering," "saving," and less ambiguously as "taking along" and "bringing back." The Ahnenerbe's thoroughness and its terminology in the field of looting directly or indirectly influenced the actions of the Nazis in their behavior in the world of art until the final debacle.

CHAPTER 2

BONFIRES AND EXHIBITIONS

IN MAY, 1936, a new law authorized the confiscation of "degenerate" art hanging in German museums. Although such art was never clearly defined by the men in power, the term included:

1. Any art, no matter in what style, created by Jews.
2. Art with Jewish themes, even if painted by non-Jews. Under this heading such works as Rembrandt's ghetto scenes and portraits and some religious paintings were "degenerate."
3. Art advocating pacifism or showing war as ugly.
4. Art with Marxist or socialist themes.
5. Art portraying ugly or deformed people, since these were members of an inferior race.
6. All Expressionist art, even if Nordic and racist in concept.
7. All abstract art (Cubist, Futurist, Constructivist) and anything not strictly realistic.

The list was comprehensive enough to cover the major art movements and styles from 1850 onward. The attack on the museums hit all the "isms" that preceded the Nazi art of the 1930's and hit where it hurt most—on the careful selections of discriminating art scholars.

The first museum raided was Karlsruhe's Kunsthalle, which lost its entire collection of modern art: 145 paintings. On July 6 the Wallraf-Reichartz Museum in Cologne, one of the finest in Germany, lost its entire collection of Postimpressionist art, most of it forever. Düsseldorf's Fine Arts Museum lost 900 works; Essen's Folkwang Museum, 1,273; Hamburg's Kunsthalle, 983; Frankfort's Städel Art Institute, 500. Vandalism also hit Berlin's National Gallery, which lost 505 pieces of art, cited in a recent book on German art museums as being "squandered by Hitler." Among the foreign artists whose works were confiscated were Van Gogh, Kandinsky, Klee, Signac, and Kokoschka. Among the Germans were Macke and Marc, both of whom had died on the battlefield fighting for Germany in World War I; Nolde, who was a member of the Danish Nazi party; and Beckmann, who barely survived the war years in Holland only to die, literally of exhaustion, soon after his arrival in the United States. The Friends of the National Gallery were so frightened by the raids that they sold works by Braque, Picasso, and Juan Gris at derisory prices to prevent their total loss by confiscation. Göring was not so disgusted with modern art that he could not cram Karinhall with works whose international monetary value was well known. By devious ruses he managed to acquire works by Signac, Cézanne, Van Gogh, Gauguin, Munch, and even Pissarro, the only Jewish artist of the French Impressionist group.

Dealers and private owners were also forced to give up any examples of modern art they possessed. About five thousand paintings and pieces of sculpture and about twelve thousand drawings and graphics were stored in a Berlin warehouse. Hitler came to look at them and made up his mind that these monstrosities must never be returned to their rightful owners, the German people.

The Germans lost almost all of these "monstrosities," but a visit to any German museum today indicates that not every private German citizen turned over every piece of modern art. Immediately after the downfall of the Reich the museums began to build up their collections again. Some of them started as early as 1945; others, such as Berlin's, which had to be rebuilt, were forced to wait until as late as 1957. In 1948 Cologne's Wallraf-Reichartz received the Josef Haubrich collection of modern art as a gift. Nolde and his wife gave to the city of Seebüll and to Munich's Haus der Kunst several hundred of the artist's own works as well as their private collection of Kandinskys and Klees. The number of paintings in each museum today is considerably smaller than it was. To cite only a few examples, for 101 museums were raided by Hitler, Berlin has 200 modern paintings; Essen, about 150; Düsseldorf, slightly more than 200; Hamburg, about 150 paintings and 40 sculptures. Some of the works that are proudly displayed today were painted by German artists under *Malverbot* who risked their freedom and their lives by painting in back rooms and hiding their works; others had been stowed away in dark closets and attics, buried in gardens, hidden behind false walls, or disguised in various ways. The small plaques attached to each painting do not indicate where the works had been hidden during the thirteen dark years, but they give the artists' names and their places and dates of birth and death. It is still terrifying to read "Died in Auschwitz" or "Died in Dachau" below a landscape full of color and light.

Two notable art events occurred in 1937. The first was the grand opening of the House of German Art in Munich, preceded by a big parade lavishly decorated with swastika flags. Hitler made a speech thunderously proclaiming that the function of art was to intensify racial consciousness and that it must be created according to set rules and free of all foreign influence. The theme of the opening exhibition was ancient Germany: it was filled with representations of Viking ships in orderly array, old Germanic gods, and such myths as that of the hoard of the Nibelungen.

With this solid national art already on view, the *Völkischer Beobachter*, the party newspaper, came out on the morning of July 17 with a headline announcing that "the hour of the rebirth of German art" was to be further ushered in by a "Degenerate Art Show" in Munich's Archaeological Museum. This was not the first propagandistic art show held in Germany. One entitled "The German Revolution," honored by an address by Rosenberg, was described by William Shirer as the "dreariest collection" he had ever seen. Nuremberg assembled an "art chamber of horrors" so that the people might see how extravagantly their tax money had been spent. The old director of the Chemnitz Museum was summarily removed for liberalism, and his successor put on a show called clumsily "Kunst, die nicht aus unserer Seele kam" ("Art That Did Not Come from Our Soul"). Dresden staged a show in the courtyard of its new city hall: "Paintings Mirroring the Decay of Art." To arouse public indignation, prices for the works were listed in terms of the wildly inflated currency of the period after World War I. One of the paintings shown was a famous work by Otto Dix showing the horrors of trench warfare. The Dresden show was brought to Munich and shown at police headquarters, perhaps to impress the police with what they might freely destroy.

But the show to end all shows was the "Degenerate Art Show" ordered by Hitler himself and arranged by Goebbels, who had been empowered to select whatever he wished from publicly owned examples of post-1910 "decadent" painting and sculpture. He chose 730 works and crammed them into side rooms in the Archaeological Institute. The entrance to the show was crowned by a sculpture by Barlach and ornamented with derisive inscriptions that "explained" the works of the Dadaists. Inside, the paintings were hung as badly as possible, usually without frames, much too close together, often simply on the floor and leaning against the wall. Occasionally a really bad painting was hung beside a masterpiece. The lighting was as poor as the hanging arrangements.

To hammer home his lesson, Goebbels prepared a catalog that was, if possible, even more disgraceful than the show. Smudgily printed, its black-and-white illustrations laid out to show the works in the worst possible way, with marginal notes and critical commentaries that were at best vulgar, at worst obscene, the thirty-two pages of the catalog were really so many pages of a tract accusing all twentieth-century art of being the decadent product of an era dominated by Jews and Bolsheviks. Among the milder comments was that "up until recently these artists had been teaching German youth." The cover was adorned with a reproduction of a stone head by Otto Freundlich, an artist who managed to escape to France. He was picked up by the Gestapo after 1940 and sent back to Germany to die in a concentration camp.

The works were divided into nine categories:

1. Those without Nazi ideas of sound, healthy craftsmanship.
2. Those with religious themes, which were labeled a brazen mockery of the religious experience. (Suddenly, the Nazis, who sent thousands of priests and pastors to concentration camps, closed religious institutions, censored Christian publications, and advocated crude anti-Christian and antireligious propaganda, posed as defenders of Christianity, "defamed" by German Expressionist artists.)
3. "Bolshevist" paintings showing starvation, exploitation, or social misery of any kind.
4. Paintings attacking militarism and chauvinism.
5. Art deriving from the arts of Africa and Oceania. (Only Greek art canons were acceptable.)
6. Art showing prostitutes and "personifications of vice."

7. Creations of lunatics, to show similarities between their work and that of Expressionists.
8. Any style of art created by Jews.
9. "Isms" foisted on the innocent German people by Jewish dealers.

The paintings of the 112 German and foreign artists represented were labeled "junk," "incompetent," "lunatic," "tortured," or otherwise opprobriously. Yet despite the catalog's ravings, the obscene signs decorating the rooms, and the adverse newspaper publicity, the lines outside the Archaeological Institute were endless. People waited patiently for hours to take a last heartbroken look at what they feared would be lost forever. One German historian remarked that "some, no doubt, found it hard to suppress their tears." Of course, a few convinced Nazis came to scoff, but they were lost in the crowd. Himmler was so infuriated by the reaction of the people of Munich that he shut the doors long before the scheduled closing date.

Like a carnival sideshow, the Munich exhibition toured Germany until 1939. During the tour period the Reich's Ministry for Propaganda prepared a six-volume catalog listing 1,290 oils, 160 pieces of sculpture, 7,350 watercolors, drawings, and engravings, and 3,360 other graphics which were all stored in a warehouse on Köpenicker Strasse in Berlin. The warehouse was needed for storing grain, and the Committee for the Disposition of Confiscated Works of Art, under the chairmanship of Reichsminister Dr. Franz Hofmann, met on February 20, 1939, to dispose of the art. Committee members included art dealers and men from Alfred Rosenberg's office. To get some art out of Germany it was decided that a few art dealers might purchase certain works for resale for foreign exchange only. No Germans might buy any of this art to keep. The prices paid by the dealers were ridiculously low and included such bargains as five Klee watercolors for $250 and fifteen by Nolde for $450. Evidence that such art had been confiscated from German museums had to be removed. Such marks always include labels or marking on the backs of canvases, plaques on frames, museum stamps on works done on paper, and catalog numbers indicating acquisition dates.

Dr. Hofmann then informed the committee that Propaganda Minister Goebbels had decided upon an international auction of the most desirable works of art and had selected Theodore Fischer, of Lucerne, to handle this auction. The proceeds would go to Hitler's special E.K. (*Entartete Kunst*—Degenerate Art) Fund. One dealer, Karl Haberstock, of Berlin, questioned both the selection of art works and the choice of Fischer. He added that there were other works that might also be auctioned, but his objections were overruled.

The warehouse would still be far from empty, however, so with the full approval of Goebbels and upon the suggestion of Dr. Hofmann, the remaining works were to be burned as "a symbolic and propagandist act" in a public bonfire. Haberstock, backed up by Robert Scholz, of Rosenberg's office, announced grave doubts as to the advisability of such an action and wanted no part in it. The rest of the committee kept silent, and it was suggested that Haberstock and Scholz pay a visit to Köpenicker Strasse to be convinced of the worthlessness of its contents. In 1939 it was very brave to question a Goebbels decision; it was also usually quite futile.

The pictures for the auction and for straight resale abroad were removed, and the remaining works were taken to the courtyard of Berlin's principal firehouse. A fanatical mob hurled 1,004 paintings and sculptures and 3,825 watercolors, drawings, and graphics into a raging fire that reduced them to ashes.

An exhibition of 125 masterpieces selected from the warehouse was held in Zurich in May, 1939, before the works were taken to the Grand Hotel National in Lucerne for the auction, held on June 30. Museum directors, dealers, private collectors, and journalists came from the unoccupied countries of Europe and from the United States. In what newsmen described as a gala atmosphere on a beautiful summer day, the distinguished bidders purchased all of the paintings at deliberately held-down prices, since it was no secret that the E.K. Fund would be used for war or for forced purchases from museums and private owners for the projected Führermuseum in Linz. Plans for the museum were already well under way, and works of art had been gathered together by Dr. Hans Posse, chief curator of the Dresden State Museum. Posse had at first opposed Hitler, for the Führer began his Linz collection by simply deciding what he wanted from each German museum and ordering such works removed and stored away. Posse had tried to save the Dresden collection, but beaten down under repeated attacks and threatened with the loss of his job, he capitulated. His reward, engineered by Albert Speer, was a meeting with Hitler and the Linz job, which he took on in addition to keeping his original post.

Prices at the Lucerne auction are almost impossible to believe. Drawings and watercolors by masters sold for seven to twenty-two cents apiece. A Kandinsky oil, now in New York's Guggenheim Museum, brought one hundred dollars. Bidding was a bit sharper for one of the masterworks of Picasso's Blue Period, which drew seven thousand dollars and went to Washington, D.C., to hang in the National Gallery. The sale was not the triumph Goebbels or Hitler had hoped, but it did strengthen the determination of other European countries to safeguard their own art, whether privately or publicly owned. The decrees applied to Jewish possessions in Germany and occupied lands were public knowledge; so were the requisitions and forced sales which stripped Vienna and Prague of art from museums, cathedrals, churches, and private collections and laid rough hands on porcelain, furniture, tapestries, and carpets.

Nearly a year before the Lucerne auction, during the uneasy summer of 1938, when war seemed imminent, the French had begun plans for the evacuation of their most valuable art from the Louvre, the principal national museum, in a sense a symbol for all French art. Everybody expected Paris to be the principal target for bombing raids when war was declared. And so, at six in the morning on September 27, 1938, several trucks left the museum for Chambord, in the Loire Valley, about a hundred miles from Paris. The 440-room Renaissance château of Chambord is the second largest castle in France, with a history dating back to 1519 and King Francis I. The story of Chambord in World War II, important thought it is, is merely one episode in a long series of astonishing historical events that occurred under its magnificent roof and behind its glorious facade.

A second, longer convoy set out for the same destination on the following day. But before the third convoy could be prepared, Edouard Daladier, President of the French National Council, returned from Munich and the signing of the Munich pact. No further trucks left for Chambord except to pick up and return, very discreetly, what had been removed from the Louvre.

Few people believed that the pact guaranteed "peace in our time," as Neville Chamberlain happily announced to the British when he returned to London. As far as the Louvre was concerned, the Munich pact provided a breathing space and the opportunity to prepare a much more detailed plan for the evacuation of art. During the strange limbo of the eleven months before the invasion of Poland on September 1, 1939, the museum staff—curators, archivists, historians, restorers, guards, and workmen—was welded into a team under the extraordinarily able direction of Jacques Jaujard, who was named Director of French National Museums during this period and so felt generally responsible for all the art in France. Jaujard, who had been responsible for the masterpieces of the Prado and other Spanish museums during the Spanish Civil War of 1936–1939, knew what to expect. Spanish art had been in constant flight before the tanks and planes of the Fascist armies and had reached safety only by crossing the Pyrenees. It was impossible to imagine that French art would be secure beyond either the Pyrenees or the Alps. Jaujard used the months of grace to prepare for a staggeringly difficult moving job whose purpose was to save French art within the borders of France.

During this time the Louvre never regained its normal aspect. Although the art was replaced on walls or on pedestals, materials for packing filled the basements and storerooms. Many of the cases used for the first exodus were left standing in exhibition halls, conveniently at hand and grim reminders of the uncertainty of the peace and the terrors of total war. The museum's personnel made endless inventories, classifying and reclassifying works of art for size, value, importance, and fragility. Small colored dots—red, green, and yellow—one or two of each, were affixed to the back of each painting. The color and the number of dots indicated priority. The "Mona Lisa" wore two red dots on the back of the panel from which she smiles. Similar brilliant dots on the exteriors of the cases enabled curators and guards to tell at a glance which cases were most important in the event of any emergency. Curators and assistants studied the best methods of packing and the quickest ways to take paintings from walls and out of frames. They carefully examined very large works to determine whether or not they were in condition to be rolled for easier packing and transportation. Jaujard and his helpers acquired fire-fighting equipment and tried to find suitable trucks that had not already been requisitioned by the army and were strong enough to transport heavy yet fragile loads safely in any sort of weather. Packers and assistants had to be recruited, men not liable to be called up for service in the army and yet not so old that they would break down under the rapid effort anticipated.

Although Chambord was to be the first resting place for all the art, even its many rooms and deep cellars could not hold, boxed or unboxed, most of the treasures of the Louvre, one-third of the contents of the Jeu de Paume and Cluny museums, one-third of the collections of other Paris museums directed by the city itself and not the central government, and important works from other municipalities. (Since it was impossible to move or find storage room for all the art in Paris, the choice was based on the importance, size, and weight of the individual pieces.) Jaujard thus had to find other châteaux suitable for the storing of art, with entrance doors wide enough to admit huge cases and bundles, with solid floors, and with adequate accommodations inside or in the vicinity for the curators and the guards, many of whom had families. Feeding all the people who would live with the art also had to be considered.

The Beaux-Arts of Paris, the group responsible for all art belonging to the city, was actively engaged in selecting the works that would move with those of the Louvre and in protecting all the city's churches (except Notre Dame, a national monument). Religious art—stained-glass windows, tombs and monuments, paintings and fixtures—also had to be protected. Sometimes works were marked to be moved from one church to the crypt of another; sometimes sandbags had to be piled around immovable stonework. City and state worked hand in hand on preparations, removals, and delicate decisions. In every museum all the members of the staffs worked at whatever task was most urgent at any given moment to be certain that everything would be ready for the day that everybody knew would come.

PART II

ACTION: 1939–1944

CHAPTER 3

MUSEUMS ON THE MOVE

ONE WEEK BEFORE the outbreak of hostilities, when it became apparent that war was no longer merely inevitable but imminent, the Louvre closed its doors to the public. The meticulously planned packing began on August 25, 1939. In each museum department, teams put the most precious objects into their cases first, packing rapidly but carefully and tacking on the inside lids a list of what was enclosed. Duplicates of these lists remained in the Louvre. The task was staggering. The Archives and Fine Books Department alone required nearly four hundred cases. The staff worked twelve hours a day, wearing smocks; the women added turbans to protect their hair; and at the end of each day everybody was as filthy and exhausted as any householder on moving day.

By the evening of August 27 the first and most precious cases were ready. The next day the "Mona Lisa" left for Chambord in the first convoy, keeping her place of honor, as she had a year before. Between the first departure and the last, on December 28, everything movable left the Rue de Rivoli in thirty-seven convoys of from five to eight trucks each. A few unimportant paintings were left in the basement, and some statuary too heavy and thus impossible to move remained on the ground floor. In the long halls where paintings usually hung, only the marks on the walls indicated that the Louvre, once a palace, had been a museum for many years. The twenty-ninth convoy carried, among other statues, the "Venus de Milo" and the "Winged Victory." The latter, carefully wrapped, had been removed from her pedestal and eased gently down the flight of fifty-three steps at whose head she always stands. The task was fraught with danger, for the "Victory" is put together out of fragments of marble held together with plaster, and one false move could have caused irreparable damage.

The convoys always left the museum in the same way after passing inspection in the Cour Carrée, the closable interior court at the southwest, Rue du Louvre, end of the museum. On ordinary days the court is open to the public, which may pass through it to and from the Seine. On these days it was closed, with chairs and tables set up for Jaujard, a few aides, and the principal trucker. The trucks filed past; the list of cases in each was carefully checked; names of drivers were ticked off; fastenings and covering tarpaulins were inspected. The trucks then got in line, surrounded by motorcycle police. The automobiles carrying personnel took their places at the front and rear, and the signal to leave was given. The convoys traveled slowly, usually at night along well-traveled roads.

The first nine trips were accomplished without incident. The tenth convoy, which left just before war was declared, ran into trouble in front of the town hall of Versailles. Géricault's "The Raft of the Medusa," one of the Louvre's largest paintings, is 23½ feet wide and 16 feet high. Since the paint was liable to crack if the canvas was rolled up, the painting was left on its stretcher and placed standing on end in a trailer used by the French National Theater for towing scenery. The edge of the canvas hit the tram lines and caused a short circuit in the town and a shower of stars in the night. The people of Versailles panicked in the dark, police whistles added to the disorder, and a mob of annoyed citizens surrounded the convoy while sparks continued to flash against the sky and against the painting. The curators feared both a fire and a riot. Luckily, technicians arrived in time to prevent both. They lifted up the tram wires and replaced them, and "The Raft" sailed on as far as the château of Versailles, where it was left in the shelter of the Orangerie, for it was obviously unwise to create such trouble in every tram-equipped town on the road.

"The Raft" left Versailles at the end of September, going directly to the château of Louvigny with other large unrolled canvases. One of the Louvre's most eminent curators, René Huyghe, led this parade of giants along a route carefully planned beforehand to avoid tram lines and low bridges. No accidents interrupted the convoy, but the telephone linesmen who accompanied it made good use of long poles to unhook and replace the overhead electric wires in several places.

The tenth convoy, minus "The Raft," continued on its way and arrived at Chambord at dawn to be greeted by its director, Pierre Schommer, and his wife, who remained the hosts of the château throughout the war. This was not a social gathering, however, and after a brief nap the museum personnel who were to remain at Chambord began to work. Strong men were required to arrange the cases in some sort of order. Once the cases were arranged, they had to be opened and their contents checked. Throughout the war the art work often had to be moved around inside the château and quite frequently had to be reloaded on trucks and moved to other châteaux, sometimes because this was the original plan and sometimes because the line of battle was drawing uncomfortably closer. For all these men and their families, lodgings were required. Chambord is enormous but icy cold except in one wing, and the temporary beds set up in small dormitories were not in the heated portion, which was being used by curators for offices and to store fragile art works. Winter posed a problem, and it was necessary to find lodgings for the guards in whatever was available in the village of Chambord and in Bracieux, another town about four miles away. Schommer took care of the handling of the cases, and his wife and another woman curator attended to the problems of housing the men.

The task was not easy, for not only was it difficult to find housing even with the help of parish priests, village mayors, and local policemen, but the lodgings to be had were not very satisfactory. The two women spent their mornings listening to complaints and making lists of urgent needs. Then they went out in the afternoons looking for vacant apartments. Everybody was as helpful as possible under the circumstances, and eventually all the guards and their wives and many children were safely housed, and a canteen was set up in the vicarage for the bachelors unable to cook for themselves.

The next job was to find other châteaux in the region where the art could be suitably resettled and retain at least a modicum of classification. Châteaux abound in the Loire Valley, but they are not all suitable for temporary museums. The three largest—Cheverny, Courtalain, and Brissac—could hold many cases and museum workers and guards to watch over them. Large-sized Greek antiquities, smaller Greek art objects, and Asiatic art went to Valençay; decorative arts (furniture, silver, porcelain), to Cheverny; the Egyptian Department to Courtalain; and private collections from the Camondo and Versailles museums, to Brissac. The directors of the Beaux-Arts of the city of Paris went to live temporarily in Chaumont, a huge ugly building on a mountain peak overlooking the Loire.

Paintings are the most delicate of all art and have to be treated with great care. They cannot be left indefinitely in cases, for without light their color alters and darkens. The decision to place them in several châteaux—Allier, Louvigny, Chereperrine, La Pelice, and eventually Sourches—in the adjoining, more westerly department of the Sarthe made it easier for curators to move from one château to another to open the cases. Many male curators were in the army, so one could not be permanently assigned to each château. La Pelice housed all the restorers, and paintings needing repairs could be brought to them. The "Mona Lisa" was to go to Chauvigny but could not leave Chambord until her next home was prepared. She traveled in a special double-walled poplar case, tailor-made for her in 1938. For the trip from Chambord, the case was placed on an ambulance stretcher provided with elastic springs to absorb shocks. The stretcher was fastened inside a truck that was followed by another in case of accident. Both trucks were accompanied by an automobile. Schommer accompanied the lady, and he was so concerned over her safe arrival that he decided not to ride either beside the truck driver or in the automobile but sat inside the truck beside the stretcher. He was half-asphyxiated from lack of air when the cortege arrived at Chauvigny. Louvre curators took no chances except with their own lives.

The Archives and Fine Books Department and the Drawings Department remained at Chambord, fairly comfortably installed in the castle's heated wing and able for a few months to resume their regular tasks. Chambord was busy and often well populated with the museum personnel who accompanied each convoy that left Paris, but most of them returned to their homes in Paris. At the end of September, the most precious cargo having been suitably taken care of, the Monuments Commission decided to empty the Louvre as completely as possible, and the packing began again. At the same time Jaujard decided that insofar as was humanly possible, he had to safeguard private collections as well. He was particularly concerned about those belonging to Jews, as they seemed to him in constantly increasing danger. To find enough truckers for this new batch of convoys, the Louvre called on everybody interested in art; artists, retired civil servants, and the societies of the Friends of the Louvre, of Versailles, and of other museums helped find trucks and accompanied the convoys. The last of them arrived shortly after Christmas. A permanent resident of Chambord described the life as "strange . . . burdensome and sad, in a fairy-tale land conceived for happiness and disfigured for us by this expectation of the worst."

The icy cold winter of 1939–1940 was the time of the "phony war," when nothing seemed to happen and the newspapers enlarged upon every incident to remind people that there really was a war going on and that soldiers were being wounded or killed all along the front. The spring offensive changed all that. The invasions and occupations of Norway, Holland, and Belgium, the retreat of the British Army at Dunkirk, miraculous though it was, and Mussolini's cowardly entry into the war—all led to the collapse of France. By May, 1940, General Maurice Gamelin, commander of the Franco-British forces, considered abandoning Paris. Many Louvre guards who had returned to Paris during the lull went back to the various châteaux with their families, and the curators who had remained in Compiègne, Versailles, Saint-Germain-en-Laye, and the Louvre itself hastened to regain Chambord and Valençay. Finally, Jacques Jaujard left Paris for Chambord to supervise another journey for the art masterpieces, since they could no longer be considered safe so close to Paris. Once the capitulation of the country was inevitable, Jaujard and his staff also had to consider what would happen to Parisian museums, empty or with partial collections, if they were left without administrative officials when the Germans arrived. Nobody knew whether disciplined troops or unruly mobs would roam the city in the first days after the surrender. An administrative curator was selected for each museum. Then, during the few final days of freedom, there was nothing to do inside Paris except wait . . . in anguish and in fear.

CHAPTER 4

KUNSTSCHUTZ AND EMBASSY

THE PERIOD OF waiting was brief. The Germans began their push to the west on May 10, 1940; on June 5 they reached the Somme. On June 10 the French Government abandoned Paris, leaving first for Tours and then for Bordeaux in long motorcades that added to the confusion already present on the roads. Millions of civilians in blind panic abandoned their cities and towns and villages, hoping to cross the Loire, to reach the south, to escape the advancing troops. The roads were a tangled jam of luxurious cars, old jalopies, bicycles, baby carriages, farm wagons, and people on foot. The trains were as packed as the roads. People slept anywhere in any fashion; they ate anything they could find, looted abandoned shops, pillaged their own countrymen's homes, and went hungry. German planes flew low over the roads and railroad lines, selecting human targets and firing at them as if trying for bull's-eyes in shooting galleries.

On June 14 the Germans entered Paris and found a silent, half-empty city upon whose roofs and facades they hung their flags and down whose deserted Champs Elysées they marched with their prisoners. On June 17 Marshall Henri Pétain asked for an armistice. Only thirty-eight days had passed, and the French had suffered the worst defeat in the history of their country. More than a million and a half French soldiers were prisoners and the Germans had taken most of their equipment. Those soldiers who had escaped capture deserted their units and joined the millions on the roads or went into hiding. On June 18 Charles de Gaulle, who had escaped to London, invited them and every other French citizen to join him in his continuing battle.

The treasures of France were caught up in the rout. Two of the châteaux, Valençay and Cheverny, stood on the route of the advancing German Army and in the path of the fleeing citizenry. Luckily, by the time the Germans reached Valençay, there seemed little use for continued fighting, and both the château, which housed the art, and its stables, which sheltered more than two thousand refugees, were left alone. Cheverny was surrounded at a slight distance by the German Army, and French civilians, true to the old tradition of seeking shelter at a château, tried unsuccessfully to storm its gates. Clearly, neither of these places could be utilized for the reception of more art treasures. The curators, like everyone else, turned their eyes toward the interior and the south of France.

The second evacuation had begun on June 3, when the first of four hastily packed convoys left Chambord and the châteaux of the Sarthe for the Abbey of Loc-Dieu in the Aveyron, a part of the mountainous heart of the country. The most important of 3,120 paintings went first, and as she had twice before, the "Mona Lisa" rode in the first convoy. The fourth convoy left Chambord on June 15 and arrived at Loc-Dieu the day before all bridges were closed to ordinary traffic. Another important lady, Isabella d'Este, Duchess of Mantua, traveled in this last convoy in her own, slightly smaller, special case. Attributed to Da Vinci, this portrait is as fragile as any 400-year-old drawing on paper. Two women curators accompanied the convoy, and Isabella rode with one of them. At night she slept between the women's cots—first at Valençay, where the sounds of bombardment were dangerously close, and then in a classroom in an abandoned primary school. Isabella had a hazardous trip. The last voyage was particularly difficult because of the crowded roads, the necessity for stopping to check the lashings of the cases in the trucks, the absence of any military authority, and the invisibility of civil government. Gasoline was extremely scarce, and the conveying party was pleased and surprised when the museum trucks received special attention.

About five hundred paintings remained in Chambord and the Sarthe, where Courtalain was soon to be occupied by the Germans. The most important Egyptian sculpture had been removed from the château and sent farther south before the Nazis moved in.

The terms of the armistice signed with the Germans on June 22, 1940, and with the Italians a few days later, created two Frances, neither of which could live without the other under the best of circumstances. Furthermore, one of them, the northern occupied one, was cut into four sections, each of which felt the presence of the German

Army and administration to a greater or lesser degree. Alsace-Lorraine felt the presence most, for it was simply annexed, its people forbidden to use the French language, the names of its towns changed, its francs replaced by marks, and its people labeled "wicked imbeciles" when they persisted in their often silent, stubborn resistance. The forbidden zone, bordered on one side by the English Channel and on another by Belgium, was treated like a colony. The reserved zone, bordering Germany on the northeast and Switzerland south of Alsace, provided a convenient buffer for the Germans and made passage into Switzerland difficult. The free, or unoccupied, zone was also partially occupied along the Franco-Italian frontier. The Germans ruled from Paris, and the Vichy Government remained south of the demarcation line, a frequently closed frontier that deliberately divided cantons, private property, and families. To pass from one zone to the other required an *Ausweis*, an exit pass issued by the Germans and of limited duration.

One road to freedom lay across the Pyrenees into Spain, which became the gateway to the democracies, a circuitous pathway along which about thirty thousand managed to escape: Frenchmen eager to join Free French Forces; English, American, Polish, and Czech pilots; and thousands of Jews. Men and women could also escape by boat from the coast of Brittany and Normandy and sometimes slip through the ring that the Germans erected around Switzerland, the favorite haunt of secret agents, a temporary haven for prisoners escaped from German camps, a way station on the road to England, and a fine place to sell art.

The Nazis helped themselves freely to French butter, cheese, champagne, meat, and silks, they set up administrative councils to control agriculture, education, labor unions, heavy industry, banks, and railroads, and they did not forget the cultural treasures they had coveted. For four years there was what Jean Cassou, a Louvre curator, called "from one end of the country to the other, a network of intrigues and dirty deals in which the most redoubtable leaders of National Socialism squabbled and defied each other in a sordid, stubborn struggle for the possession of famous paintings or valuable pieces of sculpture."

The intrigues began on June 30, 1940, when Hitler sent out an order demanding "the placing in security of all objects of art, whether they belonged to France, to private owners, or to Jews." This was explained not as an expropriation but as a transfer into

German custody as a guarantee for peace negotiations. The order went to the O.K.W., or German Military High Command, in Paris and from it, normally enough, to Count Wolff Metternich, head of the Kunstschutz, the Commission for the Preservation of Works of Art. The order also went to the Foreign Minister, Von Ribbentrop, who passed it on immediately to his ambassador in Paris, Otto Abetz.

Abetz, who entered Paris with the Wehrmacht, had been expelled from France before the war by Daladier for espionage and fifth-column activities. Trained as a teacher of art, he was rather a Francophile, had a French wife who had worked for a collaborationist newspaper, and liked French wines. An ambassador without a French counterpart in Germany, he was responsible only to Ribbentrop. A diplomat who doubled as an informer, he finally took on a third role, that of plunderer.

Metternich, by birth and education an enlightened European, was a man who disliked clumsy solutions to delicate problems. Elegant and courteous, possibly even secretly sympathetic, he was an aid to the French museum curators and by the end of 1941 had managed to convince Goebbels that French art really ought to remain in France for negotiation after the peace. He had to fight Abetz, backed up by Ribbentrop, all the way, for as early as July 16, 1940, Abetz had informed the army that "the Führer and the Foreign Minister would decide whether the art objects would remain in France or be transferred to Germany" and on the next day added that the Baron von Kuensberg, of the Secret Police, had been placed in his service and had the exclusive authority to carry out his directives.

Abetz had also ordered the seizure of all art belonging to state, provincial, and city museums, but since only the German troops could have carried out such an appropriation, his order was ignored. The census and seizure of Jewish-owned art began immediately, however, and priceless paintings were stolen from Baron Edouard de Rothschild and from the Seligmann, Wildenstein, Kann, Rosenberg, and Bernheim collections, which were picked up in a police raid on the fifteen most important art galleries in Paris. All this art passed through the doors of the German Embassy on the Rue de Lille. Since Von Kuensberg insisted that an order from Ribbentrop gave him the right to dispose of any art, publicly or privately owned, especially if it had belonged to Jews before the war, some of this treasure was put aside for the Nazis and some was marked for sale in the Paris art market. Abetz and Von Kuensberg and all those attached to their services also tried to force the removal of French national art treasures from the châteaux back to Paris on the flimsy pretext that they could care for the art better than its curators and, if necessary, more effectively control what happened to it.

Metternich was more "correct" and followed out Hitler's directives in a military manner without interpreting them as promises of national loot or personal gain. A census of the confiscated art was a hopeful guarantee that the collections would remain intact until after the peace, and it was within Metternich's power to prevent illegal transport, alteration, or transfer of ownership of all works of art. Abetz found this counter to his own aims and did his best to have the Kunstschutz made responsible for only nontransportable monuments, whereupon Metternich notified his superiors and received from Field Marshal Heinrich von Brauchitsch a decree restoring the necessary authority to his service. This decree forbade the transfer of any works of art from museums or châteaux used as repositories and ordered that notices be posted on all buildings containing such works to indicate that they were under military protection. When the High Command repulsed Von Kuensberg's final efforts to return the contents of the Louvre to Paris, Abetz gave in. All he could do was study the lists prepared by Metternich, hope for an increase in embassy power, and wait.

The Kunstschutz was helpful to the curators of French museums who consulted Metternich before moving their collections through the ensuing years, but the Kunstschutz was quite as helpful to the Nazis. Books and manuscripts from the Bibliothèque Nationale and the Institut de France were brought back from repositories to Paris by the Kunstschutz and used in the preparation of the list of works to be returned to Germany when the war ended. The Kunstschutz arranged for the opening of the German Historical Institute in Paris. It helped German military historians study fortification plans in the French Army Museum at the Invalides; it assisted German museum directors and art dealers who visited France to acquire works for their collections; and it handed over to the Einsatzstab Rosenberg all the important private collections picked up in the Paris area by Abetz and Von Kuensberg.

Jaujard's counterpart in Berlin was Dr. Otto Kümmel, General Director of German State Museums, and it was for him that the Kunstschutz provided the French books and manuscripts. Upon an order from Goebbels, Dr. Kümmel prepared a two-part list of art works to go to Germany, the *Geraubte Kulturgüter* (Stolen Cultural Goods). The list, begun in Germany long before the armistice, was completed on French soil, the first part by September 18, 1940, the second by January 20, 1941. The Nazi Minister of Education first in charge of this thousand-page document had relinquished his position in the project to that passionate collector, Reichsmarschall Göring. Göring and Goebbels were thus in agreement as to what the list should include, not only in France but in other occupied countries as well. The catalog covered:

1. All cultural objects of German origin taken from Germany during previous wars or through commercial transactions.
2. Works of art connected with the Reich, either by their inherent nature or by their history, from the fifteenth century onward.
3. Works of art related to any annexed or occupied country that had ever (like Belgium or Alsace-Lorraine) been attached to Germany during the course of its entire history.
4. Any of the aforementioned works of art that had disappeared through the years. Others, already designated, were to replace them as compensation.
5. Any other art confiscated from enemies of the Reich (Jews and Freemasons). Such art was not to be included in the overall demands of the Germans, and works carried off by the Nazis to "safeguard" them were not included as part of the German demands nor in the lists of art to be turned over as compensation.

If any of the occupied countries had really known what was planned, the general discontent would have been difficult to contain. In fact, when certain works on the list were stolen from their hiding places during the war years, the victims of the thefts created an uproar heard around the world.

Secrecy was vitally important to the Nazis. When Count Metternich received the rather mild-mannered, nearsighted Dr. Kümmel and his assistants, he was told only vaguely what their presence in Paris meant. Neither the Kunstschutz nor the French curators knew that, as the list's introductory remarks modestly stated, all of France's treasures probably would not be sufficient to meet the Führer's demands for restitution. What happened in the next four years depended to a large degree on the use made of the list by Hitler and his ministers and on the secret actions of occupying officials and complacent quislings. For four years museum personnel used whatever ingenuity they could muster to save their collections from this sword of Damocles.

The occupying army, meanwhile, tried in various ways to restore some semblance of life to Paris and even attempted to present entertainment. One of the diversions offered was a daily parade down the Champs Elysées, where the few Parisians who happened along at the appointed hour suddenly discovered interesting displays even in empty show windows or else vanished into the interiors of cafés. The German Army band give outdoor concerts; neatly lettered placards indicated that they were playing "For the French," who stayed away in droves.

The Germans persevered, however, and Count Metternich agreed with his superiors that in addition to reopening the theaters to distract both troops and civilians, it would be a fine idea to reopen some of the museums, even with their sadly depleted collections. The Louvre agreed to open its Hall of Antiquities three times a week—on opening day the officials dressed in black—and the Beaux-Arts of Paris reopened the Carnavalet and Cernuschi museums. The Germans removed some of the sandbags piled around the principal monuments and mounted machine guns on the roofs of the buildings around the Place de la Concorde. They also began to cast covetous glances at unused museum buildings and were particularly interested in the complex that clusters around the Trocadero Gardens on Chaillot Hill. The Anthropology Museum (Musée de l'Homme), which had been partially reopened, was comparatively safe (although Himmler yearned for its collection of skulls for the Ahnenerbe's research). The twin national and municipal Museum of Modern Art buildings were tempting, for they were not only empty—their collections of "degenerate" art had been removed to safety—but also not quite completed, and the collecting instincts of the Nazis could always imagine some use for large buildings. To prevent their takeover, the Louvre reinstalled the collection from the Luxembourg Palace in its building, and the Beaux-Arts turned their building over to the Artists' Aid Society for mounting exhibitions open to French artists.

When Carnavalet reopened with a show entitled "Manners and Styles of the Eighteenth Century," the French learned what German interference based on Nazi theory could mean. Dr. Hermann Bunjes—the liaison man for the Kunstschutz in charge of Parisian collections—and a German Embassy attaché examined every art object selected for exhibition and watched the installation carefully. In general, the Germans approved the choice of objects and methods of presentation; however, they refused permission to exhibit a small statue of the Jewish actress Mlle. Rachel and a portrait of Sarah Bernhardt in the room devoted to theatrical life. The French put Rachel back by the simple expedient of labeling her statue, draped in classical robes, "Tragedy." Bunjes went so far as to add a catalog in German. His name figured largely on the cover, and the titles of the works were translated into what one French curator called "revolting delicatessen," with Louis XIV renamed Ludwig. German troops came in large numbers, as their officers commanded, and learned about French traditions, a subject of little interest to most of them.

At the same time the Germans mounted an exhibition of their own in the Petit Palais. Its purpose was to show the wickedness of Freemasonry, and to accomplish this they had looted and emptied Parisian Masonic lodges, including the principal one of France. The exhibition was a pudding of Masonic symbols and equipment and resulted in complete boredom for the viewers. That show was no sooner over than the German Armaments Ministry announced its decision to move into the building and hold a permanent exhibition for French manufacturers and workers of what the Wehrmacht required in the way of weapons and machine tools. The interior was fancifully redecorated with gilt paper, fake-bronze busts of Hitler, swastikas, swastika flags, and green plants. The museum cases were filled with screws, nuts and bolts, and assorted odd bits of machinery illuminated so strongly that one night the silken curtains caught fire from the overheated lighting fixtures.

The Orangerie, across the Tuileries Gardens from the Musée de Jeu de Paume, was chosen by the French for an exhibition of French painting. The Grand Palais was being used as a barracks by the Occupation troops. During this first summer, the French also made plans to hold the Autumn Salon in the empty Marine Museum. A certain amount of artistic activity resumed in Paris. Some art dealers opened their galleries; the Hôtel Drouôt began its auctions again; a few artists returned from the country or the unoccupied zone. Some of the artists moved into the studios of absent Jewish artist friends to protect abandoned art or to confuse the Germans. A few Jewish artists took over the studios of "Aryan" artists who had preferred freedom, hiding out until they too could escape.

In the fall of 1940 several interesting German art-lovers turned up in Paris. In October the Germans seriously began to "safeguard" the collections of Jews. The central storehouse for the staggering quantities of loot was the Jeu de Paume Museum, once the tennis court of the kings of France and now for four years the headquarters of the French branch, the Dienstelle Louvre (Louvre Service), of the Einsatzstab Reichsleiter Rosenberg (Rosenberg Task Force), or E.R.R., and the site of Göring's private art fishing-pond and hunting-preserve.

CHAPTER 5

THE ROSENBERG TASK FORCE

REICHSLEITER ALFRED ROSENBERG, Nazi theoretician, was born in Estonia in 1893 and graduated from Moscow University in 1917, with degrees in philosophy and architecture. He went to Munich as a White Russian émigré in 1918, met Hitler the next year, and became editor of the official Nazi newspaper, the *Völkischer Beobachter*, in 1923. Sharing with Goebbels the honor of being chief propagandist for Nazism, Rosenberg advocated an antiquated system of education and the arts. His task force, the Einsatzstab, was originally set up for the collection of political material in occupied countries. However, as a special project of his Foreign Political Office, which focused on the struggle against Jews and Freemasons, Rosenberg also set up the Amt Westen (Office for Western Europe), which began its operation in July, 1940, with Paris headquarters in the Hôtel Commodore on the Boulevard Haussmann.

The organization and working processes in Paris were troublesome and confusing from the outset, for the task force, which now worked for the Amt Westen, had two heads, one in Paris and one in Berlin. In Paris the pictorial-arts section, called the Sonderstab Louvre (Louvre Special Staff), was technically a subsection of the entire Rosenberg action. Its staff of art historians and photographers had no executive powers, but it did have a specific job: photographing and cataloging the art works sent to Germany after preliminary judgment as to what was worthwhile. This group began its work on the collections that had been picked up for the German Embassy by the G.F.P. (Geheime Feldpolizei), or Secret Police, which, like the Kunstschutz, was subordinate to the military government. The art historians were appointed by one man in Berlin but disciplined by another, and the titular head of the Paris bureau had so much power that he could resist orders from the chief in the Berlin office. Hitler ordered the confiscations in Paris, and General Wilhelm Keitel gave the necessary military orders, but Göring dominated the operation because Rosenberg could not oppose him on equal political terms. To complicate matters further, Göring's Luftwaffe supplied Rosenberg with necessary transportation, military escorts, and other useful operational services.

Another factor made Göring's influence more easily accepted. Hitler's director for the Linz project, Dr. Hans Posse, had full authority over the disposal of all confiscated art, but he made little use of this power. Posse was seriously ill, and since he already disposed of ample funds for purchasing art, he did not wish to shoulder so much more extra responsibility, particularly from a distance, for he rarely visited Paris.

Rosenberg, not really very bright and a slippery liar who changed his testimony innumerable times at Nuremberg in an effort to save his neck, chose Gerhardt Utikal, a young man who had been a small-property owner and a minor party functionary, as his second-in-command for all E.R.R. operations. Utikal was not an intellectual giant, but he was sly enough to apply lex talionis to excuse his mishandling of Jewish property and crude enough to present this excuse in terroristic language when the occasion presented itself. His disloyalty to his immediate superior showed in his support of Göring, best expressed by his own remark to a subordinate, "Hermann can have everything he wants."

The divisional director for Paris of Rosenberg's Office for Pictorial Arts in Berlin was Dr. Robert Scholz. He was himself an artist and an art critic who had met Rosenberg in 1934. From that date until 1939, when he became director of the Moritzburg Museum in Halle, Scholz wrote art criticism for the *Völkischer Beobachter*, following the party line that all modern art was degenerate. Scholz made frequent trips to Paris, controlled the assignment and removal of all personnel working in Paris, ordered and directed the list of modern works to be sold or exchanged, and represented Rosenberg in relations with the

Reichschancellery, the party, and the military when questions of art arose. Shrewd but vacillating and hence unreliable, he minimized his own responsibility for E.R.R. operations during his questioning before the Nuremberg trials.

This triumvirate worked together in E.R.R.'s principal job of locating, confiscating, and removing to Germany the collections of art and art objects belonging to Jews. If the Jews happened to be Germans who had escaped from Germany with their possessions, the excuse given was that these people had not paid the refugee tax and so their property was liable to confiscation. However, with both Hitler and Göring actively supporting its actions, the E.R.R. had the power to take and to remove all Jewish possessions from occupied countries. The object was to accomplish this in such a way as "to attract as little attention as possible. In the event of repeated questioning by local authorities, the answer should be given *verbally* that it is a measure of reprisal carried out on orders from a higher authority; discussion is to be avoided." The E.R.R. document from which this quotation comes insisted that no receipts were to be given for removed property.

The Berlin trio had a most helpful chief-of-staff for France, the one-eyed Baron Kurt von Behr, an unscrupulous egomaniac. About sixty years old in 1940, he had served in World War I and been a British prisoner of war. He had no specific occupation between the two wars but was an ardent Nazi and often went to Italy on some kind of liaison duty with the Fascist Government. Von Behr was also a senior official of the German Red Cross, whose uniform he often wore, not to that organization's credit, for he ran what has been called a "little concentration camp in Paris." Von Behr lived an opulent, elegant, and dissolute life in Paris, gave lavish presents to his friends and to important political figures, and kept a large stock of the finest wines to serve at expensive parties encouraged by Rosenberg, who saw in them a way to ingratiate himself and to add to the prestige of the E.R.R., which the military authorities despised. Von Behr was also Göring's agent until his relations with the Reichsmarschall grew strained at the end of 1941; in January, 1942, he did not receive his usual invitation to Göring's birthday party in Berlin, apparently because he had been helping himself too freely to stolen goods. The baron engaged in a rather busy sexual life as well. He had an English wife in Berlin and a mistress, Ilse Putz, in Paris. For a while Fraulein Putz worked in the Jeu de Paume, but when the opposition to her lover grew quite serious, the young lady found herself transferred to Kiev, and Frau von Behr arrived to stand beside her husband.

Von Behr used any methods available to advance himself politically and financially. He often used criminal types to make his confiscations, which were carried out without regard for either the owners or their valuable property. Irresponsible men collected truckloads of art, took them directly to the Jeu de Paume, dumped the contents of their trucks, and disappeared. These enormous loads could not then be classified properly, for the art historians on the staff were swamped with work and handicapped by the lack of an art reference-library. (The E.R.R. confiscated thousands of books, but these all went into storage depositories elsewhere.) When the historians protested to Von Behr, he would call in Fraulein Putz, who then marked everything "Unknown" as to origin and shipped the cases to Neuschwanstein Castle, a German repository for stolen art objects. To add to this chaos, personnel inside the museum came and went; they were taken off their jobs periodically to arrange exhibitions for Göring, to go out with the S.D. to look for Jews to be shipped to concentration camps, or to accompany French collaborationist police following leads supplied to Von Behr by other collaborators—often Jews whom he forced to work for him by threats of concentration camps and forced labor.

The most disputed figure inside the Jeu de Paume was Dr. Bruno Lohse, a 1936 graduate of the University of Frankfort and a free-lance art dealer and adviser specializing in seventeenth-century Dutch and German art before the outbreak of war. He had enlisted in the Wehrmacht partly out of a sense of patriotism and partly to avoid a possible draft by the S.S., an organization he had come to dislike after having worked for it as a civilian sports instructor during his university years. He served as a driver for a field hospital and then for a tank battalion, spent a few weeks in a hospital himself, and was a private first class in a replacement unit on January 22, 1941, when he was sent, to his surprise, on a month's temporary assignment to the Special Staff for Pictorial Arts in Rosenberg's Paris service. He reported to Von Behr and learned that his job was to work on inventories of confiscated art and to select, from the mass of material picked up by laymen, the works worthy of shipment to Germany. Neither he nor his immediate superior, then Dr. Günther Schiedlausky, liked this action or the job itself. Lohse, the son of a musician in the Berlin Philharmonic and the product of an internationally minded artistic home, was not anti-Semitic and did not approve of this kind of treatment of works of art. He asked to be sent back into combat at the end of his assignment.

Just before that moment arrived, Göring came to Paris to see a collection of seventeenth-century Dutch art on exhibit for him in the Jeu de Paume, and Lohse was sent over from the Louvre, where he worked, to show the Reichsmarschall around. His performance so pleased the Reichsmarschall that Göring ordered an extension of Lohse's temporary assignment by the simple expedient of transferring him to the Luftwaffe, as a corporal, and added a special job: scouting the Paris art market for paintings in his field to be shown to Göring on his visits. The new job was an improvement only because it freed Lohse somewhat from the Rosenberg staff activities, and he asked "eight or ten" times to be returned to active duty. Göring constantly refused him until March, 1944. At that time Lohse broke his left foot and injured his right knee in an accident while on furlough, after which Göring agreed to remove Lohse from his work in the museum, although he did retain him in Paris.

Not empowered to act independently, always subordinate to Von Behr in Paris, whom he despised, and to Robert Scholz and Gerhardt Utikal in Berlin, Lohse was completely devoted to Göring, whom he loved and served to the best of his ability as a soldier obeying orders and as an art historian. Lohse, however, did not devise or profit from the Göring exchanges about which the Reichsmarschall had boasted as early as 1940. He presented paintings that Göring approved or disapproved; Walter Hofer, Göring's personal curator, suggested what paintings should be offered in exchange, as his confidential letters to his employer indicate; and Von Behr signed all the documents. For Lohse's loyalty and work, Göring returned affection and trust in the young man's judgment and behavior; he did not confide his business dealings to him.

During his years in Paris the tall, slim, energetic Lohse managed to make a few loyal friends and some deadly enemies. He had an athlete's vitality, a win-or-lose attitude toward life, personal courage, a scholarly love of art, and enough assurance to use his influence with Göring to help others—his German companions, the French with whom he came in contact, and Jews. The last category made his relations with Von Behr even more tense after the establishment of concentration camps, from which Lohse managed to save a considerable number. Once he went to Amsterdam and arranged matters so that the famous art historian Max J. Friedlaender (Director of the Prussian State Museums from 1929 to 1933) was excused from wearing the yellow star and was allowed access to libraries and museums and to keep his personal library. The Führer's headquarters did not like this, but Göring approved. Lohse's actions in Paris made him the object of suspicion to the Gestapo and the military government, but he continued to help art dealers and historians, friends of his family, and relations of his friends, whenever and however he could, with money, food, transportation, or quite literally by snatching people from concentration camps or out of police stations after predawn raids.

The Gestapo also suspected and watched Lohse for his attachment to a young Frenchwoman of Polish origin, a worker for De Gaulle and a fierce anti-Nazi. The couple were engaged but obviously could not marry during that period. Lohse had earned a large amount of money in the year before the war and, like all Germans, got a favorable rate in exchanging marks for Occupation francs. He used the money to supplement his corporal's pay and to take his fiancée along on his scouting trips and furloughs. On their last trip, when his funds had run out, the young lady sold her watch and paid her own way.

Lohse's fellow-workers, who feared his influence with Göring, watched him too, spread gossip, and supplied misinformation that went into a report made to French authorities in 1944. Full of insinuations, the document made him a complete villain, Von Behr's willing assistant, and the chief of the E.R.R., hinted that he was a coward, charged him with petty and grand larceny, and labeled his fiancée his mistress. In 1945 U.S. Army officers, questioning Lohse at length, found him totally unlike this description and among the few "decent" Germans interrogated and very forthright in his replies, which were confirmed by his colleague Dr. Walter Borchers, present during the questioning at Lohse's insistence.

Dr. Borchers, an art historian and the head of the scientific staff from 1942, was the man found least objectionable in a parallel French report, which added that he performed his duties as honestly and as well as he could and without personal gain. The American opinion of Borchers was that he was honest, learned, and sensitive but a poor judge of human character. In practice, his performance as the head of the German staff in the Jeu de Paume left much to be desired, for Borchers could not impose his goodwill toward art upon Von Behr, and he was not much of an administrator. His German colleagues found him a gossip. The Gestapo wanted to send him to a concentration camp for defeatist remarks, and he was saved from this fate only through the efforts of Robert Scholz and Lohse. Borchers did not like Lohse personally but admitted after the war in sworn testimony that Lohse had intervened in his favor several times, although the two were not friends and differed in their opinions, not only on politics but also on how the Paris operation should be handled. Borchers also antagonized both men and women staff members by accusations of theft which he then had to retract, although such remarks were less dangerous to his personal safety than were his anti-Nazi remarks addressed to party members. At one point Göring was so annoyed he wanted to send Borchers to the front. Lohse offered to go instead on the grounds that he was a better soldier, and Göring abandoned the idea.

During the chaotic summer of 1944, when it became clear that the war would end badly for the Nazis, Von Behr not only removed the sentries from the Jeu de Paume but also sent all the male members of the staff to the "Majestic" security regiment of the German Occupation Army in Paris. Borchers did not protest this any more than he attempted to stop the shipment of crates of modern art to Germany on August 1, 1944. Lohse, no longer a member of the group, was on the Normandy front and exhorting regiments of Hitler Youth to spare French châteaux and monuments.[1] He returned to Paris on August 5 or 6 and went to his apartment on the Avenue d'Iéna in the building that also housed offices of the Amt Westen. When he discovered the shocking conditions at the museum, he confronted Von Behr in a violent, noisy quarrel.[2] Lohse wanted the sentries replaced and the male historians returned to their jobs. To this Von Behr agreed, but he refused another demand: that all the art remaining in the Jeu de Paume be immediately transferred to the Louvre for safe-keeping by the French.

Lohse then decided to go to Berlin to get an order from Göring. Carrying only a briefcase and intent on speedy return, he left on August 8. In Berlin he found that the Reichsmarschall was suffering from an attack of angina and did not manage to see him until August 13. Göring gave the order for the immediate transferal of the art and for a carrier plane for Lohse's return trip. No plane was available,

[1] Sworn statement delivered in Metz by Walter Hauck, June 21, 1948.

[2] Testimony before a Bayreuth court by Arthur Garbas, clerk attached to the Amt Westen, March 21, 1950.

and after two days' wait Lohse took the train to Saarbrücken and then commandeered a car, driving into Paris against the stream of departing troops. He arrived on August 18—too late. Von Behr, aware of Lohse's Berlin trip and afraid of Göring's wrath, had transferred the art, dismissed his staff, and closed the Jeu de Paume. In the confusion of departure duplicate copies of all documents had been left behind. Lohse reported to the remaining Luftwaffe unit in Paris under Colonel von Cassel.

The staff member in Paris who knew the least about art was Lieutenant Hermann von Ingram, a hero in the early days of the war and recipient of the Ritterskreuz, the highest order of the Iron Cross, for the 1940 Belgian campaign. Promoted in the field, he was retired to inactive duty and sent to Paris, where Von Behr used him to cement relations between the E.R.R. and the military command. Von Ingram, who had been a minor customs official before 1939, was the soul of integrity, conscientious and devoid of imagination. His relations with Lohse were satisfactory until he made the mistake of marrying art historian Annamarie Tomförde. Frau von Ingram-Tomförde presented herself with expensive wedding gifts from Jewish confiscations: rugs, furniture, and a valuable silver tea-service from the David-Weill collection. Eventually Von Ingram left Paris of his own volition but carrying no loot. However, on a visit to his wife on February 13, 1943, he took twenty-two rugs. Despite two general searches conducted in inquiries on theft, temptation was great, for the example set by Hitler, Göring, and the chiefs was poor. Rosenberg "acquired" fifty-three paintings; Von Behr stole unscrupulously.

The scientific staff began to work in the Musée de Jeu de Paume in October, 1940. To indicate his independence of the German Embassy, Von Behr had asked for a separate building for his group. The German Military Command first suggested three rooms in the Louvre for storage of the art that already filled the Embassy at that date. Jacques Jaujard, unable to counter this order and thinking that Louvre storage would give him some control over confiscated art, agreed, but it was soon quite evident that the space allotted was too small. Von Behr then demanded the use of the independently located Jeu de Paume, whose site, facing the Place de la Concorde and at the far end of the Tuileries Gardens, gave him the isolation he wanted. Metternich, who had arranged for the use of the Louvre, acceded to the baron's wishes.

Jaujard met with Bunjes, Von Behr, and Metternich on October 31 and left the meeting believing that the Germans would permit a French inventory of the art collected in the museum. This agreement was verbal, but the French thought they had scored a point, which Jaujard repeated in a letter to Metternich confirming the cession of the Jeu de Paume. A copy of this letter went to the Fine Arts Division of the Vichy Government. A short while later, Jaujard received a reply indicating that "some restrictions" had been added to the problem of inventories, and it was immediately clear that any French hopes of control over confiscated art were not to come to fruition.

When the E.R.R. arrived at the Jeu de Paume, however, several French museum workers were present.[3] Among them was Mlle. Rose Valland, then forty-two years old,[4] who had been a curator at the Jeu de Paume for ten years.

On that last day of October, German trucks loaded with cases of art from the Louvre storage rooms and the German Embassy rolled up to the front door, and the place became a beehive of activity at once. Four hundred cases were opened in one day, and according to Miss Valland, valuable paintings were stacked up against the nearest convenient walls, whence some of them slipped down under army boots. (The Jeu de Paume is small as museums go, roughly three hundred feet long and about a hundred wide, with several interior walls dividing up its two stories for the display of paintings in normal periods.)

Plainly, inventory-taking under such conditions was impractical, if not impossible, but Miss Valland found herself a corner, took out a notebook, and worked all morning while the activity around her grew more and more feverish, for the museum expected a visitor. Reichsmarschall Göring would expect a very special display of art on this visit, the first in a series of twenty between November 3, 1940, and November 27, 1942.

The man who set up the exhibition for Göring was Dr. Günther Schiedlausky, an art historian born in 1907 and a one-time curator of the Berlin State Museums who had been charged at the outbreak of the war with the protection of Berlin museum art. Schiedlausky's "career" during the war was marked by considerable movement. Drafted in June, 1940, he was assigned to a motor-transport division

[3] Rose Valland, *Le Front de l'art* (Paris: Plon, 1961), pp. 57–58.

[4] On December 28, 1948, Miss Valland appeared in a French military court in a confrontation with Lohse. She stated her age then as fifty (Document 113, d'Inscription au Registre Spécial).

for four months and then sent to the Kunstschutz in Paris, at the lowest rank permitted on a civilian level but as a captain in the army. He had been there a month when the E.R.R. sent for him, and he set up ten shows of art for Göring and one for Rosenberg between November, 1940, and December 1, 1941, when he was sent to the eastern front for six months. After that he was put in charge of the Neuschwanstein repository for a short period and then sent out again, this time to the Russian front. In July, 1942, a Luftwaffe transfer sent him back to Paris until February, 1944, when he went back to Neuschwanstein and took charge of the details of the removal of some objects to Alt Aussee in Austria. He tried to bring some order and method into whatever task he fulfilled, although he worked against almost impossible odds.

At noon on the exhibition day, November 3, according to Miss Valland, "a tall, uniformed figure appeared. . . . He went directly to the notebook on which a tentative inventory was written and closed the book with a categorical gesture." The tall man was Dr. Bunjes, who also dismissed several other French curators sent over to work with Miss Valland and told them not to return.

Rose Valland did not exactly know why she decided not to leave the museum with her dismissed co-workers nor even what she would do, since the inventory she had been taking was now forbidden. She did not know what would happen to her amidst all the Germans, soldiers, policemen, and art experts, all walking around the museum as if they owned it. She stayed and watched while eight uniformed men took over the offices and others stood guard at the door, while in the exhibition rooms white-smocked experts hung paintings and arranged furniture. The only French workers that day were five guards who tended the furnaces and cleaned up and two other maintenance specialists transferred from the Louvre.

To make certain that everything was properly arranged for Göring's visit, Baron von Behr turned up at the museum later in the day. In full uniform, his cap visor shading his glass eye, the tall sexagenarian was "still in a state of euphoria over the victory." He spoke French quite well, and in what Miss Valland described as a worldly conversation, during which he tried to prove that he was not a barbarian, he graciously granted her permission to remain at her post in the museum. Only those with a pass issued by Von Behr could get past the sentries. For the next four years Rose Valland passed through the doors each morning and went home at night. Every two or three days she passed on whatever scraps of information she managed to glean to Jaujard and two other Louvre curators.[5]

Göring arrived at the museum in civilian clothes, a long overcoat reaching to his ankles and a soft hat with brim turned up to expose his forehead. He and his party, Walter Hofer and leading figures of the Luftwaffe and the E.R.R., walked in upon expensive rugs covering the floors and feasted their eyes upon walls covered with paintings that had been owned by the art dealer Seligmann and the Baron Edouard de Rothschild. Göring was so dazzled by his first examination that he prolonged his stay in Paris and returned two days later to view a fresh batch of paintings that replaced the first exhibit. At the end of his second visit he took over the Einsatzstab in the following words:

> I order the following disposition of the objects of art transported to the Louvre:
> 1. Works that the Führer shall have the right to dispose of.
> 2. Works that will complete the collections of the Reichsmarschall.
> 3. Art objects and libraries which seem desirable for use by the Höhe Schule of the party and within the sphere of Reichsleiter Rosenberg.
> 4. Works of art intended for German museums will be immediately inventoried, packed, and sent to Germany with the aid of the Luftwaffe.
> 5. Works of art intended for French museums and French and German art dealers will be sold at auction, at a time to be announced later. The money received will be turned over to the French [Vichy] Government for distribution to war widows and orphans.
> 6. Subsequent measures concerning art belonging to Jews will be taken in the manner that has already shown its value in the work of the Einsatzstab Rosenberg, working in collaboration with the head of the military government in Paris.

[5] Valland, pp. 58 and 79. Exactly how this information was presented is uncertain. When I wrote Miss Valland—now retired and living in Paris, where as late as 1969 she headed the Louvre Committee for the Preservation of Art in the Event of Armed Conflict—and asked for an interview during a visit to Paris, she refused "categorically" to see me and added that she thus rendered me, as well as others who made this request, "a greater service" (letter to the author, February 12, 1969).

I will submit this proposition to the Führer. While awaiting his decision, this procedure remains in force.

[Signed] Göring

The news of Göring's visit and edict brought immediate action from the E.R.R. office in Berlin. Rosenberg sent Scholz to Paris to determine the extent of Göring's interest,[6] and Scholz equivocally reported that he thought the confiscations were not ideologically consistent with the political functions of the Rosenberg operation. Hitler, however, did not alter the Göring proposition in any way (and possibly never even saw it). The first four articles remained in force throughout the Occupation, with a constantly growing disproportion in favor of Article 2. Göring, in one stroke, had put an end to the claims of Abetz, Von Kuensberg, and Von Ribbentrop; the Kunstschutz was entirely helpless; and the E.R.R, although under Göring's rather than Rosenberg's power, had everything it needed to take whatever it could get.

Rosenberg's discontent at his loss of power was undoubtedly increased when he received a letter from Göring two weeks later informing him that his appointment as head of the E.R.R. had been hesitantly made in the first place but that Göring had approved it. The letter continued with mention of the assistance given in the way of transport and cover by the Luftwaffe. The final blow was a reference to Göring's discovery of many secret hiding places of property owned by Jews—through the bribery of French detectives, hired agents, and an investigation of foreign exchange and the contents of bank vaults. Göring indicated that the results of his discoveries would be passed on to the E.R.R., which would then be required to take suitable action.

The National Museums and the French Treasury asked again for a French inventory and the right to have French civil servants enter homes and apartments sealed by the Germans and thus supervise the

[6] Göring was so much in command of the E.R.R. that he used the Jeu de Paume for an exhibition, "Front Line Art," which ran for twelve weeks in either 1942 or 1943. According to Bruno Lohse (in a letter to the author dated March 13, 1970), all the work was executed by soldiers, and *only* soldiers were allowed entry to the show. One German soldier who saw it recalls it as "a terrible propaganda exhibition . . . of war experiences in the style of the Nazis." The poster for this exhibition in Paris shows the swastika, the title of the exhibit in French ("*L'Art au Front*"), the dates ("1 *août*–16 *novembre*"), and the hours of admission. It must be noted that neither the E.R.R. nor the French were responsible in any way for this showing of paintings, drawings, and sculpture in approved Nazi style.

handling of the property of absent owners. The German Military Command in Paris neither answered nor acknowledged the letters written by French authorities. The Jeu de Paume remained under military guard, opening its doors only to truckloads of confiscated art. By mid-November, 1940, most of the Rothschild, Kann, Weil-Picard, Wildenstein, and Seligmann collections had been confiscated, and what followed after, in slightly smaller quantity, was of the same superb caliber. Göring returned to Paris early in February, 1941, and on February 5 announced that the Führer's choice of art objects and the pieces that he wanted to buy for his own collection were to be loaded immediately into two cars attached to his special train for the return trip to Berlin.

A Vichy law, dated October 5, 1940, gave custody of sequestered French property to France for safekeeping or sale, if necessary. The legal status of the confiscated art made Dr. Bunjes slightly uneasy, and he protested feebly to Göring. The Reichsmarschall simply announced that he would take up the matter with the Führer, adding that the objects would be taxed and sums of money equivalent to their value would be placed in a blocked account. A French graphic artist, Jacques Beltrand, valued the art at ridiculously low prices, but this was of slight importance, for no money was ever placed in any bank. Rosenberg's dismay at the impending action resulted in a hasty trip from Berlin to Paris by Robert Scholz, who arrived too late to put a stop to the proceedings, because "the cars were already loaded."

The first transport, on February 8, 1941, held some of the most precious art works in France. One special group of seven old masters—a Teniers, a Rubens, a Cranach, a Boucher, a Goya, a Rembrandt, and a Franz Hals—came from the Jonas collection and had been brought from Bordeaux by Luftwaffe pilots flying military planes. Five special black packing cases, made to order for the Rothschilds, were also included. Hitler's share of the two carloads was a select group of Rothschild possessions: fifty-three paintings and six eighteenth-century chests. (As late as July 16, 1941, Dr. Posse wrote a letter complaining that some of the pieces had not yet arrived to be inventoried for Linz.) Göring's greed is the more notable when we remember that between the first load and the last on July 15, 1944, more than twenty-one thousand works of art left the Place de la Concorde for Germany.

During their most fruitful year, 1941, the Germans seized, among many others, eleven Rothschild collections in Paris and at several family châteaux: Lafite, Mouton-Rothschild, La Muette, Dreux, Armanvilliers, and Ferrières, the last property being further spoiled when it was taken over by a Göring order and "improved" with a cement swimming-pool. At Lafitte a collection worth several million dollars was transferred to an agent of Abetz by a Judas who received a few thousand francs for his treachery. At Mouton-Rothschild two Registry Board receivers notified the prefect of the department of the proprietor's absence and the presence of his art collection. The prefect passed on the information to the German authorities because he believed that the money from sales of confiscated property would benefit war widows and orphans. Cases filled with paintings by Picasso, Braque, Matisse, and Renoir took off for the Jeu de Paume in December. Philippe de Rothschild left some of his collection in a bank vault in Arcachon. Under the ruling that such vaults were to be investigated and then sealed, all the property was seized. Hitler's reasoning entitled him to such valuables since the wealth of European Jews of German ancestry really belonged to the Reich.

One Rothschild collection, however, never reached the E.R.R. The French National Museums had moved their own paintings from Loc-Dieu, too damp and cold for the winter, to the Ingres Museum in Montauban, farther south. One day in April the Treasury Department notified the curators that a great many cases belonging to Robert de Rothschild had been found abandoned on a road in Auvergne and taken into custody as French property. Did the curators wish to handle them? Curators and Treasury officials made the necessary arrangements, and the entire lot was taken to Montauban, where several more cases belonging to Maurice de Rothschild joined them in September, again after sequestration by the Treasury. To prevent the Germans from knowing that this art existed, the National Museums and the Treasury set up a general meeting of curators from several parts of France. Each one selected what would most naturally fit into his own museum's collection (from Persian art to Picasso). The Treasury then provided antedated papers of prewar acquisition to hide the art in inventories. What the museums did not want—very little, indeed—was returned to the Treasury. As soon as the war ended, the works were returned to their rightful owners. Meanwhile they were safe in their own boxes, prettily striped with blue and yellow, the Rothschild racing colors. These remained until 1943, when a young curator with some knowledge of the track pointed out the danger of such identification being known to German visiting inspectors. A great washing and scratching removed the stripes a few days before the next inspection.

The National Museums were less fortunate with other collections stored with their own. After one German inspection tour Chambord had to hand over seven Jewish collections, and Sourches very reluctantly parted with two, one of them owned by David-Weill, of the Louvre's board of trustees. Thus, 130 cases of one of the most fabulous collections of antique silver and gold objects turned up in the Jeu de Paume to dazzle the Nazis. Other lots of art were uncovered by the Divisenschutzkommando in bank vaults in Paris and occupied France. This group, really a parallel to the E.R.R., was primarily interested in money and foreign exchange but took anything else it could find when examining strong rooms and safety-deposit boxes. In 1940 Picasso had placed his most valuable canvases in a bank strongroom in Paris. His vault adjoined two rented by Matisse for storage of his own works. Neither Picasso nor Matisse was a Jew, but both painted very valuable "degenerate" works. Non-Jews were permitted the right to be present when their vaults were inspected. When it was the turn of the two artists, Matisse, recuperating after a major operation, could not be present, and Picasso did the honors for himself and for his friend. He insisted on having all three vaults opened at once for two Nazi soldiers whom he so bewildered by double-talk and by dashing from one room to the other, and so impressed by his haughty manner, that he managed to save all the paintings from confiscation. The soldiers could not tell one artist's work from the other's, believed that they had seen everything when they actually saw the same few works over and over, and left convinced that the collections worth millions were not worth picking up.

Paul Rosenberg, the art dealer, was much less lucky. He had left for business in the United States early in June, 1940, after placing part of his superb collection of contemporary art in a bank vault in Libourne, near Bordeaux. Another group of paintings remained in his country house nearby, watched over by two devoted employees waiting to see the works packed and shipped to New York, according to arrangements the owner had made before his departure. The shipping company, after twice telephoning to inquire how many cases would be needed, finally told the employees that the customs house had closed for the duration and they really did not want to take on the job. Rosenberg's secretary wrote New York for new instructions, but before he could receive an answer, several Germans, a Frenchman, and an Italian turned up at the house, inspected the cases and their contents, and carted them off. The Luftwaffe brought most of Rosenberg's collection from bank vault and country house to the Jeu de Paume, and for the next several years the magnificent collection traveled widely as it passed from hand to greedy hand. Rosenberg's house and gallery in Paris were likewise emptied of paintings, furniture, books, and the complete photographic file of the art stolen—4,500 photographs, valuable for identification purposes. Part of the file was saved because it fell into the hands of Louise Leiris—the "Aryan" sister-in-law of Daniel Kahnweiler, Picasso's dealer—who ran Kahnweiler's gallery while the owner and his wife sought refuge in the unoccupied zone. The entire file was offered to Mme. Leiris, but she purchased only 1,200 photographs of works by Picasso, Braque, Léger, and Masson after consultation with Picasso, who urged her to buy them. The other 3,300 photographs passed through the hands of two agents before their sale to a Parisian press agency in the fall of 1943 for the derisory price of a hundred thousand Occupation francs. Rosenberg's house on the Rue de la Boëtie in the fashionable Eighth Arrondissement became the Institute for the Study of Jewish Questions.

The mountains of art and art objects arrived in a steady stream at the Jeu de Paume, turning its ground floor into a warehouse and its second floor into a gallery where constant exhibitions helped the Nazis decide what went to Germany and what to the Paris art market. Rose Valland remained, carrying on what she described as a kind of espionage activity,[7] discovering the locations of art repositories: three Bavarian castles, the Führerbau in Munich, two sites in Czechoslovakia, and two in Austria. By passing on this information to her superiors, she prevented Allied bombing of the sites.

The locations of the repositories were noted in the packers' book, which was always left on a table in the museum "for the convenience of all concerned"; above the table a list was posted daily indicating the shipping orders and the destinations of the crates of art. Also, as often as they could, the Germans left the museum for lunch, leaving promptly at noon and returning at two, and she was left there alone. Since the historians had neither locked drawers nor a safe, all of their material was readily at her disposal.[8]

During the lifetime of the E.R.R., Von Behr dismissed Miss Valland four times for reasons quite apart from her "spying" activities.

[7] Valland, pp. 78–80.

[8] Bruno Lohse, letter to the author, May 10, 1970.

Each time it was Bruno Lohse who insisted that she be permitted to return. German art historians, in general, are not experts in French art—and the reverse is freely admitted by French art historians, for the weakest spot in the Louvre collections is its paltry selection of German paintings. Miss Valland's ability to identify French art in private collections was gratefully accepted by her German colleagues, who had an unconscionable amount of work and no art reference-library at hand.

The French workers who tended furnaces, cleaned, did odd jobs, drove trucks, or packed art were also subject to summary dismissal. Miss Valland used them as her extra eyes and ears and somehow managed to retain two of them constantly, a talkative packer named Alexandre and a driver who transported crates to railroad stations or other departure points. She also listened to gossip, some of it malicious and personal, and was the occasional confidante of disgruntled members of the E.R.R. staff, none of whom particularly enjoyed the job to be done. From these bits and pieces she compiled reports for French authorities. Copies of the reports were turned over to the Americans in charge of art restitution after the liberation of Paris. They thus became part of American archives and can be compared or contrasted with American reports based on prolonged questioning of the individuals directly concerned.

Miss Valland was only once caught outright in the business of copying down addresses, but she managed to make her questioners disbelieve their eyes. She felt that after this her presence became annoying and that Von Behr had decided to liquidate her before the war ended by taking her to Germany and shooting her once past the frontier.[9]

[9] This story is told in Valland's *Le Front de l'art* on pages 83–84 and in a footnote on page 84. The footnote states that this evidence was given during a *confrontation* at the military court of Paris between "a member of the E.R.R." and herself on December 23, 1950. A *confrontation* between Bruno Lohse and Rose Valland took place on December 28, 1948, but this *confrontation* record does not include such a statement. A later *confrontation* between Rose Valland and Utikal may be the one referred to. However, Bruno Lohse denies (in a letter to the author, May 10, 1970) that anybody intended to kill Miss Valland. He adds that the only time she was in danger of being taken to Germany, she was unaware of the threat. Von Behr wished to send some of the skilled French packers to Bavaria to work with Schiedlausky on repacking art to be moved in the final days of the war, since no skilled German labor was then available. Miss Valland was to be sent along to keep her silent about the operation, and Von Behr was convinced that she would be safe in Germany because of her good relationship with the E.R.R. historians. During discussions on this idea there was never mention of "liquidation." Lohse, who thought the idea impractical and risky, finally appealed to Göring, behind Von Behr's back, and the entire idea was dropped.

Jaujard and the National Museums never ceased their efforts to save the confiscated art. On June 3, 1941, with the Ministry of Youth and Sports, they wrote the German Military Commander. Two weeks later, Admiral François Darlan, Vice-President of the French Council, also wrote. A group important in the art world asked for an audience with Fernand de Brinon, Vichy Ambassador to the German Military Government in Paris. On June 26 the Treasury wrote a letter stressing Article 46 of the Hague Convention of 1907—the guarantee of the inviolability of private property.[10] Silence answered all the letters. The General Commission for Jewish Affairs sent a letter, July 25, 1941, to Dr. Werner Best, the S.S. Administrative Chief for Occupied Paris. Finally Darlan received a reply: The seizure of Jewish property was a political rather than a military decision and should be taken up with Foreign Minister von Ribbentrop. On November 3, 1941, Utikal issued a violent manifesto that settled the problem once and for all. The French now knew that as long as Hitler remained in power, the confiscation of Jewish property would continue.

By late 1941 the E.R.R. had collected so much French art that Robert Scholz wanted the entire Paris operation to close down. Rosenberg, however, had other ideas after a trip through the eastern part of Germany, where the "terrible living conditions" of party officials suffering from the effects of Allied bombing raids affected him deeply. He wrote a letter to Hitler, more effective than asking for an audience, for the Führer found him a bore and avoided him whenever he could. Once, in fact, Rosenberg had to wait nine months to see his chief. Rosenberg, this time, suggested the seizure of furnishings in "ownerless" Jewish residences and the transport of everything into Germany. Hitler accepted this idea wholeheartedly, and "Action M"—after the German word for "furniture," *Möbel*—was born.

This action got under way in March, 1942, with Von Behr enthu-

[10] On May 16, 1942, Dr. Bunjes wrote a paper in which he stated that the 1940 armistice was made with the French and *not* with Jews and Freemasons. Thus the Reich was not bound to respect Jewish property rights. Jews and Communists had made attempts on the lives and persons of the Wehrmacht and German civilians and had to be punished severely. French protests indicated that the French Government wished to deceive the Reich and to abet anti-German subversive activities. Access to German inventories by the French would lead to espionage. The protests were motivated by a desire to stir up anti-German cultural propaganda, to resist German claims for the return to the Reich of cultural material destroyed or stolen by French soldiers, and to discount the nobility and altruism of German action to preserve French cultural material.

siastically in charge, for he saw a way to have a much freer hand without any inventories at all and the possibility that any fine art found in the homes would be his to dispose of. Scholz, however, disliked Von Behr and believed that these actions were detrimental to the reputation of the Nazi party, since the wholesale confiscations had been so disorderly that if final disposition of the works of art was referred to an international commission after the war (and he expected this to happen), German prestige would suffer. He and Lieutenant von Ingram put together a "revision" report, asking for cataloging and conservation of works of art. The report also asked for control of everything collected under "Action M" and power to withdraw and "freeze" any art objects collected in order to stop further misuse of valuable works.

On June 18, 1942, Rosenberg wrote to Göring informing him that he could make no more personal selections but that the art historians were at his disposal and Bruno Lohse might remain as the Reichsmarschall's aide for "special duties." This statement did not affect Von Behr–the man Scholz really wished to remove–who remained in power until January, 1943, when the Dienstelle Louvre became slightly less aggressive in its actions. The Jeu de Paume continued to be alternately a love nest (during one agitated period three of the men had simultaneous and tangled affairs with four of the women), a military camp, an exhibition hall, a central shipping office, and a hornets' nest of petty quarrels and grand larceny. By the time the liberation of Paris sent the staff flying in confusion, Rosenberg's task force had taken 101 large collections of art and seized the contents of 69,919 houses and apartments throughout France.

The cynicism showed by the German authorities did nothing to relieve the fears of the National Museums for their own collections. The Louvre's most valuable paintings were momentarily fairly secure in Montauban, but racial laws affected both administrative personnel and guards.[11] Most of the Jewish guards had been sent into the unoccupied zone to protect them from imprisonment and deportation, but the Vichy Government gradually weeded out such people on one pretext or another. The Louvre also protected its curators. One of the world's greatest authorities on medieval art, for example, left Montauban with the assistance of a Franco-American aid society. He

[11] Racial laws in France differed from those enforced in Germany, where one Jewish parent or grandparent sufficed to render the individual a Jew. In France an "Aryan" came of pure "Aryan" stock; a "non-Jew" might have two "Aryan" and two Jewish grandparents; a Jew was one with either all or three Jewish grandparents.

went to New York, where the Metropolitan Museum welcomed him. Other curators were affected by the laws condemning those "guilty of political actions or writings condemning Fascism." Among these, one was arrested in Toulouse and imprisoned for a year. When he was released, he joined the active Resistance.

To replace these guards and curators, Vichy sent groups of young men who fulfilled their military service by working for the museums. Thus a group of young art students from Toulouse University helped in inventory and cataloging. To prevent these students from being shipped off to Germany as part of forced-labor battalions, the museums called them chiefs but invested them with duties they performed only as assistants. Many of them became important museum personnel after the war. Many of the older guards joined the Maquis in large numbers, carrying their F.F.I. (Forces Françaises de l'Intérieur—the internal Resistance—as contrasted with De Gaulle's Free French, the F.F.L.) armbands in their pockets during the day and slipping out at night to help in acts of sabotage. According to one of them, the veteran aides were all provided with false traveling passes and papers for both France and Germany so that "if the Germans took the collections, the guards could follow wherever they went."

Ordinary life in Montauban was busy enough. Curators took paintings in and out of cases, studied them, and even made some interesting discoveries that grew out of close association with the masterpieces. Everybody was also constantly preoccupied with finding enough to eat. Nobody was ever fully satisfied with the scanty rations allowed, and the women resorted to the usual expedients of keeping chickens, rabbits, ducks, even guinea pigs, in kitchens and on tiny grass plots. The curators were faced with the problem of finding something besides turnip soup, the staple Occupation meal all over the country, to serve not only themselves but also their fellow curators who dropped in unexpectedly from Paris or other art depositories—written communication between zones was difficult and often dangerous and phone calls had to be routed through Vichy.

Other visitors—friendly, curious, or ominous—also appeared unannounced. The friendly were writers or historians; the curious were journalists eager for bits of gossip; the ominous were German and Vichy officials. The Montauban curators found Metternich polite and worldly, a bit distressed by his role, and an interested, cultivated amateur of art. As for Abel Bonnard, Vichy Minister of Education, he was "sinister," self-satisfied, and icily indifferent to the fate of less-fortunate curators whose choice of ancestors made life so difficult. When the war ended, Bonnard left the position he had so badly misused to flee to Spain. A French court condemned him to death in absentia.

Montauban was the seat of a meeting between French and Spanish museum officials which arranged an exchange of art with Spain in 1941 after long discussions that had begun in December, 1940. Although never put into words, the Spanish point of view was quite clear: Spain meant to be paid for its neutrality. Pétain, who had close ties with Spain, was ready to make concessions. The position taken by Jaujard and his aides was a compromise between the definite No that they wished to give and the realization that this was impossible in 1941. Hence Jaujard on this occasion and in the years to come always countered a question of the removal of a painting with an offer of an exchange. The one thing to avoid, each time, was rape. Spain's demands were high: the finest Murillo in the Louvre and all the crowns of the Visigoth kings, found near Toledo and legally sold to the Cluny Museum in Paris by their discoverer. One crown remained in France, and the rest went to Spain, but after long discussions with Spanish museums the French received two portraits, one by El Greco and one by Velázquez, a few drawings, and some tapestry cartoons based on Goya compositions. Since Vichy did nothing to back up its own museums, the deal was probably the best that could be made.

The Germans also wanted works from the Louvre collection. Early in 1941 Von Ribbentrop indicated his desire for Boucher's "Diana," a delightful example of eighteenth-century French nudes. The painting was taken to Paris from Montauban by order of Admiral Darlan (not always on the side of the angels) and traveled into Germany, where Ribbentrop offered a stolen Impressionist work for this exquisite masterpiece. The French invoked the principle of free exchange and asked for the Watteau paintings in Dresden and Berlin and the ceiling paintings in Potsdam's Sans Souci Palace. Of course, German curators refused to cede these works, and Ribbentrop, highly annoyed, sent the painting back to France. Ribbentrop's art holdings, established by the United States Army, included nine Gobelins tapestries, forty-seven valuable carpets, twenty-six paintings of French origin, and six "doubtful" works. His version, narrated in pretrial interrogations at Nuremberg, was quite different. He protested that he owned only "five or six cheap paintings" that he had purchased legally and furthermore did not own a Gobelins tapestry about which he was questioned, for he could not remember ever having seen it hanging on the wall of his elaborate home in Füssel—"not really his personal home," for it belonged to the Reich. He had refused the "Diana" because the French demanded two works by Vermeer in exchange, and he could not afford to buy such expensive paintings. At the conclusion of this testimony, a tangled web of lies and protests as to his own honesty, he added lamely that there was a "possibility of lack of memory" because he had "no files, no documents, and no basic information."

The Ribbentrop affair was easily handled, but the National Museums were dealt a stunning blow when Belgium's greatest art treasure, the Ghent altarpiece—"The Mystic Lamb," by Jan van Eyck—was literally lifted from its place of refuge in the Pau Museum. The Belgian Government had confided the work to the French for safekeeping in May, 1940, for it had figured prominently in the 1919 Versailles Treaty as part of German reparations. Count Metternich had guaranteed that nobody would take the painting without a document signed by himself, by the burgomaster of Ghent, and by Jaujard. With such a promise, Jaujard had been able to reassure the Belgians, who inquired constantly about their treasure.

On August 3, 1942, the director of the Munich State Museums presented himself at the Pau Museum with a paper signed by a Vichy official demanding the painting. The curator stalled by asking for time to send telegrams for confirmation. Abel Bonnard replied immediately, via yellow official telegram, ordering the curator to hand over the painting. The message sent to Jaujard in Paris never reached its destination, for it had to pass through the switchboard at Vichy, which held up even the curator's factual report until the seventeen carefully boxed wooden panels had been picked up by a German military truck and had passed across the frontier.

At almost the same time that the report reached Paris, the Belgians asked the Louvre whether they might visit Pau to inspect the work and were told what had happened. The scandal raced around the world. The Belgian protest to the French Government was politely shunted into "diplomatic channels," but the entire body of French curators stood solidly behind Jaujard, who addressed his own protest to Vichy. Bonnard was furious and telephoned the Louvre that all this fuss was inexcusable and that he would "take measures." Metternich lost his post for daring to criticize the action, and Jaujard was slightly censured by Vichy. The Belgians thanked him for his protest, but nobody knew who had instigated the theft nor what pressure had been put on Vichy to gain its complicity.

Documents found after the war revealed that Dr. Martin Konrad, of Berlin, an obscure scholar and the author of three works on Jan van Eyck, whom he considered a "Low German," had written Himmler early in September, 1941, about "safeguarding" the Ghent altarpiece in Germany for "analysis." Konrad had then gone to Pau and to Paris, failing in his mission because of Metternich's resistance. Once the work arrived in Germany, it was placed in a bomb-proof shelter, so no scholarly study could be made, either by Konrad or by any other more qualified expert. The Kümmel list made clear that the Ghent altarpiece was a prime Nazi objective as a military trophy, since it was "Nordic in inspiration" and two of its panels had been returned to Belgium from Cologne in 1919.

Very shortly after the rape of Pau the Germans let the French know that they wished to exchange some of their own French art for a long list of German works in French museums. Such an act, said Bunjes, the principal German spokesman, would contribute to better relations between the two countries. No one in France believed that the German museums had been consulted or would consent to handing over their own French treasures. The ensuing discussions led to a grotesque tragicomedy that began with Göring's sending the suggestion to Pierre Laval, who agreed in principle to the idea. The original lengthy German list included, oddly enough, two works owned by private individuals, neither of them Jews, and one item owned by the city of Rheims, whose mayor flatly refused to part with the city's property despite Vichy's coercion attempts.

Three months later, Bunjes's list had dwindled to ten items, one of them a solid-gold bas-relief, an altarpiece called the "Antependium de Bâle," the gem of the Cluny Museum in Paris. This work had not been mentioned before. Göring announced a visit to Paris—to inspect three bronzes[12] that he had ordered specially cast for the adornment of Karinhall and to inspect "the object," which he wanted taken to Paris from Chambord. When the French refused to move the bas-relief, the Germans made a trip to the château, although Vichy had announced that the altar would not be exchanged without a personal order from Pétain.

[12] News of the shipment of these bronzes to Germany caused the rumor that Göring was stealing from the Louvre and great indignation among the French people.

Temporarily balked, the Germans about-faced and pressed Jaujard for the other items on their list. The French finally agreed to exchange a rather clumsy wooden statue called "The Beautiful German" as well as one panel of an altarpiece to complete a work in Cologne for a Houdon bust and an unspecified painting. In July, 1943, a "confidential" order returned the "Antependium" to the Louvre, where it remained until December, when Göring came to Paris and demanded to see it at the Quai d'Orsay, where it was delivered by a Luftwaffe truck. A stormy high-level meeting ended when Abel Bonnard announced that the Reichsmarschall would get "the object" only if Pétain gave it to him, a statement equivalent to a flat rejection of any negotiations.

Göring's next move was an invitation to the French curators to Karinhall, on the promise of showing them what he would give them as compensation. The invitation was refused, and the Louvre swore that the "Antependium" would leave France only by force. It went back to Chambord, and the French had now only to wait for the Houdon bust and the promised painting. "The Beautiful German" and the altar panel were already in Germany. Nothing arrived in Paris for quite some time. Then a statue of the Virgin, purchased in Italy by Walter Hofer a few days before its arrival, turned up. Eventually something else appeared: a large painting still bearing the mark of the E.R.R. on its stretcher. It had made a round trip, for it was part of the Seligmann collection. The Louvre never formally accepted either work, returning both to their rightful owners after the war, and regained "The Beautiful German," minus two fingers shot off by a stray bullet.

Bunjes seemed completely oblivious to the reactions of the museums to this sham exchange and tried once more to obtain what he wanted by dangling before the French the possibility of freeing museum employees held as prisoners of war as well as the gift of a valuable medieval painting. However, at precisely the same moment, this S.S. officer disguised as an art scholar, and with pretentions to a future post as Minister of Culture, also demanded the removal of all French art to Burgundy, near the German border, a section of France that Hitler had decided in 1943 would be ideal for the creation of a sovereign S.S. state. Under the leadership of the S.S., Burgundy, having been degraded by years of French culture, would find its true place in the cultural scheme of the Greater Germany, and masterpieces of art would find themselves in a suitable environment. Luckily, Bunjes made his demand in January, 1944, and the war ended before any more exchanges or relocations could be carried out.

The Nazis also coveted the Bayeux tapestry, embroidered by Queen Matilda, wife of William the Conqueror, to celebrate the defeat of Harold II at Hastings in 1066. The Germans regarded this embroidered frieze not only as a charming work of art but also as an historical document indicative of Nordic talent and prowess in war. Although this is an idea difficult to reconcile with the defeat of the Saxons, it may have symbolized Nazi desire to land on English soil or a wish for identification with both the Norman William and the pure-blooded Saxon monarch. As early as 1940 the German High Command had photographed the whole work in color while it was still in the underground vaults of the Episcopal Palace in Bayeux, and the Ahnenerbe had set a painter to work to reproduce its principal scenes in oil for the German Historical Institute in Paris. In the spring of 1944 German interest in the tapestry became so intense that the French Historical Monuments Commission decided to bring the work to Paris under military escort on the pretext of including it in an exhibition of French art for the benefit of German soldiers. The tapestry, in its steel case, traveled on June 27, but since the Allied armies were pushing through Normandy, the exhibition was canceled, and the coveted treasure was left in the basement of the Louvre. In mid-August General Dietrich von Choltitz, the last German Commander in Paris, and the head of the Kunstschutz turned up to check on its continued presence. About ten days later, after dark, and during the fighting for Paris, two S.S. men arrived from Berlin with orders to pick up the tapestry.

Since the Louvre closes and locks its doors at night, and the gates to the Tuileries Gardens are also locked, the two messengers could scarcely have chosen a more inopportune time to enter the Louvre's vast complex, even had the city been at peace. Flashes of gunfire from the roof of one building made this night an even poorer choice. The S.S. men did not attempt to storm the Louvre, and the Bayeux tapestry remained safely inside the museum.

CHAPTER 6

PURCHASES AND EXCHANGES

BEYOND THE SEIZURE of private collections and attempts at propagandistic art exchanges, Nazi enterprise inside Paris moved into the area of contemporary "degenerate" art, which had been discovered as a source of income for the Reich at the Lucerne auction in 1939, even though that sale had brought less money than had been hoped for.

When Abetz turned over his confiscation business to the E.R.R. in 1940, he retained thirty nineteenth- and twentieth-century paintings on the advice of an aide alarmed by Von Behr's statement that such works would not be sent to Germany but would be sold or exchanged to add money to the E.K. Fund. Von Behr had merely echoed Rosenberg's belief that since the Nazi party had had to provide funds to fight Jews and Freemasons, it was only right that sale of the enemy's property should replenish the treasury. The E.R.R. considered all contemporary art coming into the Jeu de Paume as money in the bank. Von Behr even attempted a complicated deal with Portugal in which paintings would be exchanged for uncut diamonds, which would then be exchanged for raw materials needed for war industries.

Confiscated modern art was stowed away in a special back room of the museum, and its dispersal began immediately after Göring's first visit in November, 1940. Exactly whose idea it was to exchange first-rate modern art for second-rate older works has never been determined. Twenty-seven such exchanges took place: eighteen for Göring, seven for Hitler, one for Ribbentrop, and one for Martin Bormann, Hitler's private secretary, who hated both Göring and Rosenberg but was not averse to getting something for nothing. The procedure was simple enough to arouse the cupidity of several dishonest dealers: Six Germans, a Dutchman, a Frenchman, and a Hungarian helpfully unloaded dubious works of art for priceless modern masterworks.

The dealer most often involved in these exchanges was Gustav Rochlitz, and the transactions he completed indicated that perhaps he, more than anyone, received personal and material gain from the E.R.R. Rochlitz was an opportunist with no political convictions and one purpose in life: to make money. He had lost heavily twice before in crooked if unsuccessful business deals, once having to flee Germany and later Switzerland. He saw the Occupation of France as a godsend. Rochlitz's postwar story to a French court was that Bruno Lohse came to him one day asking for suitable paintings for Göring and Hitler and then came to his gallery with eleven paintings for inspection, but with a strict admonition not to look at the backs.[1] For these mysterious eleven works Rochlitz offered Lohse two unsigned oils, one Italian and one Dutch, and the deal was concluded on the spot. Rochlitz then took the paintings home, still obediently refraining from looking at anything but the fronts. Possibly he was dazzled, for the works were magnificent. That evening he invited another dealer to look at the paintings, which Rochlitz wished to exchange for others, but the unknown third party insisted on dollars and not art for what he had to offer, and no transaction took place.

Rochlitz's testimony added that Lohse told him the Matisse and Picasso paintings would be destroyed in Germany, either immediately or when the war ended, and that the paintings had come to Paris from Germany. If this last statement had been made, the first part would have been in direct contradiction to Hitler's orders forbidding the entry of such works into Germany. The second part could have been checked for veracity in any dealer's gallery reference library. In any case, Rochlitz was not disturbed enough to give up the lucrative business of exchanges, for between 1941 and 1942 he exchanged

[1] The backs would have shown him, if he did not already know it, that the paintings were marked "E.R.R." and were owned by Paul Rosenberg and Alfonse Kann. This episode refers to the first Göring exchange of three works by Matisse, two by Picasso, and one each by Corot, Braque, Renoir, Degas, Cézanne, and Sisley.

eighty modern paintings for thirty-five older works more to the taste of Reichsmarschall Göring.

The papers referring to this exchange were found in a roomful of records in the Hôtel Majestic after the E.R.R. had packed up and left. The documents list the paintings given and received; authenticity is attested to on both sides, but one document waives correct legal forms, customary in the sale or exchange of valuable paintings, and ends with the statement: "The undersigned bind themselves to hold this trade in the strictest secrecy," followed by the usual "Heil Hitler." The date is February 25, 1941. A second attached document is dated March 3, 1941. It is "between the Einsatzstab Rosenberg on the one hand and Herr Gustav Rochlitz on the other," states that "both parties declare that no further demands will be made," and is signed "for the E.R.R." It was scarcely likely that Rochlitz, who had profited enormously, would make any further demands. By the time of the Allied landings in Normandy his collection was large and important, for he operated not only in Paris but also in Nice, a center for questionable art dealings.

According to Rosenberg's figures, 150 modern French paintings were exchanged in Paris for 87 mediocre or dubious old masters by Italian, German, and Dutch artists. He was pleased with the record and gave Göring credit for the idea—basically the dispersal of stolen property through dealers acting as fences. The appearance of legality—minimal evaluations by German-selected French "experts"—was incredibly cynical. The selected experts were fearful of reprisals that might have ranged from total loss of a business to punishment of relatives in prisoner-of-war or concentration camps. In addition, experts in prints are not normally called upon to evaluate oils, nor are dealers in antique paintings automatically experts in the field of contemporary art.

Göring considered modern art so much money in his pocket and even dared to keep quite a few French moderns for himself. He had these, like those he exchanged, evaluated by an "expert" who was quite unable to judge correctly and thus innocently provided window dressing for the Reichsmarschall's pretense of payment for everything he took. Parisian exchanges were not the only ones. Thirteen took place inside Germany, for paintings forbidden entry by Hitler sometimes came in on Göring's special train or through the E.R.R. storehouse in Füssen. Göring exchanged twenty-three paintings owned by Paul Rosenberg for a Rembrandt and two tapestries.

The paintings were sent to Fischer in Lucerne for further sale. One two-step exchange brought Göring seven great Flemish works and a seventeenth-century "Vermeer," painted during the 1930's by the twentieth century's most notorious forger, Hans van Meegeren. The false Vermeer did not fool American art experts who saw it right after the war, but it did fool Göring, who would have been quite cross with Walter Hofer for having allowed him to waste some of the 150 modern paintings from the Goudstikker collection in Amsterdam which were used to pay for the lot. Göring liked a bargain, always.

Most of his purchases were made through Hofer, a Berlin art dealer before 1936, when his association with Göring began. Every morning, no matter what urgent military or political business might be waiting, Göring conferred with Hofer on the day's possibilities in the art world. Hofer received no salary–one was offered, but he refused it–and made his living buying art for Göring and himself, then reselling what Göring did not want. He estimated after the war that the Reichsmarschall had spent one hundred million marks on art in less than ten years and added that the money came from state funds. His estimate of Göring's taste was that it was "particular–developed in the course of years." Hofer was Göring's advance agent, seeking out what his patron would like, and tentatively discussing price. Göring would then bargain either in person or from photographs that Hofer brought him of works under consideration. Göring drove a hard bargain and was not above using his political power to get money back when second thoughts convinced him he had been cheated. Hofer recalled, in his Nuremberg testimony, that at one time, possibly in 1942, Göring had purchased a Flemish tapestry in Paris for three or four million francs. He then decided that he had been cheated by the middleman and commissioned "some German office" in Paris to investigate, with pleasant results: the return of six to eight hundred thousand francs. Hofer also recounted the story of Göring's projected donation of a museum to the Reich and said that the museum was mentioned in Göring's will.

Göring's testimony on the museum was slightly different. "It was my intention to build up an art gallery that I meant to hand over to the German people," he said, without drawing a distinction between an idea and a reality and adding that he bought two kinds of art: for himself and for the gallery. Gallery-intended art was paid for out of his "art budget." When pressed, he admitted that he had never turned any art or art objects over to the Government, because "How could I? Who was there to receive them?" Göring also stated that although Hofer was his principal buyer, he had agents everywhere who were paid for their efforts not by regular salaries but by the commissions they made on sales.

Hitler also had agents everywhere, and the Führer gave his men practically limitless funds. In France these were provided by the French Treasury, which by the terms of the armistice paid four hundred million francs a day for the upkeep of the occupying troops. This did not include quartering expenses, a special extra supplement also paid by France. The franc dropped from a value of nineteen cents in 1937 to five cents in 1940 and half that in 1944, yet the Occupation mark purchased twice its artificially pegged value.

Within this ruined economy the art market surged upward as the French began to buy what the Germans did not want, Impressionist and contemporary art, at prices that had never been reached before. Some bought for speculation; others for love of art. Among the latter was a dentist who quietly put together a collection of modern art that he later willed to the city of Paris in the old tradition of Frenchmen who wished to enrich their country.

German officers had plenty of money to spend and purchased such art and antiques as fit into the Nazi category of acceptable art. Buyers from Germany, dealers and museum directors, desposited large sums in the Reichsbank before coming to Paris. For this they received a receipt easily converted to the equivalent face-value of francs at the Reichshauptkasse in Paris. Since the francs were contributed by the French Government, the exchange merely seemed normal, for the money all went one way. The Germans could afford to buy lavishly, and they acquired a great many works of art that in normal times would never have been permitted to leave the country, for customs permits are never issued for historically irreplaceable art and antiques. During the Occupation a member of the National Museums staff remained, dutiful but discouraged, at his customs post. He had no authority to prevent what often happened when he refused a legal exit permit: The art took another route out of France, via uncontrollable military truck, train, or plane. The Louvre hopefully kept a list of such irreplaceable works: tapestries, furniture, statues, and paintings by such artists as Tiepolo, Lancret, Fragonard, Watteau, Rembrandt, Goya, and Rubens. A certain amount of art also left by sea, first being smuggled through Spain or Portugal. One notable instance was that of the S.S. *Excalibur*, which was stopped in Bermuda by British contraband authorities who seized, as "export from territory occupied or controlled by the enemy," several hundred paintings by Renoir, Cézanne, Degas, Gauguin, Monet, Manet, and Pissarro "from a Paris collection," reputedly that of Ambroise Vollard, the well-known art dealer.

In the autumn of 1943 France lost 284 old masters at a sale conducted by the Vichy Government in Paris. The works were part of a collection of 333 paintings, principally Dutch masters, acquired over the years by August Schloss and willed to his children. They had placed the collection in a Paris bank before the war, and the bank had moved them to what it considered a safe repository in the Château Chambon, near Tulle in the unoccupied zone. The subjects of these paintings made them suitable both for Hitler's Linz collection and for Göring, but nobody knew where the repository was. The search for the works was desultory in Posse's time; he had an ample choice of other art. When Dr. Hermann Voss succeeded Posse, however, interest in the collection revived. For some months two Parisian dealers associated with Karl Haberstock, a German dealer, traveled around France seeking the Schloss heirs, but they did not find them. Long before the paintings were finally found, Haberstock and his French aides dropped out of the race, for they could not penetrate the screen put up by Vichy.

Late in April, 1943, two of the heirs, Henri Schloss and his wife, were arrested in Nice "on suspicion of Gaullism." They were thus unable to tell the bank to remove the paintings from Chambon, where they had been tracked down by Darquier de Pellepoix, Vichy Commissioner for Jewish Affairs, through an informant, a truck driver named Neriec, who had driven the truck containing the art from Paris to the repository. Immediately after the Nice arrest a French police chief, a commissioner from the Jewish Affairs office in Marseilles, and Jean François Lefranc, introduced as the provisory administrator for the Schloss estate, arrived at the château. Lefranc had fought in World War I with Pellepoix and had been acting as an art expert for his old friend for some time. The visitors presented the bank manager with a requisition order signed by the prefect of the department. The heaviest pressure involved an ex-director of the bank, long since retired, who was a Jew. The manager resisted, called on his superiors for aid, and the current director and his assistant arrived from Paris. The struggle lasted several days, but the pressure exerted was too great, and the bank finally agreed to turn the cases of art over to Pellepoix. By the time this happened, the château had received a crowd of Vichy officials and been gratified with a Vichy administrator to assist Lefranc.

On the night after the bank's reluctant agreement to cede the collection, a police commissioner and five gendarmes watched over the cases all night. In the morning a diesel truck arrived from Paris. Lefranc swore in military court years later that he had asked for it from Pellepoix, who had obtained it through Von Behr. It was early morning, and Lefranc and the Vichy representative were not on hand to turn over the cases officially, but the truckers decided to load them anyhow and get back to Paris. Just outside of Tulle an armed French police squad, informed of what was going on and not terrified by Vichy, stopped the truck. An argument followed, and during it one of the truckers slipped away to telephone German security forces in Limoges, in the occupied zone. The arrival of security troops made it possible for the cases to be removed to a German military barracks, where they remained until another Vichy order sent them to the vaults of the Bank of France branch in Limoges. On May 8 Lefranc wrote to Germain Bazin, of the Louvre, telling him to demand his "right of preemption" so that Lefranc could legally oppose the Germans if they laid their hands on the paintings.

"Mindful of the difficulties outside of Tulle," Lefranc did nothing for nearly four months. In August, 1943, Abel Bonnard sent him to Vichy, where Laval ordered him to sell to the Germans any paintings on which the Louvre did not exercise its right of preemption. Lefranc then sent the paintings from Limoges to the Banque Dreyfus in Paris, as Bonnard ordered. A notary of the Bank of France and Louvre curators René Huyghe and Germain Bazin established an inventory; Cornelius Postma, a Dutch expert working for Vichy, evaluated the art. When the sale date was decided upon, a group of Germans was invited to be present, but they declined the invitation. Invited again a few days later, they accepted.

Present at the sale were Erhard Goepel and Lohse, as experts; Dr. Helmut von Hümmel, Bormann's deputy; a new German ambassador, Rudolf Schleier, replacing Abetz; Abel Bonnard, as Vichy representative; Lefranc; Postma; Bazin; and Huyghe. The last four set the prices (although they asked Lohse to join in this, he refused) and set them astonishingly low in German opinion. The Louvre timidly exercised its right of preemption on 49 paintings only, selecting carefully to round out Louvre collections rather than according to quality. Lohse believes that if the French had insisted that the collection's principal value lay in its being kept intact, they could have kept the entire group of paintings, for the Germans would have respected this decision. Hitler wanted the paintings for Linz but did not wish to antagonize Laval at this time, and Goepel had been instructed not to irritate the French. Göring, who had been interested in the paintings at first, had withdrawn entirely in favor of Hitler, because he had no funds with which to purchase and perhaps also because Lohse was so disgusted with the confiscation of Jewish property that he must have communicated his feelings to his chief. An anonymous buyer, acting through Lefranc under an authorization from Pellepoix, acquired 22 paintings, although the Schloss heirs received no money from this portion of the sale. The Louvre never paid for its acquisitions, which it returned to the Schloss family after the war. The remaining 262 works, which went to Hitler, cost fifty million francs, of which forty-two million went into funds for Pellepoix's service. The entire amount had come from the French Treasury's Occupation fund. The atmosphere at the sale was pleasant, and when it was over, all the participants dined together, exchanging toasts during the meal.

Hitler's paintings were sent to the Führerbau in Munich for storage. A few days before the United States Third Army arrived to set up some sort of order at the end of the war, a mob of Germans and displaced persons sacked the building. They did not know they were destroying stolen property, and a great many of the paintings vanished forever.

The indifference of the Vichy Government to France's patrimony and the split and lack of understanding between Vichy's Minister of Education, Abel Bonnard, and the Louvre curators whom he controlled are highlighted in this involved transaction. It is also an example of the fear induced in honest men who do not take positive positions or act boldly lest they be subject to reprisals. Thus the Louvre, although it might have been completely successful in its efforts to save private property, was able to achieve only slightly better results than it had accomplished earlier, when it had tried to save valuable Jewish collections by calling them gifts to the French Government. An early German decree declared that gifts made after the declaration of war were illegal, and this decision was strengthened a year later with the *Judenbüsse*, a special decree depriving Jews of the right to dispose of their own belongings. The false and antedated papers for the Rothschild collections saved by the National Museums at Montauban were the direct result of this decree.

The National Museums were also unable to stop the Germans from seizing property belonging to non-Jews when they wanted it. Göring was very fond of Gothic art, and the Nazi Minister of Finance, Dr. Walther Funk, wanted to give him a really splendid present for his fiftieth birthday. Dr. Funk decided upon two sixteenth-century Flemish tapestries belonging to the Viscount de Sèze and his wife, the daughter of the original owner, Teisserane de Bort, once French ambassador to Vienna. The tapestries hung in the Château de Bort, an obscure dwelling in a small community, so that although they had been reproduced in two books, the hangings were largely unknown and had escaped attention. Early in January, 1942, the viscount received two visitors who claimed to be inspectors of the Beaux-Arts of Paris entrusted with a mission concerning the tapestries. During their conversation the viscount heard them make a reference to an acquisition, and since he was suspicious of the men, he notified the regional police, who picked them up. They were found to be Parisian art dealers who had with them twenty million francs (identifiable as coming from the Reichskreditkasse), and they did not hide the fact that they were working for Göring.

The two men were set free but kept under surveillance until they disappeared at the end of April. Because of the zonal division of France and the vague information first received, the Beaux-Arts in Paris did not hear the story until the end of April. One of the principal inspectors of the historical-monuments section went to Bort at once, realized the importance of the tapestries, and was assured by Mme. de Sèze, by French law the actual owner of the works, that she would not sell the tapestries and would accept their classification as historical monuments. This statement was confirmed in writing, and the tapestries were so classified in a decree dated June 16, 1942. To prevent their being snatched away, they were sent to the Aubusson repair shops of National Furnishings, for almost immediately after classification Mme. de Sèze had given the works to the state, which formally accepted the gift on June 26.

When Göring heard of this, he intervened vigorously, threatening the Vichy Government with reprisals if the tapestries were not turned over to him. Pierre Laval then ordered the Beaux-Arts to put the tapestries back in the château and confirmed this order in writing on July 13. The very next day the prefect of the district sent police to take the tapestries and had them handed over to the Occupation authorities. Since a 1913 law forbade the export of classified objects, the tapestries were declassified on August 8, 1942, by the express command of Vichy. Göring sent the tapestries to Karinhall, transferred some money from one Reich cash-box to another, and closed the case.

Sometimes Frenchmen intervened to cheat the Louvre, as in the case of "The Magdalen with a Lamp" by Georges de La Tour. Camille Terff, who owned this valuable painting, was an old man, and although as early as 1937 he had expressed a wish to leave the work to the museum, in August, 1941, dangerously ill and in financial difficulties, he had to sell. He left the painting with a dealer named Laloe, who cajoled him into allowing a "negotiation" of the work for 700,000 francs. Later that year M. Terff received 630,000 francs, the original price less 10 percent commission. On November 15, 1941, however, the Louvre had taken a month's option to buy at a million francs, but when the time came to pick up the option, the painting had already been sold, and Laloe refused to name either the purchaser or the "co-owner." Determined investigation led to M. Terff, who was distressed to learn for the first time of the museum's offer and agreed to sue the dealer for "abuse of confidence." He signed the complaint, but he died a few days later.

The new owner was discovered by a lucky accident. Someone saw the director of the Cologne Museum holding the painting in a frame shop. The museum, which pleaded "legal exception," had paid 1,500,000 francs for the painting to Laloe's dummy intermediary. Laloe was fined and went to jail, but the painting went to Cologne until after the war, when it was reclaimed by and returned to the Louvre.

In 1940, after a symbolic gesture in which the French people were supremely uninterested—the return of the ashes of Napoleon's son, L'Aiglon, to the Invalides—the Germans proceeded to empty the Army Museum in the same building of military souvenirs dating back to the fifteenth century. This looting, like that of the Salorges Maritime Museum in Nantes and the confiscation of family papers belonging to the Murat family, came under a special decree affecting military, marine, and aviation museums.

Libraries were under constant scrutiny by the E.R.R. and other agencies, and it is not possible to overlook what took place there even in an account devoted primarily to fine art and art objects. Not only did the Germans appropriate Polish, Czechoslovakian, and Jewish national libraries located in Paris; they also attacked French national libraries full of rare books and manuscripts, and, it goes without saying, the private libraries of wealthy, famous, or intellectual Jews. At one point they wanted to photograph the entire collection of the Bibliothèque Sainte Geneviève, whose collection is world-famous. The purpose of this was not clear, but it may have been ordered, the curator believed, because the Germans meant eventually to destroy the library. Strong objections by the curator to Abel Bonnard led to delaying tactics, and no photographs were taken. The Military Art Commission, which demanded the photographs, had already compiled a set of seventy-six thousand others (six thousand of Rheims Cathedral alone), and since the subjects were national monuments, the question posed was whether the purpose was protective—for repair of possible war damage—or simply a record to be kept after deliberate destruction at some future date. Hitler had said that the destruction of the Reich would mean the destruction of all Europe.

Among the private libraries stolen was that of André Maurois, novelist and biographer, whose collection of ten thousand volumes was taken in 1942. Servants present during the confiscation heard the Germans remark that the books would be taken to Berlin, where a library was being set up intended for "special studies" on the Jewish brain. Standard dictionaries and encyclopedias in English and French, works by classic French writers—Molière, Corneille, Chateaubriand, Racine, and Bossuet, for example—and the writings of Byron, Shelley, Shakespeare, and Kipling were taken. Many of these books had notations in the margins by Maurois; perhaps these were what the Germans were really after for their "special studies."

Such studies were the domain of the Ahnenerbe, which had free reign in Alsace-Lorraine after the annexation of the territory. In June, 1941, Minister of Culture Wolfram Sievers set up an office in Metz for the registration and securing of cultural objects. The director of the Metz Museum managed the office, with four Germans assigned as appraisers. The four visited castles, buildings, and villages left vacant by inhabitants who had chosen comparative freedom at the time of the armistice by emigrating to other parts of France. Valuable belongings, paintings, sculptures, tapestries, furniture, and rugs were stored either in the homes of the mayors of the towns or villages or in two sites in Metz, the museum and the Carmelite Monastery. Typically native art of Lorraine was left in Metz and other local museums. The Führer decided what was to be done with larger objects; smaller ones were set aside for use as decoration of Nazi party buildings. By virtue of a decree issued by Himmler on March 19, 1941, thirty-six castles and fifty-seven towns were visited between June and mid-November, 1941, and 2,058 art objects, including valuable Gothic Madonnas and a hundred paintings, were amassed. The collecting was officially completed by the end of June, 1942, when its estimated value was 3,500,000 Reichsmarks.

On November 7, 1942, an order came to divide up the "seized cultural objects from Lorraine" which had been taken for "cleaning," "examination," "study," or "safekeeping." The dividing up included two large copper cauldrons of the kind that hang over an open fireplace, taken by one of Himmler's aides who wanted to give his boss a present. Himmler returned them to the aide in gratitude. The cauldrons had no historical value. The S.S. had acquired Peleters Castle and its farmhouse to use as a guest house for visiting officers. A request was made for the furnishings that had been removed so that the building might be suitably arranged. The furnishings included a small painting by Brueghel and a couple of old Lorraine wardrobes. Furniture from Drachenfels Castle was set aside for transfer to the district gauleiter's farm near Saarburg. Completely unauthorized people secured furniture and paintings. Valuable paintings from Mulhouse suddenly appeared in Stuttgart. Antiques from St. Leonhardt Castle—summer residence of the Baron de Dietrich, of Paris—turned up in a Baden-Baden antiques shop. Hitler's personal physician was interested in the furnishings of St. Leonhardt because, according to a letter from one S.D. officer to another, he "intends to acquire this art property for his chief." The official residence of the Metz S.S. chief contained valuable paintings and two Gobelins tapestries; six Gobelins adorned the Metz police station; a Gothic Madonna from a Metz monastery was found in the court of the Metz women's prison.

Immediately after the Allied landings in North Africa on November 8, 1942, Hitler ordered the occupation of all France, and a third very important center for illegal traffic in art promptly opened up on the Mediterranean coast, with its center at Nice. Most of the works handled were private property stolen by the Germans and purchased cheaply from the Gestapo for very profitable resale. The principal group handling such deals was headed by one Brueschwiller—owner of a Munich gallery, a Nazi party member, and a buyer for Linz—whom Bruno Lohse considered quite mad. Brueschwiller shared a villa in Villefranche, just outside Nice, with a woman and two men. One of the men, Ward Holzappel, who claimed American citizenship, was a Linz buyer and acted as intermediary between the villa, used as a temporary art storehouse, and such dealers as Rochlitz in Paris and various others of the same stamp in Nice, Cannes, and other towns along the coast. A playground of the rich, this area had always been amply provided with art galleries and antiques dealers with many foreign clients. One of the dealers involved boasted of having sent many fine pieces to Argentina via Barcelona. Another passed items into Spain, using, it was claimed, the German Consulate in Marseilles as an intermediary. This man had a shop in Monte Carlo, another run by a son in Paris, and dreams of sending his youngest son to Saint-Cyr, the French equivalent of West Point. One of his deals involved some paintings stolen from a railroad car that the Gestapo were loading for departure. He paid sixty thousand francs for the entire lot and sold one painting from it for a million.

The owners of the Maison Chaleyssin–an interior-decorating establishment on Nice's main shopping street, the Rue de France–had agreed when the Nazis occupied the southern zone to safeguard fifty-six Jewish-owned paintings worth twenty million francs. One morning in October, 1943, the shop's principal salesman discovered that seventeen paintings, sixteen owned by Jews, had vanished without any signs of breaking and entering. A police inquiry revealed that the thief was a steady customer, a Dr. Besson. The police searched his home, found the paintings, and arrested him, but he was released, still in possession of the paintings, when his family threatened to denounce the shop owners to the Gestapo on charges of withholding Jewish property. Regional newspapers publicized the theft to such an extent that both the Free French radio in Brazzaville and the German radio in Vienna broadcast the story.

The shop then rented a strong room in a local bank to protect the rest of the paintings. Among the works placed in safety were two Chardins; these were so valuable that their owner, René Gimpel, a world-renowned art dealer, had commissioned the firm to sell them for 4,500,000 francs. The shop salesman went to Paris, where he was placed in contact with Lefranc, who was so important in the abduction of the Schloss collection. Lefranc was interested and went to Nice, accompanied by a German expert who confirmed the estimated value. The sale was concluded verbally, and the two men returned to Paris. A few days later some Gestapo agents appeared and affixed seals to the Chardins. Following this, another group of agents arrived to take the other paintings in the strong room. Their leader noticed the seals on the Chardins, ripped them off, affixed his own, and took the entire lot. When Nice was liberated, a case that was supposed to hold seventeen paintings was found ripped open in a shed near the railway station. Eight of the missing works were picked up later, after having been passed from hand to hand.

Three art auctions authorized by Vichy were held in Nice. Two were conducted normally; the third, held on July 12, 1943, brought very poor receipts. On November 9, 1944, the keeper of the National Gallery in London wrote a letter to Lieutenant Colonel Sir Leonard Woolley, at the War Office, asking assistance in tracing three paintings sold in that auction, for they had been willed to the museum by their owner, Mme. Alfonse Jaffe, who had died in Nice in 1942. The pictures cited as legal British property were a Rembrandt portrait of the artist's father, a Goya portrait, and a view of Venice by Guardi, a minor work.

The auctioneer for the third sale, J. J. Terris, claimed that the paintings in the collection were not very valuable and had an exaggerated reputation, for the experts he consulted doubted the attributions of the principal works. He had therefore seen no reason to issue a catalog in which he could use only such descriptions as "School of . . ." or "Attributed to . . ." and had merely prepared one with photographs and no descriptions. The Goya was not even mentioned in the catalog. Given a tentative value of three thousand francs, it had been sold for sixty thousand to a buyer identified only as "a certain Dutey." Terris did not mention the opinion of another expert—a German in Monte Carlo at the time of the sale—who attributed the painting to Goya, since the auctioneer had no confidence in this man, who had led Göring into the purchase of a "Titian" that was later found to be a fake. Terris also declared that he had never had any contact with German buyers except for the sale of rugs. And yet the Jaffe sale was announced in German in a local newspaper.

Late in December, 1944, a French process-server went to call on Dutey in Paris, since it had been discovered that he was a lieutenant in military security. The lieutenant admitted having purchased the Goya on the understanding that its authenticity was doubtful and that that was the reason for its estimated low value. He had paid his sixty thousand plus charges but no longer had the painting, for about a year before he had exchanged it for another that he "liked better." He did not know where the painting was.

A couple of weeks later, Dutey wrote a letter to the Parisian lawyer conducting the investigation and named Gustav Rochlitz as the intermediary in the exchange of the Goya. Dutey added that he believed Rochlitz had been acting for somebody else, since he had asked Dutey to sign a paper ceding the painting to another person whom he had never seen and whose name he "did not remember." Dutey did not know whether or not the Goya was still in Paris, for Rochlitz had indicated that it would be exported. He considered it difficult to sell in France, since it was of doubtful origin. Dutey also revealed that as witnesses to the exchange he had Roger Dequoy—the Wildenstein Gallery's "Aryan" partner—and another Paris dealer; Dutey had asked the latter to sell the painting for him, but he had not been able to do so.

On February 9, 1945, Germain Bazin, Louvre curator, wrote to Albert Henraux, chief of the French group then occupied with recovering stolen art. Bazin's letter named Dequoy as the actual Nice buyer (thus indicating that Dutey had been only a front) and stated that in October, 1943, Dequoy had offered it to the Louvre for six million francs. The offer was declined, since the museum had just received a gift of another Goya portrait. In June, 1944, a "M. Dutey" requested an export license to Germany for a representative of a gallery in Chemnitz. The license was for the Goya portrait belonging to Dequoy and now attributed to "the Spanish School" and valued at nearly a million francs less than the offered sale price to the Louvre less than a year before. Permission to export was withheld, since the work should have remained in France even if the Louvre did not want it. Bazin added that he did not know what had happened after this refusal but believed that "as happened in other instances, the painting was sent into Germany without anybody's paying any attention to what the French curators thought."

The Rembrandt disappeared with less noise. The Frenchman questioned as to his possible ownership of the work denied having purchased it and said he had done nothing more than give his opinion of the work. He believed that Rochlitz had bought it but could not confirm this. When the process-server went to call on Rochlitz, the concierge of the building informed him that "M. Rochlitz was a German who had left Paris during the month of August, 1944, without leaving a forwarding address."

CHAPTER 7

EXPERTS AND AGENTS

ALTHOUGH GÖRING CONTINUED to believe that E.R.R. confiscations in France were his private property, a flow of orders from Berlin affirmed the Führer's right to govern every Nazi organization everywhere. The repetition of these orders indicated considerable confusion in Berlin, however. Some of this stemmed from the rivalry between Hitler and his Reichsmarschall—a great deal of it from the underhanded, throat-cutting tactics of large and small fry all over Europe.

Hitler's first treasures from France were the fifty-three paintings from the Rothschild collections graciously sent him in February, 1941. Oddly enough, three of the works were misdirected to Karinhall, perhaps because the cases were not correctly marked "A. H. Linz" but "H.G." The Führer's second set of treasures was the cream of the Flemish paintings collected over a long lifetime by August Schloss. These made only a brief stopover in the Jeu de Paume before going to the Führerbau. For the rest of what he acquired in France, Holland, and Belgium, Hitler, *grand seigneur*, sent out a small army of dealers and agents amply supplied with money that came from the countries that also supplied the art. No confusion existed in the minds of these underlings: They were out to get as much as they could while incidentally lining their own pockets. Hitler did have to run most of Europe and the war, and he was busier and less penurious than Göring, hence more easily served; he was content to buy from photographs or upon the counsel of his appointed advisers. During his active collecting years he spent more on art than had anybody else in the history of the world: 163,975,000 Reichsmarks, or more than 65,000,000 dollars. He never saw most of what he acquired, for paintings, sculpture, jewels, gold coins, furniture, tapestries, rugs, rare books and manuscripts, even musical instruments, were stowed away in large batches like potatoes in cellars, waiting for the triumphant show after victory.

Hitler was more interested in his scheme for the aggrandizement of Linz and the concomitant debasement of Vienna than in the art he acquired for its museum. He drew the plans for the new city, designed the buildings—in a kind of debased Attic style—and had his architect make a large room-sized model of the project, which included a grand railroad station, a plaza, a library, a theater, and an art museum. He even mentioned the project in his will, composed in the Berlin bunker, and asked that it be carried out after his death.

Before he took on the learned curators who advised him on what to purchase, Hitler's ideal museum in Linz was to have been filled with nineteenth-century German art by unimportant genre artists fond of telling morality stories in paint or depicting cozy tavern or idealized landscape scenes. Hitler also favored morbid romanticism: lovers wandering among ruins in dusky landscapes, misty vapors rising from lakes, and clouds in tatters drifting across pale full moons. For such works he would pay up to ten times the market price. Martin Bormann, Göring's successor as top-ranking Nazi after Hitler flew into a rage at the latter, paid for these expensive daubs out of Government money, entering the payments in Government records. Hitler's plan for the museum changed for the better under the aegis of Dr. Hans Posse and Dr. Hermann Voss.

The Linz arrangements were elaborate. Dr. Posse had an office in The Hague and special funds in his own name in France, Holland, and Italy. His travels were facilitated by Bormann, who gave him a special certificate obliging all German ministries in occupied lands to give him every possible assistance. When he chose to visit Dresden, the gauleiter, or regional director of the area, provided a special automobile on orders from Bormann in Hitler's name. Once, at least, he was provided with a railroad car for transporting pictures. Posse also received ten thousand Reichsmarks a year for extra travel expenses. Almost until the day of his death from cancer of the mouth in 1942, he worked fanatically for Linz. His reward was a state funeral attended by every museum curator in Germany and a eulogy read by Goebbels.

Posse had never mentioned a successor for either chief curator of the Dresden State Museum or provisional director of Linz. Dr. Voss, who was curator of the Wiesbaden Provincial Museum, received both jobs and also kept his Wiesbaden post, but without salary. The choice was peculiar, for until 1942 Voss had a reputation as an anti-Nazi. Hitler received Voss once at headquarters to discuss the museum and never saw him again. Voss spent much more money than Posse had and was generous, too, in handing out official Linz certificates for business that did not always include express purchasing trips for the museum. In spending the 150,000,000 or so marks that he disbursed to purchase three thousand paintings, however, Voss was more restricted than Posse had been. Payment for his purchases was made only in Germany and passed slowly through clearinghouses, and in the last months of the war any important purchase had to pass through Bormann's office for Hitler's approval. Bills for the Sonderauftrag Linz (Linz Special Mission) made out to Dr. Voss were paid by the Treasury through a private Berlin bank whose checks went through a clearinghouse. Agents did not receive a fixed commission, and the prices asked included their profits.

Foreign-exchange permits, which had not been required of Posse, now had to be obtained from Bormann's office. The complicated procedure required payment of extra fees. Purchases made in Paris required an authorization from the Reichsstelle für Waren Verschiedener Art (Office for Miscellaneous Objects) for which the dealer paid a fee. A second Paris bureau issued purchase authorizations and required a report when the purchase was completed. The last step was a German customs fee, later abolished. The second step required supplying the names of French collaborators, and this, according to a complaint filed by Posse's principal agent, Karl Haberstock, was not only unfair but also bad for business. *Collabos*, as the French slangily called them, took a quick personal profit that contributed to long-term national bankruptcy, and the Germans as well as the French were aware of how they were regarded.

Hitler's special adviser on art matters was a party member, his long-time friend and official photographer, "Professor" Heinrich Hoffmann, who shared his leader's enthusiasm for second-rate nineteenth-century German painting. He had acquired his purely honorary title for his work in the House of German Art in Munich. Hoffmann, who claimed no official connection with Linz and held no travel certificate, did a considerable amount of traveling inside and outside Germany taking photographs. He managed to sell 155 paintings (some of them stolen in Holland) to Linz and had significant business connections with his friend Maria Dietrich, who managed to rise from obscurity to prominence as a dealer during the war years.

Both Hoffmann and Dietrich knew very little about art, but they knew Hitler's taste. Hoffmann also knew the Führer's taste in women and had introduced his employee Eva Braun to the man who made her his lonely mistress and last-hour wife. Since Eva was a friend of Dietrich's daughter Mimi, the connections were close. Registers of paintings received at the Führerbau in Munich list paintings purchased "by Prof. Hoffmann for the Führer," "from the Almas [Dietrich] Gallery and Prof. Hoffmann," or "from the Almas Gallery by Prof. Hoffmann." Despite the Führerbau's registers, which list paintings bought from Hoffmann and sold to Linz at a profit, the "Professor" insisted that he merely acted as a disinterested middleman, accepting pictures from dealers whom he knew so well he never questioned them. Hence, he never knew whether paintings left with him were German in origin or confiscated Jewish property. He also revealed a new facet of Hitler's personality by stating that the Führer was "too shy" to walk into any art galleries except those owned by Dietrich and Haberstock.

Maria Dietrich sold more paintings to Hitler than did any other dealer. She specialized in quantity rather than quality, and despite Nazi contempt for women in a world run by men, she managed to hold her own even against sometimes difficult odds. Born in Munich in 1892, she had an illegitimate child in 1910 by a Jewish father and in 1921 married a Turkish-Jewish tobacconist named Ali Almas-Diamant. She had adopted both the Jewish faith and Turkish citizenship when she married, and from 1933 she had considerable trouble with Nazi authorities until she regained her German citizenship in 1940, after a 1937 divorce. She kept the name Almas for her gallery but otherwise used her maiden name. Her gallery income was forty-seven thousand Reichsmarks in 1937, and this figure jumped to ten times as much in 1938, when she met Hitler through Hoffmann and began selling to the Führer. Her income remained in the six-figure bracket throughout the war, during which she generally made a 50 percent profit on sales to Linz; on thirty-eight occasions this jumped to 100 percent. Most of her sales were direct ones without the intervention or approval of Posse or Voss, who could do nothing to prevent Hitler from buying what he pleased and paying anything asked.

Dietrich frequented auction sales in Germany and was well known for the high prices she paid. As a holder of a Linz travel certificate, she made frequent trips to Paris. She bought from about one hundred persons and made use of scouts: a Russian princess to whom she paid small commissions, a French dealer who ended a letter to her with "Heil Hitler," and two or three others, including Bruno Lohse, who helped her out as a friendly gesture. She denied knowing anything about E.R.R. operations, although she received from that organization a Pissarro landscape in an exchange. Since it was dangerous to keep such a work on her ledgers, she passed it on to her daughter, who scrupulously cared for it until the end of the war. Except for her overbidding at auctions and her exorbitant profits, Dietrich was more ignorant about art than dishonest. She kept careful books, even noting reduced prices for paintings that turned out to be fakes. Hitler and Bormann scolded her for careless judgment, and the head of the Bavarian State Museums once threw her out of his office for bringing him so many fakes.

In contrast to Dietrich was Karl Haberstock, a shrewd dealer with forty years of experience, important connections outside of Germany, and adept at getting what he wanted. Haberstock joined the Nazi party in 1933, sold his first picture to Hitler in 1936, and was consistently and profitably occupied for the next several years both inside and outside the Reich. Hitler liked him because he understood thoroughly what was suitable art for Nazi dogma. Also, everybody in the art world knew what Haberstock wanted, and he got so much of it that he could generously afford to skip his 10 percent commission on very large sales because he made so much on smaller ones. Posse's years at Linz were the best for Haberstock. The two men had been friends for years; they were so close, in fact, that when Posse died, his widow wired Haberstock and his wife to attend the funeral, insisting in the telegram that the couple sit beside her in the front row of the funeral hall.

Haberstock's acquisitions all over occupied Europe were spectacular, and he did business with the nobility, museum directors, and gallery owners; nevertheless, the biggest bargain Hitler ever acquired, although long accredited as a coup by Haberstock, was actually purchased directly by Posse through a Munich attorney named Scanconi—trustee for the seller—and a Munich art dealer. (Haberstock's gallery was in Berlin, and he was born in Augsburg.) The painting was the so-called Czernin Vermeer, a self-portrait of the artist which is considered the finest of the thirty-three positively identified Vermeers in the world. Before the war Count Czernin, who owned the painting, had refused an offer of $2,000,000 from Andrew Mellon, since the picture was on the list of art works considered national treasures by the Austrian Government and therefore could not be taken out of the country. Six months before the actual sale Hitler, who wanted the painting badly, found an asking price of about $500,000 too high to pay. Posse, who had full power-of-attorney for Linz purchases, paid $660,000, however. The count did not have to pay a tax on this sale, which was made directly to the Reich, and he wrote a letter stating that he considered the price satisfactory. Hence, when the war ended, the painting was returned to the Austrian Government and not to the Czernin family.

When Haberstock came to Paris (his customary hotel was the Ritz), he put a notice of his visit in the *Gazette des Beaux-Arts*, which had been taken over from the Wildenstein Gallery by a German art publisher. Haberstock also sent out printed announcements of his presence in France and called on about seventy-five important dealers, not only in Paris but also in Marseilles, Dijon, Le Havre, Nice, and Aix-en-Provence. One gallery only, Duveen Brothers, refused to see him and never transacted any business with him. Perhaps Haberstock, despite all his foreign connections, did not know that Mme. René Gimpel, whose husband and sons had joined the French Resistance, was the sister of the eight Duveen brothers.

Haberstock wanted fifteenth-, sixteenth-, eighteenth-, and nineteenth-century German masters, Italian masters, and the Flemish giants of the sixteenth and seventeenth centuries, as well as signed Dutch works of the seventeenth century. In French art he wanted Poussin, Claude Lorrain, and signed Bouchers, Fragonards, and Watteaus, although in a letter to a French dealer he noted that these were difficult to find. Recent works by Renoir, Manet, and Monet were overpriced, he said, and he "could not take the responsibility of spending foreign currency for them." Among other things Haberstock acquired in France were two large Rembrandts, a Poussin, two Courbet nudes, and seven paintings from the Wildenstein Gallery, operated during the war by an "Aryan" partner, Roger Dequoy. Haberstock and Dequoy had gone to see Georges Wildenstein, the senior partner, who had taken refuge in Aix immediately after the fall of France, and urged him to return to Paris, where Haberstock believed he would be quite safe. Wildenstein hesitated to return and eventually left France. The "Aryanizing" of Wildenstein's prevented a number of the firm's paintings from passing into the collections of the E.R.R., a serious deprivation for Göring. Mme. Jane Weyll, who often represented Haberstock at the Hôtel Drouôt auctions, tried to appease the Reichsmarschall by offering him a small portrait by Lucas Cranach owned by her friend Baron von Poellnitz, a Luftwaffe officer. Göring turned it down, and Haberstock sold it to Hitler.

Haberstock's star dwindled when Posse was succeeded by Voss as the head of Linz, for the new director favored his own friends. Bormann did not like him, either, and other, less successful dealers began a kind of whispering campaign that finally ended in denunciations to American authorities in 1946, when Haberstock and others were questioned in the Bavarian castle to which he and his wife and other bombed-out dealers had retreated after the Berlin fires and destruction. Such denunciations, common enough in the period when people were scrambling to safety by pushing others in the mud, included such petty accusations as middle-class origins, lack of university training, excessive chauvinism, and personal profit from the Lucerne auction, for which he was not responsible. The accusations so bothered Haberstock that in December, 1952, when he was seventy-four, he wrote a long memorandum to Theodore Rousseau, Jr., of the Metropolitan Museum of Art, his interrogating M.F.A. and A. officer, again taking up and disproving the points in order, with elaborations. The document is a sad commentary, behind its facade, on the debasing effects of Hitler's dictatorship.

The chief buyer for Linz in Holland, Dr. Erhard Goepel, also traveled to Paris fairly frequently. He had Ward Holzappel as adviser in a purchase of nineteenth-century French paintings not intended for Linz and also took advice from Bruno Lohse. Among the paintings purchased in Paris ostensibly for Linz were three that he reputedly took to The Hague. Lohse believed that Goepel was unhappy working for Voss and secretly coveted his position.

Another holder of a Linz certificate for Paris was Dr. Hildebrand Gurlitt, a friend of Voss's with a similar reputation for having been anti-Nazi as late as March, 1943. Gurlitt's paternal grandmother was a Jewess, and his career as a museum director in Zwickau and Hamburg had been demolished by the party in 1930. He then became a dealer in Hamburg, specializing in works by avant-garde artists later put on the banned list. He moved to Dresden in 1942, and Voss made him an accredited Linz agent for Paris in early spring, 1943. Considering Gurlitt's background, this appointment was as strange as that of Dr. Voss himself.

Gurlitt went off to Paris, stayed away from party circles, and did most of his buying through a Dutch dealer who died in 1944. In about a year's time Gurlitt had increased his normal prewar income five times. Prices in Paris had skyrocketed, and Gurlitt's bills, including his commission in prices, were high. Voss paid them without question, because, he candidly informed Allied interrogators in 1945, "We had plenty of money." Gurlitt himself was extremely nervous when questioned in 1945 and offered a minimum of information. He apparently knew a great many other Linz agents and bought principally from dealers. He stressed that he bought only what was voluntarily offered. The painting he considered the most important of those he purchased in France was a portrait attributed to Jean Fouquet. (Voss did not buy it, but the Cologne Museum did.) The conditions of this purchase—made from Count Demandolx, of Marseilles—were odd. Gurlitt's Dutch dealer made the arrangements, offering a price of sixteen million francs. Gurlitt went to Marseilles, paid Count Demandolx ten million francs, and received no bill of sale. He then returned to Paris and paid the rest of the money to his Dutch friend, who made out a bill for the entire sum. The count then announced that he had sold the work for the ten million he received from Gurlitt. Bruno Lohse learned the real price from an assistant curator at the Louvre who had filled out the export permit in longhand. (Such a method avoided carbon copies, although it did not necessarily prevent a ledger entry.)

When Gurlitt was questioned in Aschbach—Von Poellnitz's Bavarian castle, which sheltered Haberstock and other bombed-out Linz agents—he had with him twenty cases of paintings, some heirlooms and some purchased in Paris and Amsterdam during the war. This was a handsome nest-egg for a man who might easily have ended in a concentration camp.

Another important Linz agent for Voss had been a staff member for the Dorotheum, a Viennese auction house. Blondish, spectacled, fat-faced Dr. Herbst bought 250 paintings in Holland and in the summer of 1943 went to Paris accompanied by a woman named R. Begeer, a Dutch collaborationist dealer. She had been in Paris toward the end of 1940 and called on a woman whose lectures at the Louvre she had attended. She said she needed help in finding first-grade Impressionist works for a Dutch museum and works by Dürer, Holbein, and Cranach for a German museum. A few months after her visit she sent a letter to her former teacher, giving her address as Hochstrasse 133, Vienna (Perchtoldsdorff):

Vienna, 12 March, 1941

Chère Mademoiselle,

Please excuse my long silence. Instead of returning to Paris in January, I had to leave suddenly for Vienna, and that is why you did not see me again. At first I thought my stay here would be brief, but I now realize that I shall have to remain a while longer and probably will not return to Paris before the end of April.

Please do not think, chère mademoiselle, that I have forgotten what I asked you. Quite the contrary! I repeat my request. I beg you to be so kind as to find me marvelous paintings by Manet, Degas, Renoir, Cézanne, or Toulouse-Lautrec for a museum in Holland.

Price is no object if the painting is of first quality. The painting can be any place at all in France. I have a *laisser-passer* for the unoccupied zone also, and I could probably get you one if you wanted to go there.

I beg you to do whatever you can; this will be good business for you also!! Anyhow, I will be back. Perhaps you have already found something?

Please accept, with my anticipated thanks, my compliments.

[Signed] R. Begeer

This naïve document, with its confident invitation to collaborate, found its way with a covering letter of explanation to the French Committee for Restitution of Stolen Art in 1944. When the M.F.A. and A. sought Herbst in 1945, he could not be found, although he was presumed to be in Vienna. Miss Begeer might have been with him.

With the help of his many agents and dozens of collaborationist dealers all over Europe, Dr. Voss managed to spend the equivalent of sixty million dollars for several thousand paintings in two years. When questioned, he remembered only three specific works and also forgot meetings and discussions others recalled quite well. Despite his bad memory and a crusty disposition that was well known in Germany and soon revealed itself to the Americans, Voss was clever enough to know how to flatter his Führer, and his 1944 birthday gift, a thriftily refurbished acquisition from Posse's time, sent with his "deepest gratitude," may very well have spared him the disgrace that had been visited on Rosenberg a year before.

On April 20, 1943, Rosenberg presented Hitler with a thirty-nine-volume set of brown-leather photograph albums, each one containing fifty photographs of works "seized by his staff" and each one with a hand-lettered title page in Gothic lettering.[1] Rosenberg expected gratitude for making it possible for Hitler to choose conveniently what he wanted for Linz. His reply came the next day, in the form of a letter from Martin Bormann demanding that all the works be immediately turned over to the experts working for Linz: Dr. Voss for art, his address given as the Dresden State Museum, Dr. Friedrich Woffhardt for books, and Dr. von Hümmel for other collections, both of them at the Führerbau in Munich.

Bormann's letter opened a new phase in the control of the E.R.R. in France. It had now passed through two, the first when Göring took complete control at the very beginning of the Louvre operation and the second when Von Behr and Rosenberg set up "Action M" and Rosenberg took over the reins, relegating Göring to a secondary position. Now it was the turn of Hitler and Bormann. Political jealousy and personal greed were again the dominant operating factors. Bormann resented the Rosenberg-Göring alliance, tenuous as it was, and he sought Göring's place as Hitler's chief aide and heir-apparent.

Rosenberg, his back to the wall, replied immediately in a letter from Berlin, where he had moved about a year before. (It must be noted here that Nazi leaders moved about constantly. Hitler relaxed at his home in Berchtesgaden; he visited party headquarters in Munich, inspected factories, and traveled to the front lines on inspection tours. Wherever Hitler went, Bormann also went. Göring alternately stayed in Karinhall, in his hunting lodge, in his Paris apartment, or in any of his other residences. He also visited Luftwaffe installations all over. Rosenberg was chief of both the E.R.R.'s Amt Westen and Amt Östen, which handled eastern confiscations. He also visited bombed German cities to determine their needs for confiscated property, and he had to check on the many E.R.R. repositories of art. Berlin was the capital and the seat of government, but government leaders were quite mobile.)

Rosenberg's letter explained the impossibility of carrying out Bormann's order. The inventories were not completed, and only the E.R.R., which had all the information on the confiscated art, could accomplish the task. Until this inventory was completed, the E.R.R. did not see how any just distribution of the works could be carried out. Besides, a definitive catalog was necessary for the pursuit of negotiations still going on with the French Government, and nobody could prepare such a catalog before the completion of the inventory.

[1] The albums are now in the National Archives, Washington, D.C.

The delay, to be sure, was all the fault of the French, who kept hindering his operations. Rosenberg then pointed out that the Sonderauftrag Linz was a project for the future, whereas the E.R.R. had already shown its mettle by collecting the kind of art that would be suitable for Linz. He added that he had succeeded in this enterprise by tracking down Rothschild possessions all over France. (Since the photographs of these possessions were now in Hitler's hands and had no doubt roused his, or the ambitious Bormann's, lust for possessing them, it seems strange that Rosenberg called attention to them again, but logical thought was never a strong point among Nazi chieftains.) He went on bravely to point out that any works of art not selected for Linz belonged to the party and that it and its treasurer, who had financed the E.R.R., had the right to be consulted. In conclusion, since the Linz experts could not possibly make workable plans to use all this art, he believed it was his duty to explain this whole affair personally to the Führer. (If he could manage this, he could bypass and possibly outsmart Bormann.)

All he received for his pains was a period of grace in which to close down E.R.R. operations in France and at German headquarters. The period of grace was so short that when it was transmitted to Von Behr via telephone from Berlin, he exclaimed, "I think everybody in Berlin has gone mad!"

In the liquidation proceedings something had to be done about the modern paintings, for there were so many of them that they had overflowed the back room of the Jeu de Paume into the Louvre itself. Their fate depended upon how much money they could bring. On April 16 Rosenberg had written Hitler that the modern paintings would be utilized in some special manner that he would one day decide. Suddenly the military situation deteriorated, and Rosenberg had to do something, for he might be ordered to close down his operation quickly. He gave orders, countermanded them, issued new ones. The paintings were packed for departure several times, left in their cases, forgotten, recalled to mind, unpacked again. This business lasted for some time while the art historians grew more and more nervous; the paintings, wrote Miss Valland, seemed to embarrass them, as if "they were explosive material dangerous to handle."

When the E.R.R. decided to return the rooms in the Louvre that they had used for storage, they cleaned them of the debris that had collected in several years of moving paintings in and out. The trash was collected and loaded on a German Army truck and then dumped outside the Jeu de Paume in the Tuileries Gardens and burned. This burning gave rise to an unconfirmed rumor that the Germans were burning several hundred paintings. United States archives are quite precise about the fact that the only destruction of paintings by fire in France occurred at two châteaux, both in the Dordogne. The French Government did not demand restitution, as it would have if paintings had been deliberately destroyed. The Germans would have been incredibly stupid to have performed such an act in the heart of Paris, especially at a time when they were aware that they were losing the war. The German art historians, acutely aware of the honor of their country and personally extremely upset by the confiscations, were not fanatical hoodlums intent on wanton destruction. And since the "burned" paintings were said to have included works by such modern masters as Picasso, Klee, Miró, and Léger, to name only a few, and since such names had always represented money—even to the Nazis, who disapproved of such "degenerate" art—it would have been quite strange indeed for anybody to have turned such vast sums into smoke and ashes.[2]

A last effort to exchange modern art for old masters took place in

[2] This rumor is presented as fact in Valland's *Le Front de l'art* (Chapter 20, pp. 179–182), with the date given as May 27, 1943, on page 179 and again on page 182. The pages between tell of a meeting held in Berlin in July for a decision on which paintings might be saved; after this meeting Robert Scholz and Walter Borchers are said to have gone to the Louvre with other unnamed art historians, all equipped with knives for slashing canvases. The sequence of dates troubled me, and I wrote Miss Valland (August 8, 1969), asking whether there had been a second burning and if so, precisely when. On September 7, 1969, Miss Valland wrote me stating that an error had not been corrected in proofreading and that an errata slip had been inserted in her book "as early as the first edition" to the effect that "Line 17, p. 182, should read July 27, not May 27." This corrected only the second appearance of the date in the text. My own copy was purchased in Paris in April, 1969. It was secondhand, but the pages had not been cut, and the book was sealed in transparent paper. This errata slip was not attached to the copy in the Library of Congress or to that owned by Bruno Lohse or, apparently, to that used by Hildegarde Brenner in the preparation of her book in German on the general subject of Nazi art politics, published in 1963. The May 27 date appeared on wall posters during a 1962 Munich exhibition commemorating the "degenerate art" destruction, and it was repeated in the catalog, which also accepted the story unquestioningly. Scholz and Borchers were personally attacked in a German art magazine for their part in the "destruction," and they replied to the attack in a letter to the magazine, explaining that to clear the rooms for the Louvre, which wanted them back, they had burned "frames, photographs, reproductions, and unsigned works by amateurs," adding that possibly people afraid of being named collaborators had invented the story that Miss Valland believed.

I had never heard such a tale before reading Miss Valland's book and found it quite unbelievable, especially since the American art historians never mentioned it; I have never run across any mention in books on the artists named indicating that any of their works had been burned in Paris, nor is there any such reference in art refer-

1944. A carefully selected group of sixty paintings by Braque, Picasso, Pierre Bonnard, and Marquet was offered in return for a doubtful French eighteenth-century landscape and four architectural views by two Italian artists. The sixty paintings were delivered to a Parisian dealer and valued at a paltry two million francs, the accepted price of one Braque or Picasso at the time. When Robert Scholz saw what was being traded for the modern masterpieces, he canceled the transaction, for the possibility of scandal was too obvious. The sixty paintings, minus one Braque that got lost on the way, returned to the museum.

They remained there with all the others until August 1, 1944. Everything not "degenerate" had left by July 15 for inside Germany, but such entry was forbidden these modern paintings by express order of Hitler. Rosenberg had found a solution to the problem by securing storage room outside the Reich until such time as the canvases could be turned into foreign currency for the E.K. Fund; 148 cases of masterpieces were piled on trucks and taken to a railroad station. The approach of Allied forces made timing important. On August 2 the Germans sealed five cars full of paintings, set a military guard over them, and waited for the rest of the convoy to be loaded. "Action M" had forty-seven cars to load. The loaders were soldiers, inexpert and probably distracted with thoughts of the approaching enemy. The job took ten days, during which the French National Museums sought delaying action from the French National Railways. The railways agreed to help without hesitation, and the convoy broke down at Bourget, a twenty-minute run from central Paris, and had to remain there for forty-eight hours for repairs. Then the convoy was switched to a shunting line that took it to the repair shops at Aulnay to wait for a fresh locomotive. Eighteen hours later, with Von Behr poking and prodding, it seemed inevitable that the train would proceed on its scheduled journey. A rather miraculous intervention stopped this, for a detachment from General Jacques Leclerc's army, already in the area, hastened to the Aulnay yards, ousted the German

---

ence-books, which mention frequently the destruction by fire in Berlin. No artist I asked had ever heard of it either.

Except for the Scholz-Borchers letter after the Munich exhibition in 1962, this story has never been contradicted, either in Germany or elsewhere, except indirectly in United States archives, which are not generally read except by scholars or authors. There is no doubt in my mind, after reading the material prepared by the Monuments, Fine Arts and Archives officers—all careful, thorough men of art—that they could not have overlooked such an occurrence or omitted mention of it in their mountainous reports.

guards, and took over the train.[3] By a curious coincidence the detachment leader was Paul Rosenberg's son, who thus sent part of his father's collection back to the Jeu de Paume. This was the first step in the giant task of restitution, for 2,765 other packing cases reached German repositories.[4]

[3] In 1964 a Franco-Italian film company made *The Train*, a romanticized, inaccurate, and historically incorrect account of this incident which excited audiences while it misinformed them. The film was the subject of a paper (October 10, 1964) by Dr. Bernhard von Tischowitz, successor to Metternich as the head of the Kunstschutz. Although this paper criticizes the film for historical inaccuracy, it is itself inaccurate in its attack on the E.R.R. and its attempt to whitewash the Kunstschutz and the High Command in Paris, for it absolves both of any participation in the confiscations. Among other curious remarks it states that Rose Valland was on Von Behr's staff, that all the E.R.R. members were "healthy young men wearing party uniforms who should have been on the Russian front," that the operation began in the spring of 1940, and that the Musée de Jeu de Paume was completely emptied, all its Impressionist paintings having been safely stored elsewhere.

[4] Robert Scholz listed the contents of the cases as:

10,890 paintings (of all kinds)
684 miniatures
583 pieces of sculpture
2,477 pieces of historically valuable furniture
583 tapestries, carpets, and embroideries
5,825 articles of porcelain, ceramic, bronze, gold, and silver
1,296 pieces of Oriental art
259 pieces of antique art

CHAPTER 8

APPROPRIATIONS AND EXHIBITIONS

THE MANUFACTURE OF war materials demands huge quantities of copper, then found principally in the United States and Canada. Since neither country did business with the Third Reich, when the Nazis had exhausted their stockpile and needed more, they looked elsewhere—to the parks and streets of France, where a considerable amount of copper ordinarily stands on pedestals as statues cast in bronze (eight parts of copper to one part of tin is the standard mix).

As early as June, 1940, the occupants had removed two statues and melted them down: one of General Charles Mangin, a hero of the 1918 French offensives and the Battle of Verdun, and one of Edith Cavell, the English nurse shot in Belgium for her aid to the Allies. About a year and a half later, in the fall of 1941, Vichy, obedient to the commands of its German masters, issued a proclamation: "We, Marshal Pétain, head of the French State, decree the removal of all copper-alloy statues and monuments from public places and buildings so that we may turn the metals therein found into tools for industrial and agricultural production."

The eighty-five-year-old Pétain may have believed that the metal recovered would be used to aid French food production and to provide machine tools. He most certainly believed in government by decree. His original decree was followed by an order from the Minister of the Interior and the Minister of Industrial Production to the prefects of all departments, demanding the establishment of commissions to select the statues to be spared, warning that the choice must be severe, without sentiment, and mindful of the public good. As a kind of reinforcement of this order, Pétain, Laval, and Darlan (themselves already in the process of immortalization by sculpture) suggested to the prefect of the Seine, the district that includes Paris, that his commission save only the statues of Joan of Arc, King Henry IV, and King Louis XIV.

Since monuments and statues in public places are part of the ordinary business of the Beaux-Arts of Paris, the prefect selected his commission from the ranks of that fairly conservative body. The group met in the Hôtel de Ville, passing into the building between the handsome bronze lions on its front steps, and it was not long before their discussions meandered off into interpretations of the statute in a manner typically French. At length they presented a brief list of statues "susceptible" of sacrifice; all the others, and there were hundreds, had to be saved. Pawing the ground with impatience, the Germans issued an ultimatum: The whole affair had to be concluded by the end of 1941. Vichy, stung, stung Paris. The delightfully dilatory commission found itself forced into action while the collaborationist press demanded the "disappearance of all these eyesores" and handed out "certificates of ugliness" to statues representing ideas disagreeable to their politics.

The Frenchman in the street suddenly found himself deeply attached to statues he had never particularly liked or even noticed and began to worry about the small replica of the Statue of Liberty and the Vendôme column, made of twelve hundred enemy cannon captured by Napoleon's armies in 1805. At the same time the German press suggested the destruction of stone statues that "claim to beautify" the streets of Paris, and people were alarmed at the possible destruction or removal of such giants as the elaborate figures adorning the Place de la Concorde. The first tumbrel loads of undesirables, however, were the bronzes: busts and full-length statues, equestrian, pensive, exhortative, or simply decorative. Authors, philosophers, cardinals, generals, physicians, scientists, lions, mermaids, and dolphins were wrenched from their bases and sent off to the foundries. A zealot in the Ministry of Industrial Production insisted that France was dying for lack of copper and ought to sacrifice every monument in the country, including those commemorating the dead of World War I. He yearned for the ornamental bronze lampposts that adorned the city.

Suddenly the occupants recalled a World War I source of copper for German armies: church bells from the more than 150 Parisian churches. The Council of Ministers voted this down, and the bells were spared—on the condition that their equivalent weight in copper be found. Parisian priests gathered up chandeliers, sconces, patens, pyxes, crucifixes, medals, and chalices.

Time passed; statues still stood, and the occupants were not satisfied. Abel Bonnard stepped from the shadows where he had been lurking, and prodded by the O.K.W., began talking nonsense about statues setting noble examples to men of flesh and blood before admitting less poetically that the requisitions had nothing to do with growing grapes, with politics, or with beauty. In flagrant violation of the law, he drew up his own list and let it be known that the only statues spared would be those "the occupant did not demand." The mask was off. After the execution of Bonnard's order only about twenty statues remained in a strangely naked Paris bereft of bronze lampposts, fountains, statues, the chariot and its four horses on the roof of the Grand Palais, Charlemagne on the parvis of Notre Dame, La Fontaine, Victor Hugo, and dozens of other works familiar as landmarks and lovers' trysting places. Out of this melted metal the Germans did extract a certain amount of art: replicas of Rodin's "Gates of Hell" for Linz and Hitler, a replica of "Diana, the Huntress" for Göring, the hunter, and material for the masculine giants of Arno Breker, the Third Reich's favorite sculptor, who was trained in Paris.

The Nazis were not content merely with confiscating great art collections but issued a seven-part edict for the appropriation of Jewish businesses and the exclusion of Jews from the fields of education, journalism, the theater, and the arts. The edict had practically no effect upon the principal "Aryan" art dealers handling contemporary art. They neither demanded birth certificates nor imposed Nazi standards of art when they chose the artists whose works they wished to buy or sell. Such rich and powerful galleries as Knoedler's and such forceful men as Louis Carré, as well as others less famous, accepted abstract paintings or works by Expressionists and other followers or innovators of new trends in contemporary art whether or not the creators were supposed to register as Jews. These dealers saved many artists from total misery and launched many others on successful careers, right under the noses of the occupants. Avant-garde painting was an affirmation of resistance to totalitarianism, not only because artists continued to produce it but also because the French never stopped buying it.

The exhibition of art by Jews or persons on the banned list in art shows organized by the French museums and supervised by German authorities was another story. Artists wishing to submit works to the official *salons* had to sign a paper, swearing on their honor that they were not Jews. The assumption was that every Frenchman was a Jew, and it was up to him to prove otherwise. This often caused a scramble for birth and baptismal certificates when phone calls from organizers demanded positive proof. Artists from small villages across the zonal lines who lost contact with their hometowns and relatives sometimes could not furnish the required proof of indisputable "Aryan" origin. They were then in serious trouble, for the Germans preferred imprisoning six perfectly good Catholics to losing one wicked Jew. World War I orphans, brought up at the expense of the French Government, found it difficult to believe they could not exhibit art at French Government shows simply because they were Jews as well as orphans. The distress of such individuals was shared by the French organizers, who were powerless to overcome the regulations.

Collaborationists took advantage of the situation to submit sentimental plaster statuettes of wounded French soldiers held up by solicitous German soldiers, apotheosized visions of German soldiers surrounded by rainbows, and similar trash. Refused permission to exhibit, such artists complained to the German authorities, accusing the jurors of Germanophobia, and once in a while were astounded to discover that German experts agreed with the jurors.

The 154th Salon d'Automne, held in the Museum of Modern Art, indicated just how far the occupants would go to assert their authority. The inauguration was always a grand affair, opened by the President of the Republic and attended by notables. Since there was no longer a republic or a president, the Germans took over the museum. So many uniformed personnel surged in that civilians could not be noticed and the artists were absolutely lost. The Germans were quite pleased with the show and displayed definite interest in some of the paintings. One wanted to purchase a nude and bargained for it. The artist refused to reduce the price for a German officer and the next day had to remove her painting from the wall, for it had been slashed from top to bottom. Another German wanted to purchase an Indo-chinese work that was on loan. When informed that the painting was not for sale, he left in a rage, threatening requisition.

No exhibits were damaged and no requisitions even suggested at an art exhibition put on by the propagandists for the Germans. Entitled

"France and the Jew," its avowed purpose was "to show racial characteristics of the Jews" in text and image and to point out the evil the Jews had accomplished. The exhibition hall was the Berlitz Palace, a small building on one of the wide boulevards in central Paris. These wide avenues are much frequented by large crowds of people who like to take long walks on sunny days, window-shopping, stopping off for a drink at sidewalk cafés, even visiting sideshows. The sideshow arranged for the education of the French was about as disgraceful, although on a much smaller scale, as the 1937 Munich "Degenerate Art Show." Large signs announced that the people must all defend themselves against Hebraic influence and that the best way to do this was by learning to recognize Jews. They could do this rapidly by looking at the hideous exhibits. Small glass cases contained "models" of "Jewish" ears, fingers, noses, eyes, and heads. Large cards described the exhibits. The art shown was all abstract, and although only one of the paintings was created by a Jew, large cards under each work explained why it was Jewish art. One French abstract artist who saw this "art exhibition" shook his head slowly from side to side as he described it nearly thirty years later and qualified it as "unbelievable."

Equally unbelievable was an announcement posted in all the German prisoner-of-war camps: "An exposition will take place in Paris showing works of art made by prisoners. Give us your work; it will be sold to help your needy comrades." The announcement of the show was made in July, 1941, and the city of Paris decided to put the Galliera Museum at the disposal of the German services, which were eager to show their generosity and the sweetness of life inside their camps. The German sponsoring committee went so far as to set up an additional committee made up of liberated prisoners whom they kept well supplied with drinks. The French also had a committee, appointed by Vichy, to work hand in hand with the Germans. A flood of amateur paintings and drawings, tableware made of tin cans, hand-carved Gallic cocks and cottages, engraved canteens, and the kind of bric-a-brac with which bored men while away endless hours poured into the museum. The men's families planned to come in large numbers, especially since the committees made it known that visitors who entered the exhibition hall could purchase a special postcard to send an extra message to the prisoners, whose correspondence was strictly limited.

The German committee spared no expense, draping the museum in velvet and illuminating it with masses of colored lights—absolutely dazzling at a time when electricity was so rationed that it was a miracle the French did not all develop severe cases of eye strain. The installation of the works was marked by constant backbiting among the committees, all of them intent on their own propaganda. Preparations were thus extremely slow and marked by painting slogans, removing slogans, repainting slogans, waiting for coats of paint to dry, and general indifference on the part of the workmen. In the midst of these petty quarrels Japan bombed Pearl Harbor, and the German High Command knew that the United States would immediately declare war on the Axis. Every time the Americans did anything, the Germans punished Paris by arresting Jews or cutting rations. On December 7, 1941, the curfew was moved back to six in the evening. Workers in the museum would have to leave at 4:30 to get home before the night patrols began. If they left, the exhibition would never be ready. The German committee offered a fat overtime benefit if the workmen would remain in the museum and work all night. To help them make up their minds, the committee brought in piles of food, magnums of champagne, and bottles of good red wine, undoubtedly better rations than any of the men had seen for a long time. They stayed.

The opening day of the Prisoners' Salon was notable for the absence of ranking Germans and the increased number of guards. That same day there was whispered news of the arrests of two university professors and a radio announcement telling of the shooting of one hundred Jews and the deportation of hundreds of others in reprisal for recent attacks on German soldiers. The families of war prisoners came by the hundreds, waiting in long lines to see what the hands of their men had touched, perhaps to recognize a pair of initials or a special sign.

By the constant scheduling of exhibitions in all the available museums the French usually managed to keep the Germans out, with one notable exception whose ramifications extended far beyond museum walls. Directly across the Tuileries Gardens and facing the Jeu de Paume is a small building called the Orangerie. Today a museum primarily devoted to the exhibition of Claude Monet's "Waterlily" paintings, it was once the hothouse of the French kings and—like the Jeu de Paume, its almost-twin—is really a part of the Louvre. Monet's paintings were made to fit the walls of the two main-floor rooms (the Orangerie added a second story in 1968), and since removal of the works is difficult, they remained in place throughout the war years. The Louvre did not want the E.R.R. to take over the Orangerie as a storage warehouse—it would have been extremely convenient for Von Behr and his staff—and Jaujard was quite distressed when an order came from Berlin demanding the use of the museum for a German exhibition in the spring of 1942. Luckily he could reply that the exhibition could take place from March 15 to May 31 only, because another French exhibition was scheduled immediately thereafter.

The artist to be honored with an exhibition at the Orangerie, a site usually reserved for the greatest masters, was Arno Breker, whom Hitler called his Phidias. Breker's speciality was the sculpture of gigantic male nudes in heroic, slightly uncomfortable poses, often exhibiting sexual organs more suitable for bulls than for men. Breker was fairly well known in Paris, where he had studied with both Bourdelle and Despiau, lived in Montmartre, and married a Greek model. He was also known for his profound belief that the only people in the world without any faults were the Germans. During Hitler's one visit to Paris, Breker acted as a sort of expert tour-conductor and courtier. He himself visited the city so often as a representative of the artistic culture of the Third Reich and as an incidental assistant for the Linz project that he felt the need for a suitable residence. He selected the Île St. Louis apartment of Mme. Helena Rubinstein, the cosmetics queen, who was so unfortunate as to have exquisite taste and plenty of money and to have been a Russian-born Jew and an American citizen. Breker decided that her handsomely furnished apartment with its beautiful view over the Seine and the city should be "Aryanized," and he set out to get it. He went to Abetz, who considered this idea superb and sent out a requisition order.

Once set up in quarters suitable for his artistic temperament, Breker wanted a Paris exhibition of his monumental males. The German Institute, set up in the ex-Embassy of Poland, went to work on the project, softening up dozens of Parisians in various ways, which included gifts of sacks of coal and bags of ersatz coffee. The Vichy Government added its support to the project by announcing the patronage of the exhibition by its Secretary of State in a letter inviting "the most representative personalities of Paris" to lend their names to the patronage committee. (The committee was set up quite late, four days before the actual opening—"regrettably," according to the Secretary.) The publicity for this affair was enormous; the receptions given, countless. Laval made a speech at a banquet and compared Breker to the greatest artists of all time.

In their desire to surround Breker with a suitable artistic aura, the Germans cast a lure to notable French artists: an invitation from the Führer to visit Germany officially while German artists visited France. The trip for the French would include all kinds of public homage, elaborate banquets, visits to museums, and welcoming committees composed of the greatest German artists, who would invite their French brethren to their studios and accompany them on sketching trips. Since the greatest German artists either had left the country or were unable to work, this phase of the visit struck an ironic note. A feather attached to the lure promised the liberation of prisoners of war as the crowning event of the projected visit. Any artist who embarked on this trip would be helping his unfortunate compatriots.

About twenty important painters and sculptors, their scruples wiped away or buried, took down their valises and prepared to make the trip. Among them was André Derain, who had previously refused an invitation to travel to Germany to paint the portraits of Ribbentrop and his family. Derain had been bitterly grieved by the destruction of a large canvas with a classical subject from Greek mythology which he had left in his country studio; German soldiers, billeted in the building, did bayonet practice on its figures. He naïvely believed that he would see Hitler during the trip, however, explain the situation in Paris, and tell the Führer what he thought. Derain believed firmly in the release of prisoners—the number to be set free for each artist on the trip varied from "some" to 200 and as high as 250, depending on which German official was promoting the idea. Others who went along were Vlaminck, Derain's ex-friend to whom he had not spoken for several years, and the sculptor Despiau, who had also let himself be inveigled into affixing his signature to the preface of a book glorifying Breker and his work.

Since it was really only a propaganda stunt, the trip resulted in nothing at all. No prisoners were released, Hitler did not receive the artists, and the French were intolerably bored. Among the invitations extended to the group was one from Albert Speer, then still merely Hitler's architect, who knew several of the men and asked them to his office to look at the models for the improved Berlin to rise after the war. Speer was not present, but the artists must have said nothing at all when they looked at the plans for a triumphal arch large enough to contain the Arc de Triomphe forty-nine times and a Chancellery dome greater than St. Peter's, for the architect's office journal recorded no comments on November 11, 1941, the date of their visit. Speer had helped several of this group with commissions from Germany, but even this moved nobody to ecstatic approval of the designs.

Derain's comment about the entire trip when he returned was, "It was long, very long." He then retreated into complete silence and never mentioned the journey again. Vlaminck echoed Derain's bored comment, adding that they had done nothing from morning to night except visit museums. Despiau, his friends say, was so depressed by the way he had been taken in that he never recovered. He died shortly after the liberation of Paris, weighing so little, his friends said, that "it was pitiful to see him." Possibly the sole benefit gained by anybody was the reconciliation, even though somewhat tenuous, of Derain and Vlaminck.

The elaborate opening of Breker's exhibition was attended by an audience dressed predominantly in gray-green uniforms, among which was a light sprinkling of French officials and a few artists. German propaganda whispered that the initiative for the whole show was really French and that this proved that they were all much more in favor of Hitlerism than they pretended. The Spanish painter Sert was baffled by the choice of locale and thought that the National Museums sponsored the exhibition. He telephoned one of the curators to ask, "Is it the Louvre that organized this garbage?" One French artist remarked that Breker's claim to love France frightened her, as this kind of love ate one alive. The prefect of Paris sighed over the buffet served at the opening and remarked that at least he had taken that from the enemy. One of Breker's old Montparnasse friends, it was said, met the sculptor on the street and asked him what he was doing parading around Paris while his pals were being slaughtered on the Russian front. Breker had his exhibition, and Paris had a bit of gossip to enliven the dreary days.

Various collaborationist groups and individuals also besieged the museum directors with requests for odd or impossible exhibitions. A group of French colonial officials wanted to show one about the colonial influence in French decoration—paintings, sculpture, tapestries, silks, wallpaper, furniture, faience, porcelain, clocks, and other furnishings showing colonial influence from the time of the Crusades to 1940. The idea was pleasant but unrealizable. Most of the public collections were in storage, and most of the private collections had been confiscated. What little remained was either impossible to obtain or completely without interest. The colonials were quite distressed and insisted on their plan until the curator in charge of decorative arts lost his temper completely. He named the works absolutely essential for a successful exhibition and followed each work with the name of its owner: Rothschild, David-Weill, Weil-Picard. This so infuriated the spokesman for the colonials that he protested that there must be some collectors who were not Jews. The meeting ended abruptly when the curator asked, "Do you know of any? Very well, name them."

Another collaborationist-inspired brainstorm was "an international salon for music and the arts it inspired." Its object was the reappraisal of moral and artistic influences, the regrouping of national talents, and help for unappreciated artists who thought the "right" way.

The General Commissariat for the Family wanted to do something about the birth rate and proposed an exhibition that would do honor to Vichy's slogan: "Country, Family, Work" (which replaced "Liberty, Equality, Fraternity"). The exhibit would exalt domestic and family virtues and vilify unmarried men and women, divorce, pornography, venereal diseases, and contraceptives. One could hardly have picked a worse time to plan such an exhibit. Almost every French family had one or more of its male members in prisoner-of-war camps; thousands of young men were being drafted into forced labor in Germany, and others were hiding in the Maquis to avoid such drafts. The French family was on a near-starvation diet. Six months of the projected dioramas and demonstrations of how to bring up babies and be a good housewife might very well have brought on the rebellious explosion so far avoided.

CHAPTER 9

ARTISTS' LIVES

ON AUGUST 6, 1942, Göring complained that the French ate too much. It was true they ate too many sausages stuffed with sawdust, too many cheeses made of old melted-down ends, and definitely too much turnip soup, flavored with last week's bone if one were lucky enough to have had a bit of meat. The French also drank too much questionable fruit juice to replace the wine they could not find. After their gourmet meals they might relax with a cup of hot liquid brewed from a mixture of one part coffee to two parts dried beans or chick-peas. Smokers might enjoy too many cigarettes made of corn-husks or eucalyptus, linden, or tomato leaves. The French family could wash with a sliver of soap that felt, smelled, and cleaned like plaster.

The French had eight categories of ration cards, labeled A to V, bread tickets, and pink and blue coupons for household equipment, clothing, shoes, school notebooks, and detergents. A special ticket marked in large black letters indicating the months of the year brought special foods at specific seasons: January, figs; November, oranges. Most adults were classified in ration category "A" and had the right each month to 18 pounds of bread, 4½ pounds of potatoes, 1¼ pounds of meat, and 4½ bottles of wine . . . in 1942. In 1939 the same adult had eaten, per month, 30 pounds of bread, 66 pounds of potatoes, nearly 8 pounds of meat, and drunk 12 bottles of wine.

Since the cost of food increased in direct proportion to its decrease in availability, actual prices paid had quadrupled by 1942, although legal prices had only doubled. Although ordinary salaries of white-collar workers had increased by from 30 to 35 percent between 1939 and 1942, against a cost-of-living rise of 70 percent, everybody able to afford it traded on the black market, where a pound of butter cost twice a day's pay for a clerk or shop-girl.

The Germans encouraged the black market, another method of ruining the French economy and lowering morale. They did not encourage the flourishing trade in forged ration cards, bread tickets, and coupons. The forgeries, created by artists, cost slightly less than genuine cards, which were stolen by the hundreds in raids on city halls all over France. Artists also made false passports, travel vouchers, and identity cards for Resistants or people trying to escape. Sculptors created the rubber stamps needed to make the false papers credible.

Artists, unless they were already firmly established or sold constantly to dealers during the Occupation years, suffered with the rest of the population. Many of them struggled along on the fourteen-francs-a-day allotment for the unemployed. The sale of a painting cut off the dole for as many days as forty francs could be divided into the net price received. (This was an indication that nobody believed fourteen francs a day was enough to live on, although this sum was never increased as the cost of living mounted.) Artists have starved in Paris garrets for generations, usually helped over the lean times by their more affluent comrades; but during this period the more affluent had, in general, left Paris. Picasso's wartime still-lifes showing pitchers of water and two or three undersized fruits are accurate reflections of that grim era. Picasso, however, never complained, and when the Germans offered him extra coal and food, he replied haughtily that "Spaniards are never cold and never hungry."

Picasso could not keep the Germans out of his studio. They visited him constantly on the thinnest of pretexts, asking about Jewish artists who had long since left the country, inspecting his work with a view to purchase, or simply observing as if he were some sort of tourist attraction. This bothered him considerably, for he feared they might be planting an incriminating paper among the hundreds of sketches lying around in the crowded room. He worried, too, about his small sculptures made of metal scraps that his friends brought him. One German officer remarked that the sculptures were too small to make cannon but were large enough for revolvers. None of the works was confiscated, however. Picasso soon grew bored with these visits and to amuse himself had some postcards made of "Guernica," his anti-

Franco, antiwar painting commemorating that atrocity. These he would press on the soldiers as "souvenirs." When asked by a Nazi, pointing to a replica of "Guernica" on the wall, if he had done that, Picasso retorted with his now-famous quip, "No, you did."

Many artists, to forget the world around them, drew and painted landscapes, figures, and scenes of the world that had been. Many more, haunted by the miseries of war, painted a decomposing world or an exaggeratedly hungry one. The spiky, angular painting of Bernard Buffet was born during the war, the work of an adolescent so poor he used bed-sheets for canvas. The impulse toward abstraction moved strongly ahead also; in an unbalanced universe artists played with subtle balances of forms and colors.

A considerable number of artists joined the Resistance, manufacturing fake rubber stamps, altering photographs for false papers, camouflaging installations of the Maquis,[1] making posters to be hastily stuck on walls between Nazi patrols after curfew, or drawing cartoons for clandestine newspapers. Others performed acts of sabotage, acted as spies, or joined De Gaulle's army. Many not actively Resistants themselves shielded those who were, hiding men and women sought by the Gestapo, taking in Allied aviators forced to bail out over France, and sheltering the hundreds who disappeared from view to avoid deportation as forced laborers.

Dozens of clandestine newspapers began to appear, put together by small groups working secretly to pass on scraps of information censured out of official papers, advice for raising morale, and hints for improving living conditions. *L'Art Français*, typewritten and mimeographed, appeared four times, once each year of the Occupation. Its editor was Edouard Goerg, a painter and printmaker well known in France. Its articles were unsigned, and it is possible that Goerg wrote most of them himself. Issue Number 2 (1942) advised artists on the dole not to declare their sales and so avoid loss of their fourteen francs a day or, if this were impossible, to falsify professional expenses by tripling or quadrupling the quantities of paint, canvas, clay, paper, and brushes used in order to cut down on net profit. The advice continued with an urgent warning to those skilled in the handling of metal—sculptors and printmakers—to switch to other art

[1] *Maquis* means "brush" and refers first to Mediterranean scrub land covered with bushes and briars. *Prendre le maquis* is to hide out in such land; hence the use of the word to indicate the remote areas where Resistants lived together in camps. A *maquisard* was anybody who hid out in this manner. *Maquis* eventually came to refer to the underground organization itself.

forms and hide their talent. Skilled metal workers were especially subject to deportation to forced labor in Germany, and there, the writer assured them, they would be killed by British bombs dropping squarely on the factories. Since information about bombing raids was censured out of official newspapers, this last served a double purpose.

Other bits of gossip, news of forced sales of Jewish property to Vichy ministers, descriptions of modern paintings damaged by moisture from storage in cellars, reports of prominent artists who refused to exhibit as long as the Germans occupied the country, an account of the arrest and imprisonment of a Louvre curator, a plea to French artists to risk liberty and even life for a free France—all were calculated to arouse anger or pride and stir readers into action.

Underground newspapers were delivered at night, slipped into mailboxes by men who sauntered casually along deserted streets long after curfew, stopping occasionally to scrawl *V*'s and the Cross of Lorraine on walls with a scrap of chalk. Wehrmacht patrols walked the streets regularly, their boots loud and frightening; Wehrmacht patrol cars drove around and around. Encounter with a patrol could be dangerous: The presence of a piece of chalk in a pocket was evidence of guilt; possession of the newspapers was a serious offense. Yet the newspapers were regularly or irregularly delivered all over France. Before the occupation of the entire country, editorial rooms were usually in the southern zone. After the take-over, many became mobile. It was quite possible to hide in the forests of the Maritime Alps or to change residence every night, hiding out with friends or friendly sympathizers.

The beginning of the war was the occasion for the formation of the Artists' Aid Society (Société d'Entraide des Artistes), which accomplished the difficult feat of allying diverse tendencies into a single force for mutual assistance. The society was based, ironically enough, on a gift from the Salomon Rothschild Foundation. The Baroness de Rothschild had left her large Parisian mansion, its outbuildings, and its spacious grounds to the French Government on condition that the property be used by the Beaux-Arts. She also endowed the gift with a yearly income of one hundred thousand *gold* francs. The governing body of the foundation included people from the Beaux-Arts, the Sorbonne, art dealers, collectors, and curators. They agreed unanimously, as soon as war was declared, that some sort of unified aid to artists was imperative, and the foundation gave the Artists' Aid Society about four hundred thousand francs to set up immediately a kind of thrift shop and lunch canteen. Voluntary assistance by members of important artistic groups made it possible for needy artists to purchase clothing and one good meal a day for a minimum outlay of money.

The Occupation of Paris and the enactment of racial laws forced the disappearance of several foundation members—Georges Wildenstein, David-Weill, and Paul Léon among them. The result was a further tightening of the links between all artists' associations. The society agreed unanimously to add the mounting of art exhibitions in the vacant museums to its functions. The governing committee met every Wednesday in the Rothschild house, not daring to call it by its name any longer but referring to it simply by the street address: Rue Berryer.

The meetings always began in the same way, with a reading of letters: from prisoners, from families looking for a lost member, from poverty-stricken artists, or from Vichy, commenting on the society's efforts to provide assistance. When art materials began to disappear from shops, artists turned to the society for help in finding them. Often the committee did not recognize the name of the person writing and had to find out whether a real professional was in need. It became necessary to take a general census of artists and set up a file. This made it possible to decide properly who was truly entitled to aid and who was simply trying to get something for nothing or who simply practiced art as a pastime.

Vichy eventually sent out official directives for the proper behavior of artists and the production of edifying, moral art. Nobody in France paid any attention to such announcements, however, for they were seldom followed by specific decrees or actions. The collaborationist parties were not really consistent or united on the kind of art and literature to be desired. Many admired Cézanne with as much enthusiasm as they praised Céline, the most fascist of French authors. The Catholic Church embraced both pure classical art and the work of Georges Rouault. The Communists were less enthusiastic about Picasso than other French art lovers, because acceptable art in "Bolshevik" Russia was exactly the kind Hitler extolled: realistic, nationalistic, and propagandistic. The aim of the Vichy Government was to let its artists do as they liked but to regiment them at the same time by organizing them into corporations like medieval guilds.

The Artists' Aid Society was called in by the Government as consultant on the best way to set up such corporations. Vichy had already organized one for architects and could not wait to start on the artists. The name envisaged was the "Order of Graphic and Plastic Arts," and the first thing to be done was to define the "profession." Vichy suggested that "anybody who makes most of his livelihood from the sale of his works is to be considered a professional." (An artist like Henri Rousseau, who made most of his money as a customs officer, was not a professional under this definition, nor was Van Gogh, who sold only one painting during his lifetime and was supported by his brother.) Each accredited member of the order would swear to practice his art conscientiously and perform his professional duties honestly. When presented with this idea, working artists responded with hilarity, ribald laughter, and sarcastic questions about "professional duties."

The proposed regulations, requiring only originality as a basis for censure, provided for disciplinary measures to be enforced by the "Council of the Order." A public scolding of the "guilty" artist in the council chamber was the first step. Persistent misbehavior would add a written report to the artist's file. The next step hinted strongly at Germanic practices: a ban on exhibition for a stated period. The last step was an indictment by the Minister of Fine Arts and the removal of the artist's name from the lists of the order.

The proposal was so ridiculous that no artists approached to handle it would touch it. The Government let the idea die. The one useful result was the establishment of an official file that became a general listing of all the artists in France, a mild enough form of order in a chaotic milieu of fierce individualists.

French curators continued to run exhibitions and so keep the museums out of the hands of the Germans, with the exception of Breker's show, until late in 1942. One day the concierge of the twin national and municipal Museum of Modern Art buildings telephoned a curator to warn him of some new German claims. They had asked him to open the communicating door between the basements of the two museums for easier passage of their trucks. The curator hastened to the museum, which was kept closed part of the time, and discovered that the Germans had accumulated large quantities of "merchandise" inside the national building. From time to time they sorted out this stockpile and sent off whatever Germany needed. If they could open the basement door between the buildings, their trucks would not have to back out but could move along in regular file and reach the street. The "merchandise" consisted of the contents of homes and apartments belonging to Jews.

Although the curator forbade the opening of the door, his ban was useless. Higher authorities intervened, and both basements were soon filled with loot, some of it brought in by soldiers. The municipal building was used for storing heavy cases; the national building held furniture. The cases were neatly arranged by size in a gridiron pattern reminiscent of a dreary modern suburb. Placards, hung from the ceiling, marked lettered "avenues," and slight narrower ones marked numbered "cross streets." Each case had an identifying label carefully nailed on: "SHOES," "WINDOW CURTAINS," "TOYS," "MEN'S SHIRTS," "DRESSES," "MEDICINE." The combination of letters and numbers made it easier to get to the desired counter in this department store for stolen goods. Cases came and went constantly until the liberation of Paris, when the museums were left with their basements still stocked with the kind of property not ordinarily put into display cases.

The artifacts of French-Jewish life arrived in the museum basements after a preliminary selection at the warehouse of the Gare d'Austerlitz, the principal merchandise station in Paris. The sorters were Jews subject to "semideportation" because they were married to "Aryans." "Semideportation" meant either permanent internment on the English Channel island of Alderney or temporary internment in the station's large wooden building normally used for storing merchandise. The raids that always began at four in the morning removed whole families of Jews to deportation centers: horribly overcrowded camps, sports stadiums, or synagogues. Empty homes and apartments were then stripped of everything but the walls and windows. Miscellaneous objects were tossed into large wooden cases, and the cases and furniture were taken to Austerlitz. The Jews unpacked the belongings of their fellow-sufferers, the men doing the heavy work and the women sorting and arranging in "departments": watches, books, furs, jewels, china, furniture, and so on. The privileged customers were German officers, who were permitted to take whatever they liked for themselves or their families back home. After bombing raids on the area around Paris, French militia men also had this privilege. What remained after these riflings went to Germany about twice a month or was repacked in cases for museum storage.

The museum basements full of packing cases and the shipments from Austerlitz were part of "Action M," which was at first confined to furnishings taken from middle-class and poor Jews. In 1943 "Action M" enlarged its scope to include the contents of the homes of the wealthiest Jews. Their furnishings had originally been left in place to accommodate and comfort German officials and officers who lived in the vacated dwellings. Rosenberg asked the military command for a special order making such seizure possible, for he wished to make certain that nothing of value would be forgotten in the event of a headlong departure before an Allied advance. The order was issued on October 17, 1943, but even before it had become official, the Paris home of the David-Weill family was emptied of everything it contained in five days. The furnishings included 176 pieces of antique furniture and family souvenirs that were simply labeled "origin unknown." These objects remained in the museum long enough to be exhibited and then were carefully packed, so carefully that they returned to France after the war's end in their German cases.

Stolen property, whether priceless or more commonplace, was not all that left France during the Occupation years. High-ranking officers and common soldiers used Occupation francs to purchase whatever they desired. The Reichsbank received one or two shipments a week—sometimes truck convoys, sometimes entire freight-car loads. Quantities listed on shipping invoices turned over to the French Government after the war indicated that even those who were not in Paris could purchase such things as antique desks, silken quilts, yards of woolens, honey, canned meats, and paradichlorobenzene. The Reichsbank itself removed enough gold and silver ingots from the Banque de France's vaults to create a vermeil table service for 150—the largest and most elaborate ever made. It was created in France by French workers, who also made elegant cabinets to contain the silver, embroidered dozens of cloths and napkins to use with it, and if they were more unfortunate, were sent to Berlin to work on the installation of a luxurious private suite for the Reichsbank's directors and their display of wealth. In the end, however, the Götterdämmerung of the Berlin fire destroyed everything.

The principal difference between the constant purchasing of the Reichsbank and the confiscations of the E.R.R. and "Action M" was in the surface legality involved in the exchange of currencies. To the demoralization of visible German buying on the black market (with resultant scarcity and even higher prices for the French population) were added the exportation of goods and materials essential for survival, the removal of gold and silver reserves vital to postwar stabilization of devalued currency, and the utilization of French labor, already in short supply because of measures set up by the Germans and agreed to by Vichy. Food shortages continued in France for years after 1945; the last item to be taken off the ration list was coffee in January, 1950. Fabrics urgently needed for reviving exhausted wardrobes could not be woven fast enough. All sorts of materials necessary for postwar housing repairs were difficult to acquire. The French economy needed years to recover from the constant drainage of everything from garden spades to kitchen pots, glass, roofing materials, and feather beds.

CHAPTER 10

ADVANCE AND EVASION

THE BEGINNING OF SEVERE Allied bombing raids along the northern coasts of France and the interior from the Channel to Paris caused the directors of the National Museums to decide upon evacuations of art from provincial museums. (A Vichy decree on August 10, 1941, had centralized responsibility and delegated different powers to city and state authorities. Provincial museums became more dependent on the state and less on local authorities. As a result, about a year later the National Museums elevated some provincial museums to national status so their collections could be better protected during the Occupation.) The principal museums affected were those in Amiens, Caen, Lille, and Valenciennes, and their collections were removed between May and December, 1942, to châteaux in the south and center of the country. The museums were all located in cities and towns occupied by important German military installations whose commanding officers had frequently decorated their own quarters with whatever they fancied in the way of painting and sculpture. The curator in charge of the museum at La Rochelle, which was to be one of the last centers of German resistance to total defeat in 1945, remarked that he would have considerable difficulty in evacuating the best paintings in the museum, since they had been taken out to adorn the commanding officers' offices and lodgings. The curator's own house had been sacked, and the new quarters he had found near the museum were also inhabited by three German soldiers, whose presence he found obsessive.

The sacking of private homes and the quartering of soldiers often took bizarre forms. The daughter of one artist received permission from Metternich to return to her occupied home for the removal of her father's paintings. When she arrived, she found a soldier who invited her in to pick up her pictures. She found the paintings hanging exactly as she had left them, but everything else in the house had disappeared. One woman artist returned to her country house to find a group of German soldiers packing her last finished painting. All her other works had long since crossed the frontier into Germany. When she looked at her remaining painting, she discovered that a German signature had replaced her own.

Other brazen or mysterious thefts occurred. In May, 1942, the Nemours Museum found itself without five large tapestries, which had been "removed under curious circumstances." Part of a collection left in a house not far from Paris vanished when occupying troops left the house. Three important paintings disappeared from the Mulhouse Museum during its occupancy by officials of the Ahnenerbe. Clocks, rugs, furniture, tapestries, sculpture, books, and art were removed from homes occupied by German troops, who occasionally took whatever they fancied and went off leaving gates and doors open so that any other light-fingered persons might finish the job they had begun. In one château not far from Paris a group of experts or dealers went through the rooms taking everything they found valuable. Among them, noted the château's owner, was "a woman in boots" who remarked after the going-over that "nothing of any interest remained."

When part of the Salorges Maritime Museum was destroyed by bombs, a French officer helplessly watched German soldiers tear eighteenth-century Indian prints from the walls and use them as wrappings for ship models removed from intact sections of the museum. A German Air Force commander in charge of the Château de Sassy supervised the removal in July, 1940, of three hundred letters written by Kings Louis XVIII, Charles X, and Louis Philippe. The city architect of Fribourg removed several antique vases from the Colmar Museum, claiming that he would use them to decorate an "artists' shelter," but kept the vases for himself. From the piles of documents listing such losses—each perhaps small in itself but contributing, finally, to a staggering total—comes an inexorable impression of the weakness of the Vichy Government, which protested not at all or so feebly as not to be heard or, worst of all, frequently went beyond German demands in an effort to ingratiate itself with the conquerors.

When the Germans invaded the unoccupied zone in November, 1942, the prefect of the department in which Montauban is located notified the curators of the imminent arrival of German troops. The curators of military age put on their uniforms and presented themselves at the French barracks. They expected military retaliation by Vichy for this breach of the armistice and wished to join the regular army or whatever was left of it. They were thanked politely, informed that Vichy had sent no orders, and told to come back the next day. When they returned, the French had gone, and the Germans had arrived and taken possession of the city without firing a shot. The French garrison had left behind a quantity of essential foodstuffs–sugar, chocolate, coffee, and dried foods–which had been put aside for distribution to the general population in the event of dire necessity; the Germans preempted the entire supply. The troops had moved in smiling, happy, and extremely pleased with themselves, with the landscape, and with the rosy-pink buildings of Montauban and the surrounding towns. Their principal weapon was the camera, and they snapped away as if they were welcome tourists. The effect of this triumphal entry was to depress and alarm the Louvre curators, who watched from the windows of the Ingres Museum and realized that they were now in the battle line and that their illusory peace and freedom had completely vanished.

The day after the arrival of the enemy troops, the curators decided that they could not move the 3,500 paintings in the Ingres Museum while the German Army was moving to its positions, but they could prepare the paintings for a move at the proper moment. They replaced the paintings in their crates, beginning with the smallest and most fragile, and began to move the packed crates to the cellar of the building. They knew that they would have to move but were not yet definite as to where. Montauban is situated on the Tarn River, over which runs an important bridge vital to transportation both by road and by rail. After a consultation with Paris the order was definite: The paintings had to be moved to places far from communications centers, out of the reach of bombing raids.

The directors of the French National Museums had kept in close contact with the Allies and with the Free French forces in London from the beginning of the war. Their first suggestion had been a kind of International Red Cross to protect works of art, an idea that both Vichy and the Germans opposed and never allowed to materialize. Radio contact between Paris and London continued, however, with messages passed to London via the Resistance and replies given during the British Broadcasting Corporation broadcasts to the French in the form of cryptic personal greetings. Whenever the museum collections changed their repositories, the news reached London, and when it did, the answers came: "The 'Mona Lisa' smiles," or "Van Dyck salutes Fragonard"–the second phrase referring to the Flemish artist's position as court painter to King Charles I and to Fragonard's having worked in the Louvre. The references in the messages could not have been misunderstood by the Germans, who monitored the broadcasts and tried to scramble them, but the enemy did not know to what information they replied. (Some French curators believed that one of the reasons for German interest in museums as storage places for their own loot stemmed from the idea that the Allies would not deliberately destroy art museums.)

Once the order had been received from Paris, it was necessary for the curators in Montauban to move as rapidly as possible. They began by temporarily transporting the most precious cases to the Château de Loubéjac a few days after the new occupation began. Since the museum's request to use the château immediately preceded a requisition order from the Germans, who wanted it as General Staff headquarters, the owners were delighted to have accommodated their own people first. Loubéjac is a fairly small, unpretentious building, just large enough to hold the contents of a single hall in the Ingres Museum. Once the precious crates arrived, they simply remained in place, unopened because of lack of space and a shortage of personnel. The curator-in-charge was André Chamson, whose curator-wife supervised the packing of the remaining art in Montauban and joined her husband at Loubéjac on weekends.

When everything in Montauban was packed, the curators, accompanied by Jaujard, started on a tour that lasted several days in an effort to find one château large enough to contain all the collections and suitable lodgings for everybody. By this time, the museum staffs were experts in this type of work. They scrutinized a number of châteaux, checking humidity, measuring doorways for height and width, testing floors and ceilings for solidity, and inspecting heating facilities, outbuildings, and sources of food. Châteaux were also much in demand for purely military purposes like the quartering of troops and centers for communications, but owners or estate managers were generally pleased to receive the museum people, whose request promised peaceful occupancy; nevertheless, happy welcomes sometimes soured as the complexities of storage intruded on private living. The curators realized that this forced communal living was difficult for all concerned. Estate managers and servants were confused, proprietors were inconvenienced, and the curators felt like intruders.

Loubéjac was completely abandoned when the Department of Paintings was moved to the Château de Montal, a beautifully restored building that belonged to the daughter of a former president of the Council of National Museums. Montal was too small, however, for the opening of cases; two neighboring châteaux, Vayrac and Bétaille, were requisitioned for this purpose. The major part of the Egyptian collection, drawings and archives, art objects, and the Rothschild art objects went to Latreyne, on a rocky point above the Dordogne River. The Chamsons were in charge of Latreyne, which was not far from Montal, whose curator-in-chief was René Huyghe; thus the staff of each repository could help the other in the event of an emergency.

The Louvre collections remained in these repositories for the remainder of the war, and the curators again settled down to lives as full of expedients as they had been at Montauban. At the beginning, finding dietary additions was slightly less difficult. The region of the Dordogne, a combination of wooded hills and flat river-lands pitted with chalky caves, gives an impression of being less fertile than do other regions of France. The area is considered sterile, and the Germans satisfied their greed in richer territory. Curators on marketing expeditions were therefore astonished to find eggs, real white bread, and cheese purchasable from small farmers who sometimes had more on hand than they could eat or keep themselves and no safe market for the surplus. To send an additional supply of such food into any sizable town would have attracted the attention of German authorities and soon impoverished everybody.

The extra nourishment was welcome, for all the National Museum curators now had extra and quite heavy duties. In March, 1942, a Government decree had reorganized all French museums, putting them all under the watchful guardianship of the National Museums. When the institutions of the Mediterranean region, the Rhone Valley, and the Atlantic coastal region were removed to shelters in the interior, each Louvre curator was responsible for regular inspection tours to the repositories. André Chamson, for example, was answerable for the surveillance of nine châteaux, scattered over a fairly wide area. He made his first tour of inspection to two of them, both belonging to the Order of the Benedictines. At Sainte-Scholastique, a cloistered convent, the nuns opened the doors normally closed against male visitors to allow the inspection of the cases. At En Calcat the curator was invited to share the monks' midday meal.

At Saint-Guilhem, also under Chamson's jurisdiction, the repository chief was the village priest, and the abbey hid not only cases of art but also cases of machine guns parachuted down by the British, as well as an English parachutist. Somebody informed Jaujard that the Gestapo knew of the latter cache and planned a raid on the crypt. He telephoned Chamson and sent him on an immediate inspection to see to it that the Gestapo found only cases containing works of art. The priest did not know the curator and was afraid he was being tricked into an admission of guilt. Until his suspicions were overcome, he swore that only art was hidden in the crypt. When Chamson left, the priest immediately ordered the removal of the cases of munitions to another shelter in the mountains and found another hiding place for the English soldier. The priest's original fears would have been stilled sooner if he had known that the curator of Latreyne was also Commandant Lauter, of the Maquis of the region, an alias taken from the Lauter River, which separates France from Germany and where he had spent the winter of 1939–1940 as a soldier in the French Army.

CHAPTER 11

ALARMS AND EXCURSIONS

THE SPRING OF 1944 was a time of hope and a time of dying. Allied pressure upon French ports and Norman and Breton cities and towns, the inevitable and necessary softening-up process before the invasion, took the form of saturation bombing: 1,284 raids on 793 localities in May, 2,307 raids on 1,572 sites in June.

The Allied pressure inside France also extended into Germany, where the raids were more frequent and heavier and destroyed not only people and property but civilian morale as well. Inside France the Wehrmacht and the Gestapo clung tenaciously to their customary raids; their behavior, in many instances, was more insensate than ever.

In the Dordogne, spring comes early. On March 30, 1944, in a place not very far removed from the châteaux used by the Louvre, a particularly spiteful and wanton act of looting and burning took place at Rastignac, the home of an Anglo-French family named Lauwick. The head of the house, dead before the incident occurred, had been an English naval officer. Living in the château were his widow; one of his sons, Jacques; his daughter, the wife of an English Indian Army officer; and her young son. In addition to family treasures, the house contained twenty-seven Impressionist paintings belonging to the Bernheim family, Parisian collectors and international art dealers. The paintings were not displayed upon the walls but were well hidden. The location of the château, which was built in the style of the White House in Washington, was enviable for its view but not for its wartime situation, since it was between Gestapo headquarters for the region and those of the Wehrmacht.

At about eight o'clock in the morning of March 30 the Lauwicks saw a large column of Germans moving along the valley road below the estate. The men were from the Gruppe Brenner, a unit commanded by General Brenner, and came from Wehrmacht (Army) headquarters. At about nine o'clock a car marked "Police" arrived at the château from the opposite direction. An Obersturmführer (three stars on his collar), a two-starred officer, a noncommissioned officer, and two S.S. troopers got out. Young, thin, dark, arrogant, and wearing thick, rimless glasses, the S.S. officer in charge ordered the family into the courtyard, where their servants were already assembled. All of them remained standing for three hours, guarded by two S.S. men, while they listened to the sounds of pillage inside the house: doors smashed in, furniture overturned, bureau and desk drawers pulled out and tossed on the floors. At about eleven o'clock they heard the sound of gunfire and learned later that the Germans had executed the mayor's assistant and his secretary.

At about noon the Obersturmführer came out and ordered the removal of the three younger members of the family to Gestapo headquarters. The servants and Mme. Lauwick were ordered to Wehrmacht headquarters. Mme. Lauwick's request to enter the house to get identification papers and some money was refused.

The Lauwicks stood against the wall at Gestapo headquarters for another three hours, this time six feet apart and guarded by a sentry. At some point during their waiting for what must have seemed inevitable death, they heard another fusillade: the execution of a farmer and his fifteen-year-old son. Eventually, the time came for questions. The Gestapo were troubled because they had found only a few thousand francs in drawers. The Lauwicks had a safe hidden behind false doors, and this had not been discovered during the looting. The S.S. officer then asked when the château had been built, a question that Jacques Lauwick found peculiar at this moment, since the German knew that the house was a replica of the White House and must, therefore, have been built after 1800. He would have found this architectural interest incredible if he had known that the château was then burning to the ground.

They learned later that shortly after their departure five empty trucks pulled up to the front door and left soon after, no longer empty. Large Flemish tapestries and the antique Persian rugs that the senior Lauwick had brought from Turkey when he was naval attaché there in 1895 were rolled up and loaded onto the trucks. The family silver was parceled out to Wehrmacht soldiers at their headquarters, bedding and linen were carried away, and clothing was distributed to civilians. The doors to the wine cellar were smashed in, and the soldiers enjoyed a collection of fine wines and liqueurs. Then a special group in asbestos garments set fire to the farm buildings, the barns, an eighteenth-century greenhouse, the estate manager's house, and the château itself. When the Lauwicks returned to poke about in the ruins of their home, they recognized countless valuable objects that had escaped looting and died twisted in the heat of the fire.

The Bernheim paintings—works by Cézanne, Renoir, Matisse, Manet, Toulouse-Lautrec, Van Gogh, Sisley, Bonnard, and others—had apparently perished, unfound, in the fire. Nobody had seen them taken out, and no trace of them could be found. The looting, moreover, was not the work of connoisseurs; its ends were utilitarian, a fact amply proved by the remains found in the ashes.

The reason for this spiteful destruction remains unknown. The Lauwick family is not Jewish and was not accused of anything except possibly being wealthy, partly English, and having the bad taste to live in an American-style house. The destruction of the Bernheims' property was purely incidental, as incidental as the loss of several important old masters during the conflagration at another Dordogne château, belonging to Mme. de Vedrines.

The Normandy landings sent the people of France and the other occupied countries into paroxysms of joy. Many believed that the end of the war would come within a few days, but the trainloads of helpless prisoners still poured into the concentration camps, the crematoriums still belched forth columns of smoke, and the reprisals became bloodier and more insensate.

Exactly four days after the landings on Omaha Beach, on June 10, 1944, a detachment of the dreaded S.S. division Das Reich, under the command of Major Otto Dickmann, herded the population of Oradour-sur-Glane into the village square. Within a very brief space of time all but 10 of the 652 inhabitants of the village were dead, machine-gunned and burned—the women and children in the church and the men in the barns. The survivors were badly burned and escaped only by feigning death when the S.S. checked on their handiwork.

The mysterious massacre of Oradour almost had a sequel in Souillac, the principal city of the area in which were dispersed the châteaux housing the contents of the Louvre. One of the most heavily traveled roads leading to the north, where the Germans moved masses of troops after the Allied landings, passes through Souillac. Just opposite the château of Latreyne is a bend in the road, called La Gréselade, overlooked by craggy hills from which the *maquisards* could shoot down upon the German soldiers with ease. The technique was simple: The French moved down the hills partway, hiding in the rocks, did their shooting, and then climbed rapidly back to the tops, escaping return fire and pursuit. (The German name for La Gréselade was "Little Russia.") Villagers whose towns were perched along the hills would come out to cheer the sniping, sometimes daring to sing the "Marseillaise." The spectacle for the curators on the terrace at Latreyne was strikingly theatrical and considerably worrisome, since German reprisals, with frequent looting and fires, always took place the day after the attacks.

The consternation of the curators may be imagined when they learned that the Das Reich unit had herded the inhabitants of Souillac into the town square and threatened summary execution of them all. Nothing happened, however. One explanation for this happy ending was the action of one of the town councilmen, who brought out several bottles of wine to divert the soldiers. Another explanation might be found in the presence of the local collaborator, whom the Germans wished to preserve for future denunciations.

The Gréselade road also runs along the border of the land belonging to the château of Lanzac. That repository and all the others were uneasy, since any incident involving one château could spread to the others. If they could have, the curators would have abandoned Lanzac, but without trucks and gasoline they could do nothing.

On the evening of June 20, after the more or less commonplace firing on the road, a wounded German soldier dragged himself to Lanzac's front gate. One of the two curators was absent; the other was a woman, too softhearted to turn the man away. She took him in and dressed his wounds. Before he could be removed to Souillac's town hall, where he would not endanger Lanzac and its staff, a group of *maquisards* came to the château and took the man prisoner. When German reprisal troops arrived the next day to search for their wounded comrade, the officer-in-charge, informed of the Maquis action, arrested the chief guard and his three assistants, blamed them for the incident, and threatened to burn down the château and its contents, the precious Ingres drawings from Montauban.

The woman curator spoke German well and managed to convince

the officer that he was perhaps acting hastily. He relented slightly and was on the point of removing the men to Cahors for questioning when the other curator returned. When he realized the imminent danger, he insisted upon being treated as their superior, responsible for their actions, and was taken prisoner with the guards. The men were taken to Cahors via Souillac. Several times along the way they were taken out of the car, lined up, and menaced with death as terrorists. (Actually, most of the guards at Lanzac and the other repositories had some contact with the Maquis, but the Gestapo never managed to prove this conclusively.)

News of this incident reached the chief curator, André Chamson, at Latreyne late in the day. Since the information he received told him only that German troops had entered the château with guns drawn, remained for a lengthy period, and then departed, taking five men with them, he did not know whether all the Germans had left the château or what had happened to the drawings. In order to find out, he had to see for himself. To get to Lanzac without passing through Souillac, which was full of spies and troops, perhaps even those who had attacked the château, he went by boat along the river after dark. One of the Latreyne guards handled the boat and remained in it while Chamson climbed up the riverbank to the château, where he found only distraught women convinced that the men taken away were already dead. Chamson could do nothing that night except find a few young men at nearby farms willing to ensure temporary guard of the repository.

Morale among the regular guards was quite low, for they now realized that their work was dangerous and that they had agreed to remain with the collections under all circumstances. Lanzac underscored a danger that had first manifested itself at Montal two weeks earlier, when a German patrol moved toward an ambush set up by the *maquisards* behind the stone wall surrounding the property. If fighting had broken out at that point, it might well have spilled over onto the grounds. The curator-in-charge, René Huyghe, also a member of the Resistance, used his authority to persuade the French to move their ambush to a farm situated farther down the hill. The eventual battle lasted for an entire afternoon. The Germans retreated, only to return the next day with forty light tanks that moved along the road toward Montal. Resistance was crushed, and the next day the Germans shot three peasants in reprisal and threw their bodies into a ravine. Bétaille and Vayrac were also caught in this action. Bullets flew all around, although none of them damaged the châteaux.

The Montal incident and the imprisonment of the Lanzac guards made it necessary for Chamson to intervene actively not only to save those men but also to prevent the loss of others who might take to the hills, leaving the art unprotected. Consultation with Maquis leaders led to a decision to go to Cahors and demand the release of the guards. He was responsible for arms, ammunition, and tracts found within the sphere of his activity, so if the Gestapo had discovered anything suspicious at the château, he was in more danger than were the men. Nevertheless, he decided to go and brazen it out.

When he reached Cahors, he went first to the prefect, who admitted that he had no authority, even though he was a Vichy appointee. However, the prefect sent a French officer who spoke a little German to accompany Chamson to Gestapo headquarters, where they found superficially debonair officers, a female agent, and brawny soldiers. Chamson talked, expanding lyrically on the value of museums, which protected masterworks of every country, including Germany, extolling his guards, who were interested in nothing in the world except protecting art, and ending with an impassioned plea for the now-unprotected Ingres drawings. The Gestapo officers listened and then asked countless questions, accusing the guards of terrorism, for their quarters had been searched, and the Germans had found maps, a compass, and some letters–fortunately not very damaging. Finally, the Gestapo told Chamson that the men would be judged fairly and advised him to return the next day, when they might give him some more information on the case.

The officer-translator, however, warned Chamson that he would be arrested if he did return. He told him to leave for Latreyne immediately and suggested sending the Gestapo a pile of official papers lavishly adorned with official stamps, always impressive to the Germans. He felt that the visit had prevented the killing of the guards, for the local Gestapo could no longer pretend that they did not know who the men were and would hesitate before doing something that Paris headquarters would not like. Chamson, having played with fire long enough, returned to Latreyne. He prepared a bulky dossier on the guards and sent it back to Cahors with another curator.

Chamson's bravery revived the morale of the guards in the châteaux for which he was responsible and encouraged the prisoners, who learned of his visit through the prison grapevine. Four of the men were released on August 10. The fifth man stayed in prison two more weeks. He had made the mistake of referring to the wounded German as a "prisoner," and since the Maquis was an illegal group and could not take prisoners, he was accused of collusion and thus merited the extra term.

Even before the return of the prisoners, Chamson had decided to evacuate Lanzac at any cost, for its location was too dangerous. He hired a truckman in Souillac, and on the first day that the road was clear the entire contents of Lanzac were divided between Latreyne and Cieurac.

During the period that began on June 6 and ended with the liberation of Paris on August 25, governmental authority in France was practically nonexistent. Vichy had no power, and no new Government had been selected to take its place. Paychecks for all museum personnel still arrived in Cahors, however, and to get them, a guard traveled the more than ninety-mile round trip. On August 15 General Jean de Lattre de Tassigny and his French troops arrived in Provence. The Germans kept control of the large cities but gradually lost their hold on the countryside except when their troops moved. The Maquis became increasingly visible, requisitioning automobiles and trucks, which appeared in growing numbers on the roads as Resistance leaders began to show their authority. Sometimes villagers thought they had been liberated and displayed flags that had to be withdrawn when German troops entered behind the "liberators." In some towns power shifted from one group to another, and the curators moved about very little to avoid running into trouble.

While the telephones still functioned, the Louvre called Chamson at Latreyne and Huyghe at Montal to inform them that the Germans had decided to take the art treasures as a form of hostage (since they knew they had lost the war) and that they wanted all of it stored beyond the Maginot Line, nearer Germany. The Germans were quite serious about this mad plan and had asked that each repository give them the cubic size of the cases in storage. The idea naturally horrified the curators, who envisioned the works they had tried so hard to preserve placed right in the middle of the final battle. The Louvre had a counterplan, however, and advised the curators to reply as if the moving were a monumental job that they seriously planned to carry out. They thus began by requesting so many trucks that the project became unrealizable at once. While Latreyne and Montal busied themselves with huge calculations, Paris warned both Vichy and the Kunstschutz about the danger of traveling on roads subject to bombing raids and suggested Switzerland as the only suitable place of refuge. Time passed, and the whole idea was forgotten.

The situation in the area around the repositories eventually became safe enough for Chamson to rejoin the French Army, which he had left immediately after the Vichy armistice. He rounded up enough *maquisards* to form a battalion and went to Aix, where he met De Lattre and asked for transportation to bring the group to the army under his (Chamson's) command as Commandant Lauter. The general gave him trucks and jeeps, and Chamson returned to Souillac, picking up his men on the way. After a brief visit to Latreyne he was off again. A few miles outside of Souillac an automobile belonging to the Maquis led him to Aubazine, where he found Colonel Berger (André Malraux), who had two battalions of volunteers for De Lattre's First Army. Three battalions add up to a brigade, and the two men, who were old friends, decided to bring them all to De Lattre, who must have been delighted to have so many volunteers at once and to have among his officers two distinguished writers.[1]

Montal, Latreyne, and the other southern repositories, in spite of some further minor alarms and the problems of food, heating, communication, and transportation, came through the remaining period of hostilities with no damage to the collections. The situation was much more critical at Valençay, the shelter for such famous Louvre statues as the "Venus de Milo" and the "Winged Victory." Constructed in 1540, the château is a handsome Renaissance building and belongs to the Talleyrand family, one of whose members, the Duke of Valençay, remained in residence during the war.

In August, 1944, the château's two great towers were gravely menaced several times. First, on August 12, a skirmish between the Maquis of Loches and Vichy militiamen in the streets of the town just outside the estate gates attracted a column of German tanks, which blazed away. One shell just missed one of the towers and set fire to the stables. Museum guards extinguished the fire during the continuing bombardment.

Four days later, on August 16, the German command at Romorantin, about twenty miles away, sent three hundred men from the Das Reich division to Valençay on a punitive expedition. About fifty soldiers burst into the château, breaking down doors to seek out the guards, whom they forced out of the building and onto the lawn, where they were made to lie down on the grass. Three officers ques-

[1] Chamson is well known as a writer in France. One of his wartime books, *Le Puits des miracles*, appeared in July, 1944; some of the manuscript was carried to Paris in Mme. Jaujard's toothbrush-holder.

tioned the curator-in-charge, who responded by asking whether they wished to go down in history as the destroyers of famous statuary. Quite clearly they did not, and it was fortunate that they did not know that Valençay also sheltered the French crown jewels, much easier to steal and transport than huge stone and metal statues.

The guards remained stretched out on the lawn during the interrogation of the curator and the Duke de Valençay, who narrowly missed a summary execution on suspicion of anti-Germanism. Then a new fire suddenly broke out, lit by bullets striking inflammable material. The curator asked that his men be allowed to extinguish it before it spread, and the guards rose to their feet. The German officers promised that they would not shoot, but despite their promise a burst of machine-gun fire struck down and killed the chief guard.

Germans and Resistants carried on their struggle outside the château walls until August 29, when a German battalion took up its position inside the park. The curator and guards breathed a sigh of relief when the Germans left, but their relief was short-lived. No sooner had the Germans gone than the *maquisards* came in, determined to remain until the last bullet. Informed of this in Paris, Jaujard called this dangerous occupation to the attention of General Pierre Koenig, commander of the F.F.I., and Koenig ordered the evacuation of the troops and saw to it that Valençay was not menaced again.

The situation at Brissac was dangerous not only because the château stood near the city of Angers and almost exactly on the original demarcation line between the occupied and unoccupied zones but also because the repository sheltered many private Jewish collections. Protective notices set up by the Kunstschutz were constantly disregarded by the military. On September 4, 1942, the Germans set up a target range on the château grounds and thoughtlessly placed a munitions dump near it. Repeated protests to Paris and to local German authorities were useless. The Germans then set up a trenched defensive camp immediately outside the château's grounds and laid out a special section for storing mines. Then the château, in the midst of all this dangerous explosive material, was designated a *Rastplatz*, a rest home for troops. The *Rastplatz* contained Angers's fabulous Apocalypse tapestries, the royal tapestries from Versailles, the decorative art of the Trianon Palace, and other easily inflammable objects.

At last the Kunstschutz obtained some concessions; the first was the opening of a road beyond the minefield to make access to the château possible. On July 16, 1944, four days before his participation in the futile attempt in Berlin on Hitler's life, General Hans von Stülpnagel, the senior German Army officer in Paris, forbade the parking of army cars on the château's grounds and allowed only small detachments of soldiers commanded by noncommissioned officers inside the gates. Less than a month later, however, a retreating German company tossed grenades into the streets near the château, and a handful of drunken soldiers burst inside, shot at point-blank range one of the guards who was trying to protect the collections, and fled. Once the Germans had gone, the village population, terrified by bombing in the vicinity and fearful of further incidents, rushed toward the castle gates in a movement as old as the days of feudalism—when castles opened their doors to the peasantry during times of war or siege. Brissac's doors were not opened this time, however, for the collections had to be protected. Fortunately, there were no more incidents, and very early in September the last Germans disappeared from the region. The Kunstschutz notice protecting the treasures was torn down, and a new one, ordered by the Allies, took its place: "OFF LIMITS."

During the summer of the liberation, guerrilla warfare raged around the château and the streets of the small village of Chambord. The Maquis of Blois joined in on August 21, and the Wehrmacht held the Louvre guards responsible. The Germans retaliated by burning down a small inn where the guards used to gather in the evenings. They then chose forty of the villagers as hostages and took them into the grounds of the château under military guard. German soldiers combed the huge building from cellar to roof, searching for arms. They found none.

During the hours of the search the commander of the German detachment questioned every man in the repository, using a German-speaking guard as an interpreter and in the presence of the chief curator. The interpreter, the curator, and the village priest pleaded for the guards and the prisoners, offering themselves as hostages instead. The Germans refused, and four of the villagers were shot inside the park within the hour.

The next day a German patrol approached the château again, marching slowly and solemnly up the long tree-lined avenue that leads to the front portal. They stopped at the top of the stone steps leading to the door, and standing rigidly at attention, witnessed a military funeral service held on the terrace for one of their own men. The soldiers then left as they had arrived, in splendid military order.

They left behind a platoon that remained in place to guard and to watch the château.

In Paris, windows shuddered as bombs fell all around the city. Everyday life continued, and the municipality issued instructions to the curators still watching over the empty or half-empty museums. One instruction, a request for more copper and bronze, arrived with a curious note that the objects selected must not have any historical, aesthetic, or utilitarian value. Such a demand received the negative response it required. One museum curator used his half-empty building to shelter family members belonging to the secret army. In another museum a curator's office was the first stage on the Pyrenees route to freedom. A steady stream of visitors, some of them thinly disguised, came in to meet a Spanish "passer" with a minimal interest in art.

Museums and galleries tried to continue with business as usual, but public interest dwindled, and the urge to attend or present exhibitions grew less pressing in the face of external events. The May Salon of 1944 was almost ready to open at the Museum of Modern Art when the Germans arrived at the door in a convoy of trucks holding ten thousand cases filled with the loot of "Action M." Since the museum basements were already full, they wanted storage room in the exhibition halls upstairs. Faced with strong objections from the curators and the organizers of the show, the Germans withdrew and took their trucks to the Petit Palais, which they had taken over—with the exception of the offices of the museum's staff—in 1940. One evening the German cases were set on fire. Parisian firemen restricted the blaze to the wooden crates, and the museum's walls were only slightly damaged.

In May, 1944, the curator of the Galliera Museum was sent to the Sarthe to replace a colleague at the Château de la Gidonière, the shelter for the collections of the municipal museums of Paris. His trip, like all others in 1944, was difficult. Constant Allied bombardments wrecked trains and destroyed bridges and sections of track. Passengers had to change trains unexpectedly, wait hours for lines to be cleared, and carry their luggage across railroad bridges. French forced-labor gangs were in no hurry to complete repairs for the occupants. Everything mechanical functioned badly; the telephone was exasperatingly slow or went completely dead; telegrams took three days to arrive. When the curator reached his destination, he found the region's inhabitants grimly determined to refuse to aid the

Germans; the countryside was alive with Resistants. The château itself was calm and undisturbed by the bureaucratic visits or frantic requests from Paris which had previously required constant moving and opening of cases. The end was in sight, but the form it might take was doubtful. The curator requested weapons for the guards, but his request went unanswered.

Allied planes flew over the château daily, for it is only about a mile from the railroad line, which they sprinkled liberally with bombs. Since a miss might strike La Gidonière, the château's personnel dug a trench shelter in the lawn, and the concierge arranged his cellar to protect his family. Many inhabitants of the village abandoned their homes and took to the rock caverns with which the area is amply provided.

Between June 6 and August 8 the Germans sent out night trains that slipped along without lights. They did not go far, for the *maquisards* blew them up. One day a British plane fell in flames, destroying a good section of vineyard not far from the château. Its occupants, clearly visible in the bright afternoon sunlight, parachuted gently down. To the village's stupefaction, no German patrol sought to find the flight crew, a complete turnabout from previous zeal. Finally, on the night of August 8, the village and the château awoke at midnight because of a continuous rolling sound from the main road. The Germans were moving out in automobiles and trucks. With them went their equipment, vaguely camouflaged with leafy branches. The men were unshaven, bare-headed, unbuttoned, perhaps slightly more human than when they had arrived four years before, and slightly less like mechanical dolls than during the years they had stood on guard all over France.

CHAPTER 12

PARIS SET FREE

DURING THE LIBERATION of Paris the Louvre reverted to its original function—that of a defensive stronghold against an enemy.[1] Mined by the Germans, in imminent danger of being totally destroyed—with Paris—to satisfy Hitler's maniacal desire to pull all of Europe down with him in defeat, the Palais du Louvre and the Tuileries Gardens were vulnerable from three positions: from the hotels sheltering German headquarters across the Rue de Rivoli, from the Hôtel de Crillon across the Place de la Concorde, and from the bridge across the Seine along one long open stretch.

On the morning of August 19, 1944, Rose Valland was at her post in the Jeu de Paume when she was called to the Louvre for a meeting.

[1] The present buildings of the Louvre are the work of several centuries of construction. Begun at the end of the reign of Francis I, it was designed by Pierre Lescot, who raised its southwestern section on the Square Court to replace the feudal fortress of Philip Augustus and Charles V. It was then enlarged by Catherine de Médicis and Henry IV, who added the Great Gallery, which links the building to the Tuileries. Kings Louis XIII and XIV ordered the completion of the buildings of the Square Court and the elaborately beautiful Colonnade. The Louvre was then deserted in favor of Versailles as the official royal residence, and no further work was done on it until the time of Napoleon I. Napoleon III finally completed the structure. Its use as a museum was first planned by the Marquis de Marigny, director of the king's buildings to Louis XV, and continued by his successor, the Comte d'Angevillier. The Revolution of 1789 interrupted the project, which was first realized by the National Convention on August 10, 1793, when the Central Museum of Art, made up of the royal collections plus revolutionary confiscations, was opened to the public. The collections were increased by Napoleon, diminished by the return of many pieces to the Allies in 1815, and have grown steadily and legally ever since. Not constructed to be a museum, the Louvre presents problems of arrangement, but the buildings are so handsome and so beloved by the French that every effort and every possible modernization suitable to the fabric are worth the loving labor of its curators.

She had barely crossed the Tuileries when she heard the first shots fired in the Place de la Concorde and on the Pont du Carrousel. It was eleven o'clock, and the six-day battle for Paris had begun. At the meeting the curators wisely planned no overt acts of resistance and decided to concentrate instead on taking protective measures for the next few uncertain days. Jaujard gave Miss Valland some instructions, and she returned to the Jeu de Paume, which was in a position that made it very useful for German defense tactics.

Situated on a slight diagonal from the corner of the Rue St. Florentin is a flight of stone steps leading up to the terrace of the Jeu de Paume; the front door faces the Place de la Concorde. As soon as the insurrection began, German patrols kept a close surveillance of the corner of the Tuileries upon which the Jeu de Paume stands, for the museum would have plainly been an ideal place for a Resistance ambush. The windows of the Hôtel de Talleyrand, directly across the Rue de Rivoli from the museum, were used as sniping posts for soldiers who reinforced the patrols. A few days earlier, the Germans had set up an observation post, opposite the museum's front door, from which soldiers could watch either the museum or the important intersection of the Rue de Rivoli and the Place de la Concorde.

On the afternoon of August 20, the day that General von Choltitz had agreed to a cease-fire, guns bristled when Miss Valland and a guard checked the outside water points, vital in the event of a fire. On August 23 the huge Grand Palais on the Avenue Alexandre III (now the Avenue Churchill) belched forth smoke. The elaborate iron structure, built for the 1900 Paris Exposition, has stone facings and colonnades and appears as solid as a rock. During the summer of 1944 the Paris police rallied strongly to the side of the Resistants, and the attack on the building was German reprisal for a police ambush that killed all the passengers in a German squad car. An explosion—engineered with a mechanical, radio-propelled miniature tank—and a rain of incendiary bombs nearly totally destroyed the palace and sent clouds of smoke into the hazy summer sky. The incident alarmed Parisians, who had suffered countless night alerts requiring descent into cellars but no saturation bombings or tank actions inside the city.

During that night a storm broke. The ordinarily quiet and peaceful Rue de Rivoli was alive with German soldiers busy coming and going in precombat confusion as commands flew. Under a pouring rain, soldiers set up barricades formed of wooden sawhorses connected with multiple strands of barbed wire. By morning the entire terrace between the Jeu de Paume and the tall iron fence surrounding the Tuileries was covered with these hastily built defenses, which made it possible for the Germans to fight with their backs against the museum walls so that French troops or bands of Resistants could not take them from behind. Miss Valland and two guards, who remained in the museum all night, were inside a German armed camp.

General Jacques Leclerc's tank attack on the hotels housing German headquarters began early in the afternoon of August 25, and in two hours, although six panzers were called in to help them, the Germans were defeated. At the Jeu de Paume they fought behind the museum's iron shutters and from behind the statuary in the garden. Nine of them died, one spilling his blood on the museum's steps; 350 other Germans surrendered and left the terrace to join other soldiers in the Square Court of the Louvre, which was converted into a mustering center for prisoners taken by Leclerc's men. The museum that had sheltered looted art was strewn with other German souvenirs: helmets, belts, and other equipment.

When the battle ended, Leclerc's tanks lined up behind the terrace balustrades, and an exhausted, jubilant Paris mob streamed after them to acclaim the victors and cheer for General de Gaulle. Suddenly snipers on the roofs began firing into the crowd, which immediately scattered in panic. A mass of frightened people from both the Place de la Concorde and the terrace poured into the museum through smashed windows and doors. Rose Valland, found inside, was forced to defend herself from the furious crowd, to whom she seemed just one more collaborator. As such, her position was extremely perilous.

During the exchange of shots with the snipers, the tanks on the terrace sprayed the walls from point-blank range; chips of stone flew. Miss Valland expostulated with one of Leclerc's officers, who put a stop to the firing. The crowd, however, still found both her actions and her presence suspicious, and when she tried to prevent entry into the basement, where some of the museum's own art was stored, she was accused of hiding Germans in the cellar. To prove that the basement contained only art, Miss Valland conducted a search accompanied by a group of Resistants, one of whom held a machine gun pointed at her back. Luckily for her, no Germans were hiding in the basement. Eventually, when Miss Valland's good faith was established, French soldiers cleared the museum of the crowd, which took with it all the German equipment left behind at the moment of surrender. None of the paintings was touched.

Across the garden, on the Seine side, an exhibition of contemporary art was still hanging in the Orangerie. A shell had gone through the wall and one of Monet's paintings before exploding inside the room, which was filled with German prisoners who had surrendered to the chief guard of the museum, mistaking his cap and the gold stripes on his uniform for those of an army officer. One of the men was killed, and several were seriously wounded.

The fighting in the gardens miraculously spared the many statues that adorn the lawns and flower beds, and the Louvre itself was quite untouched. Leclerc's army was careful, and the Germans fought only a halfhearted, face-saving battle. An elaborate system of fire prevention and control had been set up for the Louvre, which was dangerously flammable because of its old wooden roof.[2] A kind of general staff headed by Jaujard and composed of seven permanent members of the curatorial staff had settled in to live inside the museum. They were assisted by a group of sculptors who had made the Louvre their home throughout the war.[3] Their constant presence inside the huge building was a guarantee that somebody responsible was always present. Museums are lonely places when emptied of the public, and the size of the Louvre and its physical construction, stretching out in long, many-windowed galleries and corridors, would have made it not only vulnerable but also tempting as a hide-out during the Occupation years and the liberation period.

The need for precautions was well illustrated on the day after the liberation. Firemen had been stationed on the roof during the battle, and there was a question as to whether or not shots had been fired from it.[4] An angry crowd, suspicious of the Louvre's immunity to damage and the affiliations of its directors, gathered outside the museum. Temporary policemen, hastily appointed by Resistance leaders, entered the building and took Jaujard and several curators to the town hall of the arrondissement in which the Louvre is located.

[2] Fairly recently, the old roof, no longer considered safe, was replaced with a new one, raised high enough to add to the height of top-floor ceilings without disturbing the external architecture, thus permitting the installation of new windows and adding more light for offices and galleries.

[3] Living in the Louvre is not unusual; artists lived in rooms or flats either as squatters or as government pensioners until well into the nineteenth century. French kings had had artists-in-residence before the palace became a museum.

[4] There might have been shots from the roof of one of the buildings, since the Ministry of Finance, which then occupied one building on the Rue de Rivoli side between two sections of the museum, was sealed off from the rest and had a separate entrance.

The trip did not take long (the building is on the Place du Louvre, about two minutes' walk from the museum's Square Court), but it was made unpleasant by insults and threats from the accompanying police. The mayor, who had been installed that morning, was an old friend of one of the curators, and the affair was cleared up in a matter of minutes, with apologies flowing as freely as had the threats.[5]

The accusation was serious enough, however, to make Jaujard fear that his authority might be weakened. He took the opportunity to demand a supplementary guard of fifty policemen to watch the museum and, if necessary, to defend it. The guards were almost immediately useful, for the loud, angry threats of the hostile crowd around the museum reached the ears of the German prisoners inside the Square Court. Fearful that the crowd meant them harm, the prisoners forced open museum windows, entered the building, and spread out through the long galleries. They were picked up one by one in the sculpture halls on the ground floor, the luckier ones comfortably ensconced inside the Egyptian stone coffins.

[5] The number of extralegal settlings of accounts in the years immediately after the liberation of Paris varies, according to authoritative French sources, from 10,000 to 100,000. The French are not proud of either number, and as the years pass, the possibility of setting an exact figure grows less. Twenty-seven war-crimes courts had heard more than 50,000 cases by December 31, 1948: 4,397 were condemned to death in absentia, 2,640 in actuality; 2,777 were sentenced to hard labor for life, 10,434 for shorter terms; 2,173 were sentenced to solitary confinement, 24,116 to prison, and 665 to "national degradation." Civil courts condemned another 48,486 to "national degradation." Presidential intervention cut the number of death sentences to about 25 percent of the total. Resistants found the court action too lenient; Vichyites and collaborators found them too harsh.

The general cleanup and trial of collaborators was called the purge. There were purges by professions: doctors, lawyers, military officers, writers and journalists, artists. Of the people concerned with art, Abel Bonnard and Darquier de Pellepoix were condemned to death in absentia; Lefranc went to prison; De Brinon and Pierre Laval were executed. The purge commission for artists was made up of other artists. Most of the sanctions were taken against political cartoonists who had worked for collaborationist newspapers. The one prominent artist sanctioned was Maurice Vlaminck. The action taken against him was purely symbolic. Its date was June 24, 1946, and it forbade the exhibition or sale of his work for one year beginning September, 1944. Presumably this would have been a black mark in the story of his life; however, when Vlaminck died in 1958, French newspapers did not mention it.

Aboard Hitler's special train during his trip to France, Spain, and Italy in October, 1940, Hitler (left) meets Pierre Laval (center), Vice-Premier of the Vichy Government. Also present are Von Ribbentrop (center) and Dr. Schmitt (right), official interpreter. (*U.S. Army Photograph, from Von Ribbentrop's albums*)

Hermann Göring with Bruno Lohse, a corporal in the Luftwaffe who had been an art dealer before the war and was assigned to scout the Paris art market for Göring. Inside the Jeu de Paume.

Hermann Göring leaves the Jeu de Paume with Luftwaffe General Hanesse at Göring's right; behind him are Baron Kurt von Behr (hatless), Göring's physician (in white cap), and Dr. Hermann Bunjes, of the German Historical Institute in Paris, liaison officer for the Kunstschutz.

Arno Breker (right), Hitler's "Phidias," shows Hitler the sights of Paris, October, 1940. At left is Albert Speer, Reichsminister of Armaments and War Production. (*U.S. Army Photograph*)

A party at Berchtesgaden. Eva Braun is fifth from left; Martin Bormann is second from left. At right is Heinrich Hoffmann, Hitler's photographer. (*U.S. Army Photograph, from Eva Braun's collection*)

Walter Andreas Hofer, an art dealer whose association with Reichsmarschall Göring began in 1936, plays a game of chess with himself in his cell at the Nuremberg city jail, where he is being held as a witness for the Nuremberg war-crime trials. (*U.S. Army Photograph*)

Left, Karl Haberstock, an art dealer with forty years of experience who understood what was suitable art for Nazi dogma, plays chess in his cell at Nuremberg while awaiting the trial at which he was a witness. *Right*, Alfred Rosenberg, head of the E.R.R., sits in his cell at Nuremberg, where he changed his testimony innumerable times. (*U.S. Army Photograph*)

The Louvre Museum and its gardens (*French Government Tourist Office*)

The 440-room Renaissance château of Chambord (*French Government Tourist Office*)

Valençay, a château on the route of the advancing German Army (*French*

Schloss Neuschwanstein, built by Ludwig II, was included in Hitler's "scorched earth" order. (*German Information Center*)

Two of the Rosenberg Task Force files. Bruno Lohse made three trips to Kogl to place them in safety at Neuschwanstein. (*U.S. Army Photograph*)

German civilians remained underground for two weeks to escape American bombing in the mine at Siegen, where art treasures from all over Europe were stored. (*U.S. Army Photograph*)

Edouard Manet's "Jardin d'Hiver," owned by the Berlin National Gallery, was discovered by American soldiers in the Merkers salt mine. (*U.S. Army Photograph*)

Valuable stained glass was removed from the windows of Strasbourg Cathedral and hidden in salt mines at Heilbronn. *(U.S. Army Photograph)*

Military officials in Regensburg, Germany, examine bells stolen by the Nazis from French churches. (*U.S. Army Photograph*)

These Jewish books were found in Heidelberg. The open volumes were published in the eighteenth century. (*U.S. Army Photograph*)

Neuschwanstein Castle was turned over intact to the U.S. Army in May, 1945.
This is a room full of antique Rothschild chairs. (U.S. Army Photograph.)

A Rubens painting, "The Graces in the Gardens of the Hesperides," was found in its own frame by units of the U.S. Seventh Army when they explored tunnels under Neuschwanstein Castle. (*U.S. Army Photograph*)

Some of Göring's art collection: figures, candelabra, and goblets of solid gold and a sword presented to Göring by Generalissimo Francisco Franco (*U.S. Army Photograph*)

When Göring turned himself over to the U.S. Army, he carried nothing but his marshal's baton. These are his last worldly possessions on a table in his Nuremberg cell. Even the frames on his family photographs were removed. (*U.S. Army Photograph*)

The Kapelle at Alt Aussee held Archduke Ferdinand's collection of Spanish

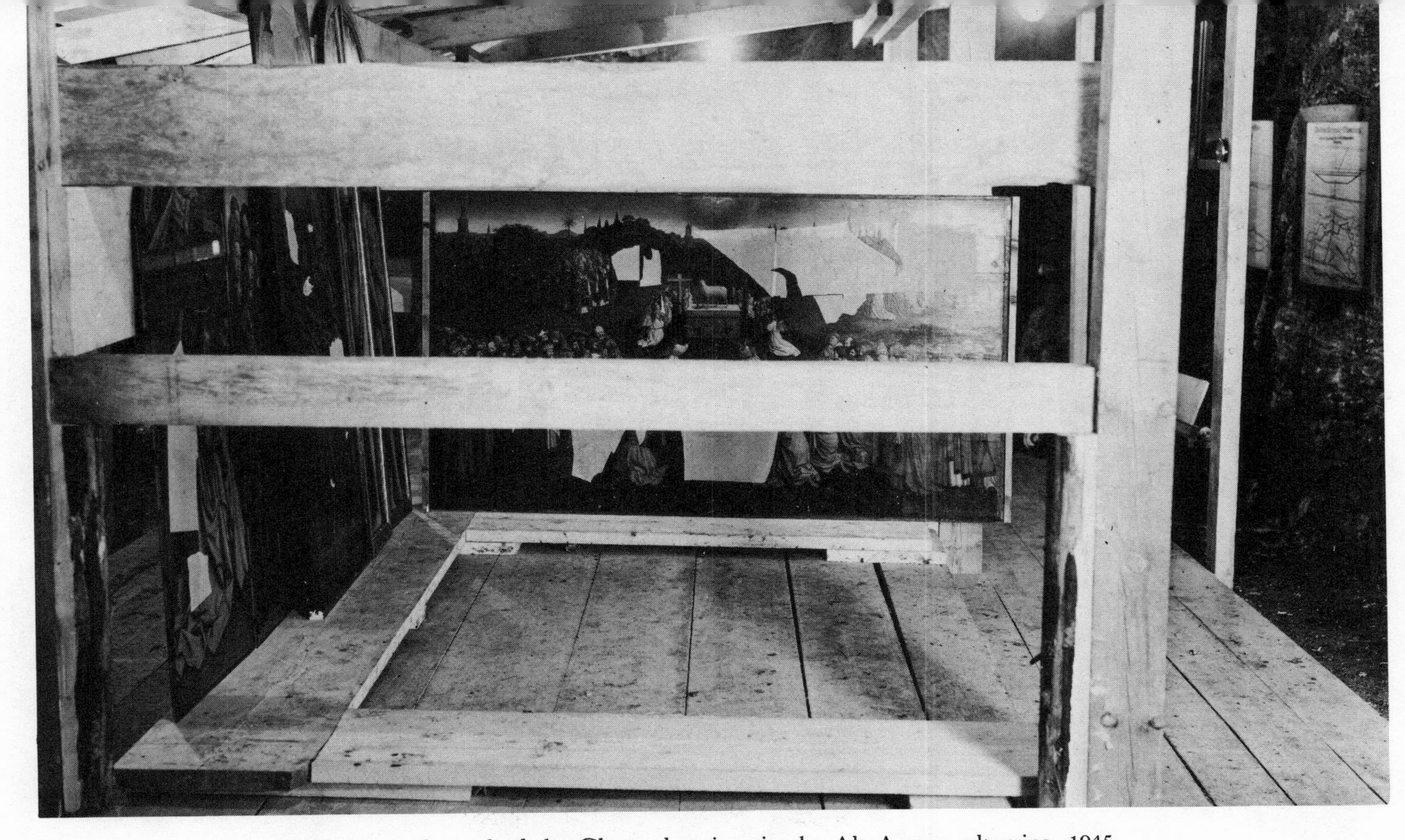

The central panel of the Ghent altarpiece in the Alt Aussee salt mine, 1945. The pale-gray patches are restorer's tissue, applied to prevent flaking of paint. (*Hans Schedelmann*)

"The Nazi cave of the Nibelungen", paintings, furniture and murals in

PART III

COUNTERACTION: 1944-1969

CHAPTER 13

MONUMENTS, FINE ARTS AND ARCHIVES

THE AMERICAN OFFICER in charge of fine-arts affairs in the Seine area was Lieutenant James J. Rorimer, whose civilian status was that of curator of medieval art at the Metropolitan Museum of Art in New York. One of his first acts in Paris was to see that the military equipment placed near the Louvre by the Allies was removed, for it was too tempting a target for the Luftwaffe. On September 4 he gained Miss Valland's gratitude by preventing a second occupation of the Jeu de Paume as a field post for the U.S. Army.

James Rorimer was a member of the smallest, most distinguished group attached to the Allied armies: Monuments, Fine Arts and Archives (M.F.A. and A.). Its members were, in civilian life, professors of art and architecture, museum curators, painters, sculptors, architects, and knowledgeable amateurs of art. Intrepid and ingenious, talented and tireless, the men were responsible to SHAEF (Supreme Headquarters Allied Expeditionary Forces) through their superior, Lieutenant Colonel Geoffrey Webb, adviser to SHAEF on matters of art and Slade Professor of Art at Cambridge University.

M.F.A. and A. was first conceived early in the war when the American-Defense Harvard Group and the Committee of the American Council of Learned Societies, interested in the protection and preservation of works of art in battle zones, drew President Franklin D. Roosevelt's attention to the probable danger to European art and architecture in the event of an Allied invasion. Roosevelt's response was a letter to Chief Justice Harlan Stone (December 28, 1942) suggesting the need for what became on August 20, 1943, the American Commission for the Protection and Salvage of Artistic and Historic Monuments in the War Area. Nobody could invent an acronym for its lengthy title, and the governmental agency with the smallest staff in Washington took its working name from its chairman, Supreme Court Justice Owen J. Roberts. The Roberts Commission had headquarters in the National Gallery and worked with experts from such institutions as the Metropolitan Museum, Columbia University, and the Fogg Museum at Harvard. The experts worked with the War Department to draw up a large military guidebook to historic buildings—churches, monasteries, châteaux, libraries, cathedrals, museums, forts, town halls, and other architecturally outstanding edifices—to be protected from bombing, burglary, and billeting, if possible. Charts showing these sites were eventually prepared for bomber commands and field artillery units, but because they were so scholarly and so detailed, printing difficulties held them up until after the war had ended.

The Roberts Commission also planned a military staff to implement the guidebook: M.F.A. and A. The original plan included an Allied advisory staff headed by a lieutenant colonel with sixteen majors under him, each of the majors assisted by several field outfits of a minimum of twelve junior officers each. These top echelons were to be mostly American. In addition, an officer was to be attached to the G-5 (Military Government for Civilian Affairs) headquarters of each army, each of these with three subordinate officers and six enlisted men on the front lines. The plan provided lavishly for transportation—trucks and jeeps—and typewriters and cameras for sending back "a constant flow of reports and information" in fifteen categories. Like many other grandiose plans, this one never materialized. The average number of M.F.A. and A. men eventually attached to G-5 was fifteen, and the largest active group was eighty-four officers and men, shortly after the German surrender in 1945.

Between the end of June and the end of August, 1944, M.F.A. and A. had first three and then eight men moving with the troops. The first three, two Americans and one British officer, arrived in Normandy about two weeks after the landings with none of the equipment imagined in Washington by the Roberts Commission. Their mission was to save and salvage art and to prove the value of their unit to top army officers, some of whom were ready to abandon the whole idea before it started. Without their own transportation, without either typewriters or cameras, they were to inspect damaged monuments and provide temporary life-saving repairs, but they had no materials to work with; they were to prevent billeting in historic monuments or oust troops incorrectly billeted, even though field commanders had the Roberts Commission guidebook, often unopened, with them.[1] Reports after the inspection of monuments on the preserve-if-possible list had to be sent back also. M.F.A. and A. men were generally unpopular and frequently had to explain who they were under actual fighting conditions, but hitching rides and borrowing typewriters, they went about their work. By the time the fighting in Europe had ended, these eight men had inspected 3,145 monuments and archives or their devastated remnants in France, Belgium, Holland, Luxembourg, and Germany.

A handwritten letter from Lieutenant Colonel A. J. L. McDonnell, the British M.F.A. and A. officer, to Colonel Webb in London gives some indication of the uncertain status of M.F.A. and A. at its outset. Dated September 23, 1944, from the unit's mission-to-France headquarters, the letter begins: "We are now installed in offices, but our files, our typewriter, and our luggage are still sitting on a boat somewhere. . . . The journey from Prince's Gardens [London headquarters] took some considerable time, and at one stage we all expected to end our days under the trees of the forest of Rambouillet [thirty-two miles from Paris]." The writer goes on to discuss the appointment of Jaujard's assistant, Pierre Billiet, as director-general of the Beaux-Arts. McDonnell believed that both men would be "extremely helpful . . . though it will take a good deal of quiet insistence and tact to get the list from them of private property taken away by the Germans through their clearinghouse at the Jeu de Paume. I think they are inclined to feel that it is a matter for the French committee which is being set up, but no doubt they will come

[1] On May 26, 1944, General Dwight D. Eisenhower issued a letter to field commanders. It began: "Shortly we will be fighting our way across the continent of Europe. . . . In the path of our advance will be found historical monuments and cultural centers which symbolize to the world all that we are fighting to preserve. It is the responsibility of every commander to protect and respect these symbols whenever possible." It is not possible to believe that the invaders of June 6, struggling to get beyond the beaches, had much time to consider churches and museums and châteaux as they blasted their way along under German fire, or that many exhausted commanding officers stopped to check billets against the guidebook list when their men needed rest and reasonable shelter. Furthermore, no M.F.A. and A. men were present to "check and protect."

to see that this information will be extremely useful in the hands of the people who are first on the spot."

The French did, indeed, feel that return of private property to French nationals was their business, but they finally managed to work out a method of cooperating with the Allies. The French committee mentioned by Colonel McDonnell was the civilian Commission de Récupération Artistique (C.R.A.), instituted in Paris on November 24, 1944, under the direction of Albert Henraux, vice-president of the Council of National Museums and a longtime Resistant who had lived in the Louvre throughout the Occupation. Rose Valland became secretary of the committee, whose headquarters were in the Jeu de Paume. The first works returned to the museum and thence to their owners were those saved from the train at Aulnay in late August. Other works were picked up in abandoned German warehouses in Paris. A few days after the liberation, several hundred paintings arrived from the Amt Westen—works left behind in favor of others considered more valuable.

The war was not over in Europe, and the art treasures in the German repositories were still in danger. Between the liberation and the end of 1944 neither the French nor the British and Americans were sure of the location of any repositories. The most secret repositories did not exist in Germany until it became obvious to the High Command that the Reich would lose the war and that the country would be bombed, so some less-important objects were not stowed away in the final repositories until as late as April, 1945. Miss Valland knew where the final sites were located but delayed so long in passing on her information that, according to Rorimer, even her French friends began to doubt its value; Colonel McDonnell was skeptical as to how much she really knew. Rorimer, who had been highly impressed with Miss Valland's knowledge of the exact contents of the fifty-two cars at Aulnay, believed that she had accurate information. Albert Henraux was willing to allow Rorimer to try to extract such knowledge, for although the SHAEF list of protected monuments inside Germany was firm, art objects were constantly moved about so that the repository list was "possible and probable."

Until January or early February, 1945, Rorimer cultivated Miss Valland's friendship, visited five E.R.R. administrative centers with her, and saw four garages used for storing furniture and books. One evening she invited him to her apartment on the Left Bank and showed him photographs she had acquired by sneaking negatives out at night and returning them early the following morning. He saw photographs of E.R.R. personnel (and heard her descriptions of them), a list of repositories—including two castles, Neuschwanstein and Hohenschwangau—and the watchman's logbook, which gave the names of all visitors to the Jeu de Paume. Although Miss Valland indicated that she distrusted military channels, considering them another form of bureaucracy, she promised that she would give this material to the French mission at SHAEF, where Rorimer himself saw it considerably later in the files. The mission checked her information against other material constantly being received and so compiled a more complete list.

Miss Valland urged Rorimer to go to Germany to save the art "before the S.S. could destroy it," since she could not go herself. Rorimer, under orders to remain in Paris, then a "rear" communications zone, could not go either. While he remained in Paris, he attempted some amateur "spying," checking on Bruno Lohse, about whom he discovered nothing more than he had already heard. Parisians did very little talking about the Occupation years for a considerable time after the liberation lest they be accused of collaboration for the slightest contact with or knowledge of Germans.

Between January and May 8, 1945, in the confusion of a fluid battlefront, the American Third and Seventh armies raced across Germany. The small force of M.F.A. and A. officers could not be everywhere at once, nor even in the front lines, but they continued to struggle with a constant communications problem and to work as well as they could. With the discovery of the Merkers mine on April 7, headquarters became seriously interested in finding stolen and lost art property, and it was at about that time that the O.S.S. entered into the picture and established a special section to investigate the looting of art objects. Rorimer was not sent to Germany until April; he arrived in the Füssen area near Neuschwanstein after the castle had been turned over to the Seventh Army.

During these months the French C.R.A. began to function as letters of reclamation poured in to be classified and copied for the use of other governmental agencies. Reclamations came in every form, from dignified, scholarly catalogs and lists, through lengthy letters telling extremely involved stories, down to handwritten notes asking for a few precious objects. Many of the simplest notes were heartbreaking. One, for example, described three small paintings, clearly not of any extraordinary value, which must have hung before their owner's eyes for years: His letter included tiny line drawings of a portrait, a still life, and a landscape. Other letters identified furniture by noting broken chair-caning, fitted slipcovers left behind by the looters, keys that fit drawers and cupboards. This breakdown into great and small individual losses gave some indication of the magnitude of the German looting operations, and it showed a touching belief in the goodwill of those trying to make some order out of chaos even while more losses occurred.

In September, 1944, the war had seven months to run. The fighting was bitter, and fifteen Monuments officers had one objective: to protect whatever they could along the paths of the advancing troops. They carried a list of thirty-six depositories of "collections from the Louvre and provincial museums . . . believed in the main to be accurate" and dozens of other châteaux, churches, and monuments in Normandy and the Île de France. "Off Limits" signs, "Protected Monument" signs, even large "X" marks of white tape indicating the imaginary presence of unexploded mines were useless as protection against bombers, blasts, shrapnel, and bullets when a building stood in the fields of battle or was near the target of a bombing run. Châteaux near the fighting lines sometimes passed from Allied hands to German hands and back again within the space of twenty-four hours. M.F.A. and A. evaluated destruction in France at about 45 percent. (The destruction rose to 90 percent in Germany, where 60 percent of the great historical monuments were entirely obliterated.) Following the armies through Normandy, Alsace-Lorraine, Belgium, Holland, and into Germany, M.F.A. and A. sent back detailed reports that read like gloomy tourist guides to places that would never be the same again: blocks of centuries-old houses totally destroyed, interiors of churches gutted, facades crumbled.

The greatest single problem of the M.F.A. and A. as long as American troops remained in Europe was the protection of European art from "spoliation and damage," the quickest way to destroy the American image and the prestige of the armies. M.F.A. and A. men, who knew perfectly well what châteaux were, carried directives defining them. They are well-built, stately homes with many rooms, elaborate interiors, multitudinous fireplaces surrounded by carved-wood or marble mantles, rich woodwork, and inlaid floors, and to officers and men they were the best places for shelter unless the M.F.A. and A. got to them first and posted signs. Letters of complaint and reports from French inspectors poured in. Sometimes a château owner praised a particular unit but requested no further billeting for fear that the next troops might not be so respectful.

Accidental fires were frequent. The winter was cold, and GI's were uncertain of the handling of ancient fireplaces or used them for cooking and set fire to the roofs. In one Alsatian château, cases full of loot stored by the Ahnenerbe were broken up, and soldiers used the sofas, their cushions, and chair cushions to make beds. In the same château a French museum inspection discovered "many small frames" in the mud of the courtyard, empty of their contents; the frames "proved" that the unit had carried off the miniatures as "souvenirs." The unit did not seem to care for a pile of eighteenth- and nineteenth-century prints and drawings left in a heap in their smashed frames in an outbuilding. If one château lost all its furniture to a group of bombardiers, an M.F.A. and A. report from another, occupied for four years by Germans, showed its occupants had carried off, according to the owner, 700 valuable paintings, 147 antique Oriental rugs, seventeenth-century tapestries, and quantities of rare old silver. The damage to châteaux was equally great in Belgium, especially during the Battle of the Bulge (December 16, 1944–January 16, 1945). This was understandable enough in a struggle that resulted in eight thousand American dead, forty-eight thousand wounded, and twenty-one thousand captured or missing, for the freezing troops took shelter wherever they could.

Even before hostilities ended, M.F.A. and A. officers were as concerned with discovering smaller pieces of art as with protecting monuments and describing destruction. When the Germans invaded northern and eastern Europe in 1940, many people hid precious objects in strange places. Like squirrels, they often forgot where their caches were or found that their improvised safe-deposit vaults had vanished. Cellars, gardens, and barn lofts disappeared under piles of rubble; owners died during the war years, naturally or unnaturally, leaving behind no clues as to what might be found where or no surviving relatives or friends to search for things easily discovered by others. Immediately after the liberation and as each town or sector was freed of the occupants, minor archaeological digs were standard procedure for civilians returning to their homes—or what was left of them. The officers kept lists of claimed objects lost and unclaimed objects found, circulated the lists among themselves, functioned as an inquiry department, and followed up clues.

One clue caused the death of one of the two Monuments men

killed in action. The first, an Englishman, died in a bombing raid. The second was an American art professor, Walter Huchthausen. Informed one evening that a "great" painting, possibly even a Da Vinci, had been found in a barn, the professor, in his enthusiasm for saving a masterpiece, borrowed a jeep and a driver and set out hastily without checking the battle lines in the area. As the jeep rolled along the autobahn in the Ruhr region, crossfire from hills on either side of the road forced the men to leave the car for shelter. Huchthausen rushed up the wrong hill and was instantly killed by the Germans. The wounded driver rolled into the roadside ditch and recovered. The "Da Vinci," examined later by another officer, proved to be a worthless daub.

French, Belgian, and Dutch reports indicated that large stores of art were hidden in various secret repositories beyond the Rhine. The first site discovered was a large underground sandstone chamber near Maastricht, Holland. There the Dutch had placed their most valuable paintings under the approving eyes of the Germans, who planned to pick them up easily after the war. American soldiers went on "museum tours" to view the Maastricht Rembrandts. Many young men learned about the artist for the first time in their lives. Their enthusiasm led to constant calls on M.F.A. and A. for identification of every painting in any Dutch attic or cellar as a possible Rembrandt.

Hidden art treasures first made sensational news across the Atlantic on April 5, 1945, when *The New York Times* carried the story of the discovery of more than four hundred valuable paintings, Charlemagne's crown (in fact a modern copy), the manuscript of Beethoven's Sixth Symphony, and other objects behind a locked door in the depths of a copper mine in Siegen, Westphalia. An officer studying an annotated Nazi art catalog in Aachen had discovered that the Aachen cathedral's art treasures were hidden someplace in Siegen and had notified headquarters to look there for a possible repository of art. The 8th Infantry Division found the mine, and when M.F.A. and A. personnel and the cathedral curate entered it, they found first the stench of sulfur and the effluvia of a large, recently departed German civilian population. At about the time (March 19, 1945) that Hitler issued his "scorched earth" directive—"If the war is lost, the nation will also perish. . . . Besides, those who remain after the battle are only the inferior ones, for the good ones have been killed."—the German radio announced that American soldiers murdered children. The people in Siegen had remained underground for two weeks, choking on the bad air, because they were so terrified of American bombers and advancing troops. (They might have been more frightened if they had known of Martin Bormann's March 23 decree. Its purpose was the concentration of the entire population of Germany—prisoners of war and slave-laborers from all over Europe as well—into the center of the Reich, which they were to reach by walking. Bormann made no provision for food or shelter for these masses en route. Both the Führer and his second-in-command had apparently lost all concern for their beloved people. Fortunately neither decree went into effect; the first would have wiped out the nation's economy for endless years; the second, most of the population.)

Behind the mine's locked door were a German caretaker and treasure from French Metz and from Vienna, Münster, Aachen, and the Rhineland. Among the paintings were some of the finest French moderns in Germany and several fifteenth-century masterpieces by Stephan Lochner. Some of these were still neatly packed in cases; others, slightly damp, were already speckled with a velvety green mold, for American bombers had wrecked the mine's dehydration plant in January. The 8th Infantry, a bit disappointed to have found property belonging principally to Germany, made the best of it and set up an art museum. They named it after their insignia, "The Golden Arrow," and put up a sign at the entrance telling what was inside. Soldiers happily tried on "Charlemagne's crown," and examined a tenth-century cross studded with jewels.

Four days later, the 347th Infantry Division of General George S. Patton's Third Army discovered a salt mine full of gold at Merkers. What looked like a sawmill on a hill was really the entrance to a mine so filled with gold that dozens of slave-laborers had worked seventy hours to carry it about 750 feet underground. The officer who entered the mine first found a Prussian State Museums curator and a British war prisoner who had helped move the gold and knew just where it was. Within a few days the area around the mine looked like a modern version of a medieval besieged city. There was a tank unit around the minehead; a rifle company was dispensed about the mine's four other entrances; jeeps, military police, and Intelligence, Special Details, and Reconnaissance men swarmed all over. An American banker, a gold expert, was flown in from Paris to inspect the prize with several officers. The gold was there in 550 canvas bags, each holding a million Reichsmarks, and in 400 smaller bags containing gold ingots. Off to one side was another source of Nazi gold: dental fillings and wedding rings taken from Jews in Auschwitz and Buchenwald. Officers from G-2 (Intelligence) found some German bankers in the vicinity who declared that the mine contained all the gold reserve of the Reichsbank. The American banker set a value of $250,000,000 on the loot. Since the Nazis had begun the war with a $50,000,000 reserve, this was a considerable profit. Eventually, part of the cache was discovered to belong to Belgium. Passed on to France for safekeeping in 1940, it had gone to Dakar, whence Vichy had ordered it turned over to the Germans.

A further look around Merkers disclosed some art, worth at least twice as much as the gold. There were 202 paintings from Berlin's Kaiser Friedrich Museum, appraised at $80,000,000.[2] Great works from fifteen other Berlin museums and the priceless head of Queen Nefertiti were also in the mine.

After a visit by Generals Eisenhower, Bradley, and Eddy, who went down into the mine with Patton in an elevator run by a German, the gold was removed to the Frankfort vaults of the Reichsbank for temporary storage. The value of the gold and the even greater value of the art changed the attitude of the army toward the M.F.A. and A. men, who ceased to be "those guys with their goddamn art." Art repositories were henceforth "targets," not taking priority over winning the war, but not to be disregarded.

Patton's Third Army hit the third target also: Alt Aussee, a salt mine not very far from Salzburg. Information about it leaked first in Trier, hometown of Dr. Bunjes, the Kunstschutz liaison man with French museums. Bunjes himself tipped off an M.F.A. and A. team attached to Patton's army. Shortly afterward, Bunjes hanged himself to escape arrest. His suicide was less elegant than that of Von Behr, who maintained his sybaritic posture by joining his wife in a drink of vintage champagne heavily laced with poison. Von Behr also accomplished a good deed before his death by turning over to the Americans the E.R.R. files in his possession.

Bunjes's information made Captain Robert Posey and Private Lincoln Kirstein, of the M.F.A. and A., extremely eager for Patton to push his way forward to the mine site, hopefully before the Russians, approaching from the opposite direction. The situation was even more perilous than either man knew.

[2] The bulk of the Kaiser Friedrich Museum's treasures had been placed in one of the gigantic flak towers constructed in Berlin to withstand heavy attacks of all kinds. The museum tower came through the bombing and tank attacks barely chipped. Two days after V-E Day, S.S. troops broke into the tower and set it afire, thus totally destroying part of their own heritage in a senseless gesture.

Very early in April, Gauleiter G. Eigruber received a perplexing letter from Martin Bormann. According to Hitler's specific wish, this repository was under no circumstances to be captured or damaged. Eigruber was puzzled, for if he destroyed the mine, it would not be taken, but its contents would be lost or seriously damaged. Hitler's orders in the last months of the war were baffling to all his subordinates, and Eigruber was no exception. Accustomed to following orders blindly and faced with a dilemma, he decided to steer a middle course so that he could move in either direction in the event of further orders.

Three large wooden crates, marked "Marble—DO NOT DROP," arrived by truck at Alt Aussee on April 10, transported by Mine Inspector Glinz, of the Upper Danube area. He made two more visits, one on April 13 and one on April 30, finally depositing the last of eight cases, or nearly half a ton, of explosives. These were placed inside the repository rooms and in such strategic spots that detonation would guarantee total destruction or heavy damage to various sections of the mine and the delivery of a knockout blow to the pumping system that ordinarily kept the mine clear of constant water seepage. Objects not blown to bits or damaged by fire would be irretrievably damaged by flooding.

Alt Aussee was the Nazi cave of the Nibelungen. It contained, besides other objects, 6,700 paintings, among them Hitler's Linz collection and art stolen in Italy in 1944 by the Hermann Göring Division as a birthday gift for the Reichsmarschall. To watch over these masterworks, Hitler had installed a small, quiet man, the Berlin art restorer Karl Sieber, whose principal interest in life was the application of his craft. Although he cared nothing for politics and less for violence, Sieber had joined the Nazi party in the 1930's because a Jewish art dealer suggested that the move would be good for his business. Since the party took care of its own, Sieber's business flourished, especially after stolen art, which was sometimes damaged in transit, began to pour into Berlin. Sieber's job was to restore the art to its original condition, and his work was so fine that when the Germans took over the mine from Austria in 1943, they moved Sieber and his family (he had a wife and young daughter) to a small house nearby. He continued his work inside the mine, doing such tasks as the invisible repair of a crack in one of the panels of the Ghent altarpiece where the wood had split during the work's removal either from Ghent or from Pau.

On April 4, 1945, Hans Schedelmann, an internationally known weapons expert, once an adviser to William Randolph Hearst, arrived at the mine with a collection of weapons, armor, and old flags from the Vienna Heeremuseum. The objects had been sent to the mine for storage by order of Dr. Leopold Ruprecht, a Linz curator and head of the Vienna weapons collection. As Ruprecht's agent, Schedelmann met Karl Sieber on this occasion. Moreover, Schedelmann did not return to Vienna but remained "in a small house near the mine" for the rest of the month. On April 14 he paid a visit to Sieber in his office in the mine and learned from him about the presence of the explosive bombs inside the repository rooms and about Eigruber's orders to a special military group to explode the bombs upon the approach of Allied troops so that the works of art would be entirely destroyed. Sieber added that Dr. von Hümmel had a certain measure of supervision over the stored art, as did Ruprecht, and that both men had agreed to the explosion.

Schedelmann immediately assured Sieber that he could count on his personal cooperation and planned efforts to prevent such a crime, further promising to maintain complete silence under all circumstances as to the tenor of their conversation. Schedelmann added that he would do everything he could to change Dr. Ruprecht's stand on this matter and would try to convince him to use his position as supervisor of goods in the mine to prevent the explosions, no matter what happened. (He had already managed, at the end of March, to change Ruprecht's mind about blowing up the Vienna Postal Savings Bank building in which the Vienna weapons collection was stored.) Schedelmann and Sieber agreed that if it was impossible to stop the explosion in this fashion, they would enlist the aid of the supervisory board of the mine, whose powers had been transferred to Dr. Ruprecht when the bombs were put in place, so that the explosives would be moved and detonated in such a way that the entrances to the repository rooms would be so cluttered with debris that the military commandos could not get near them.

Schedelmann then sounded out the political attitudes of the local police chief, a man named Jakob Merle, and told him as much as seemed feasible of the plot so that if it was necessary to prevent the blowing-up of the art works by armed force, the conspirators would have assistance. Merle immediately agreed to help. On April 24 or 25 Schedelmann telephoned Ruprecht, who was in Zell-am-Zee, and asked him to come to the mine at once on urgent business. Ruprecht arrived on April 28 and announced that he had the authority to act according to his own judgment, showed Schedelmann his order to this effect, and added that he was in favor of blowing up the art treasures. Schedelmann then explained fully the consequences of such an act and after long discussion managed to convince Ruprecht that the works of art were really the heritage of the entire civilized world and must be saved no matter what the eventual consequences might be for the conspirators, since an explosion could never be justified from any point of view.

When Schedelmann informed Sieber that he had won over Ruprecht, the two men conferred with Dr. Hubert Seiberl, of the Vienna Institute for the Protection of Monuments, and with the aid of still another conspirator, Seiberl's secretary, Linde Schrader, they began a selection of the most valuable pieces of art which they hid away in a secret place unknown to anybody else. Thus, if Eigruber's commandos managed to get into the mine before the group could prevent the great explosion, at least these precious works would be saved. Then the boxes of bombs were taken out of the repository rooms and placed elsewhere. The conspirators were afraid to let Dr. Ruprecht out of their sight, lest he switch back to Eigruber's side at the last moment. Until an order could arrive from Berchtesgaden making it possible for the mine directors to prevent the explosion, Schedelmann, quite literally, did not leave Ruprecht alone for a moment; he relaxed his vigilance only when he knew that a messenger had been dispatched to bring the order to Alt Aussee. The plan was to blow up sections of the mine tunnels so carefully that the art in the storage rooms remained intact while the passages through the tunnels were blocked enough to make entry into the rooms difficult and slow, for news of the rapid American advance made only a brief delay necessary.

Alt Aussee mine burrows horizontally through a mountain. From its main tunnel branch others, the smaller ones ending finally in caverns or chambers resulting from the removal of salt. Through the tunnels ran a miniature train pulled by a gasoline engine and provided with flatcars—called *Hünde*, or "dogs." Two feet wide and five feet long, with low wooden sides, the "dogs" accommodated two men if they sat with their arms wrapped around their knees and kept their heads down to avoid the protruding rocks of the uneven ceiling. Heavy iron doors set into the tunnel sides led to the treasure chambers.

The conspirators pored over a plan of the mine, put together by the meticulous Sieber, and marked points where small dynamite charges could bring down the tunnels' roofs and block access to the chambers without damaging their interiors.[3] The conspirators knew what they had to do and how to do it, but before they could accomplish the task, there were some minor details that had to be completed outside of the mine.

Quite early on the morning of April 30, Ruprecht, Schedelmann, and their driver, Karl Kluge, appeared at the mine to receive from Sieber a large box of gold coins to be delivered to Dr. von Hümmel at Berchtesgaden. The coins had recently arrived at the repository from Hohenfurth Monastery in Austria. Ruprecht signed the receipt for the treasure. Schedelmann accompanied him on the journey primarily to examine a document held by Von Hümmel which would give authority to prevent blowing up the mine. The three men put the chest in their vehicle and drove the approximately forty miles to Berchtesgaden. They did not hurry with their precious cargo and arrived at high noon, in time for the first Allied air attack on the Obersalzberg.[4] Schedelmann and Kluge brought the chest into the Plattnerhof Hotel; Ruprecht went to report their arrival to Von Hümmel, for nobody entered the Hitlerian compound without permission; and the air-raid alarm sounded. Everyone disappeared into the cellars, but Schedelmann, too conscientious to leave the gold unguarded in the hotel lobby, sat out the raid above ground. The hotel was struck, and from his vantage point he had the opportunity to watch men and women come swarming in to help themselves to whatever they could grab in the ruins of the hotel, the liquor stores, and the barber shop.

After the raid, while Ruprecht secured a copy of an early Hitler order stating that art works were not to be destroyed, Schedelmann turned over the chest of gold—about four feet long and containing 2,200 valuable coins—to Von Hümmel and was given a receipt for it. The next day a messenger took the Führer's order to Alt Aussee. Schedelmann, certain that Sieber would carry out the tunnel block-

[3] The Kaiser Josef chamber held Michelangelo's Madonna from Bruges; the Mineral Kabinett held the Ghent altarpiece; the Springerwerke, with double ranks of shelves around three walls and through its center, held more than two thousand paintings; the Kapelle held Archduke Ferdinand's collection of Spanish armor; and the Kammergrafen, largest in size and farthest from the minehead, held the cream of the Linz collection in a careful arrangement of balconies on different levels containing tightly packed rugs, furniture, tapestries, books, paintings, and sculpture.

[4] The Americans did not bomb the Alps as a prime target. The 9th Fighter Air Force did some strafing in the last week of the war against some of the last German holdouts in southern Bavaria, the foothills of the Alps. The Royal Air Force bombed Hitler's retreat at Berchtesgaden for psychological and architectural reasons.

age and now relieved of watching Dr. Ruprecht, went to his mother's home in Bad Reichenhall, twenty-four miles away; Ruprecht drove to Zell-am-Zee; and Kluge returned to Alt Aussee.

When an American lieutenant appeared at Schedelmann's home a short time later and asked for him, the Austrian thought the visit might refer to an incident that had occurred the night before when a group of GI's had manhandled his brother, who found them "raising hell in his house and politely asked what they wanted." The officer had come to inquire about the coins and received the receipt signed by Von Hümmel. This ended Schedelmann's part in the business.

Eventually, Dr. von Hümmel was arrested and told his captors that when he left Berchtesgaden he had transferred the chest to the Archbishop of Salzburg. The chest was found in Salzburg, and it and its contents were returned to its rightful owners, the Hohenfurth Monastery. Thus the reports that the chest was "lost" or sunk in a lake were completely unfounded and as mythical as the rumor that Martin Bormann took the chest from Dr. von Hümmel, his secretary, and carried it away with him.

Bormann was still in Berlin on the night of April 30–May 1. Hitler and Eva Braun committed suicide on the afternoon of April 30; Goebbels, his wife, and their six children followed their Führer at 8:30 on the evening of May 1. Their bunker went up in flames within a half hour. Bormann and several hundred men of Hitler's special guard—principally S.S.—were last definitely seen at 9 P.M. in the New Chancellery; they planned to pass through the Russian lines north of the Spree River by following the subway tracks from the station across the street to the Friedrichstrasse exit, where they could cross the river. The plan did not work for the entire contingent. Bormann's group tried to follow a German tank that received a direct Russian shell, which demolished it. One survivor believed Bormann was killed. Another man testified in a sworn statement that he had seen Bormann's body under the railroad bridge; it was clearly visible in the moonlight and appeared quite dead, though there was no sign of any wounds. Cyanide capsules were standard issue for Nazi leaders in tight situations, and this story presumed that Bormann had bitten down on his. The body disappeared, however, and lack of positive identification has led to twenty-five years of speculation as to what really happened to Bormann, always so careful to avoid photographers.

When Dr. Ruprecht returned to Zell-am-Zee after the trip to Berchtesgaden, he turned his responsibility for the mine back to its actual director, the engineer Dr. E. Poechmüller. On May 4 the director prepared the charges necessary for the accomplishment of the plan. On Saturday, May 5, 1945, anybody in the vicinity of the mine heard a long series of explosive noises. Each of the seventy-six charges went off without a single misfire, and the results were what had been expected. The entrances to the five principal chambers and the secret hiding-place were blocked with rubble.

When word of the explosions reached Eigruber, he flew into a rage and ordered a roundup of all suspects. They were to be shot whether guilty or not. Nobody suspected Sieber. Luckily for the other suspects, the U.S. Third Army had sent tactical units ahead of the main body of troops in order to reach Alt Aussee ahead of the Russians, who had taken Vienna. The Americans rushed through Bad Ischl, stopping only long enough to take prisoners—the Germans were now in a great rush to surrender—and found the last resistance in Alt Aussee village from the S.S. troops who had been guarding the mine. S.S. resistance was not very strong at this time, and the Americans took a few more prisoners before reaching the mine in time to stop Eigruber's plan for wholesale execution.

The 80th Infantry Division reached the mine on May 7 and set a heavy guard around it before Posey and Kirstein arrived on the next day. The two Monuments men, using acetylene lamps to see their way through the darkness, hastened along in the principal mine tunnel for about a quarter of a mile until they were brought up short by a rockfall; they had reached the site of one of the explosions. U.S. Army Engineers and Austrian miners managed to clear a path through the rocks in twenty-four hours. When Posey and Kirstein moved through the mine after all the tunnels were cleared and pulled open the first iron door, they saw—in heaps, piles, and racks—the accumulated cultural wealth of six centuries of artistic and literary effort, more than a hundred thousand items: enough paintings to fill several museums,[5] the contents of whole libraries, rugs to carpet acres of floors, tapestries to cover hundreds of walls, sculpture, armor, silver and gold objects, fabulous antique jewelry, furniture. The M.F.A. and A. had had some inkling of what the mine contained, but its impact was stupefying—to them and to the world, which finally realized the extent of Hitler's looting.

[5] The National Gallery in Washington, D.C., displays about 1,100 paintings from its collection of slightly more than 2,000.

In the months that followed, the Allied armies found fifteen hundred repositories: mines, castles, monasteries, schools, and public and private buildings of every description. Just before V-E Day the American First Army inspected the salt mine at Bernterode in Thuringia. Here in a shaft nearly a mile underground, soldiers discovered a cement chamber so freshly constructed that its walls were still damp. Four bronze coffins lay inside this vault: Frederick the Great and his father, Frederick William I, and Field Marshal Paul von Hindenburg and his wife slept here. Frederick William, called the sergeant-king for his prowess in battle, was honored with a wreath bearing a red ribbon with Hitler's name on it, a tribute from the king's admirer. This vault was to have remained undiscovered and unseen until the revival of the Third Reich, and paper labels bearing the occupants' names were attached to each casket. Over them hung the battle flags of famous Prussian regiments, swastikas hobnobbing with eagles, and around them were portraits of all the German field marshals from the eighteenth century onward. Around the coffin of Frederick the Great were his treasures from Sans Souci in Potsdam, boxes of scarlet-bound books and great eighteenth-century French paintings. The Hohenzollern imperial crowns, the royal scepter and orb, and a collection of royal swords, one of them three feet long and blazing with rubies and diamonds, completed this freshly buried monument.

In contrast with this exhibit of Prussian glory was the example of Nazi corruption found in a brick factory in Hüngen, Rosenberg's warehouse of texts for his projected Höhe Schule course in scientific anti-Semitism. The holiest Jewish books, records, and synagogue paraphernalia taken from all over Europe were piled up in the kiln; with them were priceless illuminated-parchment Torahs, cut up into typewriter covers or shoe linings, and boxes full of Jewish identity cards, thousands of simple death certificates for Jews who had died in concentration camps. Although the order had been for such cards to be destroyed, they kept turning up, often by the trunkload, with other loot sent to the collecting points. Americans charged with the redistribution of stolen property also traced survivors or helped complete the records of families wiped out completely.

The personal collections of Nazi leaders were found in various hiding-places. Göring's collection, only two hundred pieces in 1939, had swollen to two thousand by the end of the war and had been stored, as he acquired it through the years, in his collection of residences. He never lived in Mauterndorf, the home he inherited near Salzburg, for he had given it to his sisters, who furnished it with their own belongings and the family collection of ecclesiastical robes, which had led to Göring's own career as a collector. A Berlin town house contained splendid furnishings, a suitable background for official dinners and receptions. After 1937 it held only less-important art, and after 1942 most of the finest furniture was moved to Wildpark, near Potsdam, where the Luftwaffe school had a new air-raid shelter. In the Bayreuth area was Schloss Veldenstein, a sixteenth-century castle with the typically small rooms of the period. Göring was renovating Veldenstein, which held some of his Gothic tapestries and a collection of modern German paintings. The model farm near Berlin, Gollin, was richly but inappropriately fitted out with valuable French furniture. Hofer also kept some of his own collection there. Not far away was Ringenwalde, an eighteenth-century country house that Göring never occupied and left in the care of Dr. Walther Sonneman, his wife's brother. Ringenwalde had a ceiling painting from La Bagatelle, the château built for the Comte d'Artois at the edge of the Bois de Boulogne in 1801. The work, reputedly by Fragonard and Greuze, was worth a quarter of a million dollars. Its luscious females smiled down on Göring's bombed-out Berlin friends, invited to take shelter slightly away from danger. Rominten, Göring's hunting lodge on the Prussian border, was elaborately furnished and had a splendid library but no paintings. At Berchtesgaden, not far from Hitler's own house, the Berghof, Göring had a small farm where his wife usually lived from January, after her husband's birthday, until early summer. It was Karinhall, his favorite home and official residence, sixty miles southeast of Berlin, that was really so packed with art and art objects that it resembled a huge, many-roomed antiques shop.

Göring's collection was so huge that he employed Hofer as a full-time curator after February, 1944. Hofer was assisted by his wife, a restorer who had studied in Rome and New York and who was kept busy keeping the Göring paintings in good order. Hofer also consulted with other experts and employed framers, cabinetmakers, and other experts when necessary. The 1,375 paintings, 250 sculptures, 108 tapestries, 75 stained-glass windows, and 175 objets d'art usually arrived at Karinhall either in Luftwaffe trucks or in planes, which could land nearby. Longer trips were made in private two-car speed trains. Occasionally, the use of "diplomatic pouch couriers" bypassed customs barriers. Karinhall had two bomb shelters: One was for Göring and his wife and child, his most valuable paintings and sculpture, and his personal safe, containing jewelry; the second shelter had three floors, the first and third for tapestries, sculpture, and stained glass, the second for employees. The Stabsamt shelter near Berlin was for temporary storage only; the Kurfuerst, near Potsdam, supplemented Wildpark.

From February, 1945, when Berlin became an inferno, Göring was much more preoccupied with saving his art than with helping to fight the war. His plans for saving his property were wildly confused, and orders, counterorders, and secondary orders flew. He first wished to move everything out of Karinhall and the air-force bunker. Then he had to decide what art had priority and consulted Hofer about his idea of sending out everything he had purchased, setting aside E.R.R. confiscations (more than a thousand paintings) for a later shipment. Hofer suggested a combination of the best purchases and the best E.R.R. material in the first load. Göring's choice for a safe place was first Veldenstein and then a new air-raid shelter in Berchtesgaden. He had to give up any grandiose plan at once, for Veldenstein's doors were too narrow to permit the entry of large objects and the shelter was not yet completed. The one thing he had no problem with was transportation; four personal trains and their engineers and crew were at his beck and call.

One train removed the first shipment from Berlin during the first week of February. A second shipment left Hamelsprink Station near Karinhall on March 13. April's selection emptied the Berlin bunker and almost emptied Karinhall. The train was loaded at Vogelsang Station and ready to move when Göring issued a stop order and sent Hofer to Veldenstein to repack everything there for another move. After a week in Vogelsang the train went to Bad Reichenhall, about twenty-five miles from Berchtesgaden, where the first two loads from Veldenstein joined it. This triple load proceeded to Berchtesgaden and waited in the station tunnel for the completion of the bomb shelter. Hofer and two guards remained with the train. A day or so later, Göring ordered eight carloads of his most valuable art moved to Unterstein, near the Koeningsee, about twenty miles away. The art was unloaded into a shelter in Unterstein, and when it could hold nothing more, the excess was stored in a grocery store run by a friendly Nazi. Two or three cars loaded with furniture, his art library and records, and some fine paintings remained in the Berchtesgaden tunnel. One lot of twenty-four paintings "of French origin" by Dutch, Italian, and French artists disappeared at some point on the road from Karinhall to Berchtesgaden.

Göring made the trip to Berchtesgaden himself shortly after most of the collection had moved to Unterstein. His purpose was a further selection from the art left in the tunnel, and his artistic zeal put him temporarily into Martin Bormann's power. Shortly before dawn on April 25 the Berchtesgaden S.S. arrested the Reichsmarschall on a charge of "high treason." Two days before, acting on a decree of June 29, 1941, he had sent Hitler a cautiously worded telegram asking whether the Führer "agreed to his taking over the total leadership of the Reich as his deputy." Cut off from both military and civil branches of government, Hitler was clearly incapacitated as a ruler, even if he had not proved to all who saw him in the last weeks that he was emotionally unfit to make decisions. Göring's wire asked for an answer by ten at night. When the message arrived, Bormann held it for a short while and then gave it to Hitler, commenting that it was an attempt at usurpation of power and a treasonous ultimatum. A brief discussion followed. During it Hitler accused Göring of being "corrupt and a drug addict," a remark that shocked one witness to the scene who wondered, sensibly enough, why such a monster had been allowed to hold so many high positions for so long. At length Hitler sent a telegram telling Göring that he had committed treason but offering to spare his life if he immediately resigned all his posts. Göring's reply to this message was to be either Yes or No. Bormann, present during the composition of the telegram, found it too soft and sent off a wire himself to S.S. headquarters in Berchtesgaden, ordering the immediate arrest of Göring, his staff, and the State Secretary of the Reich Chancellery, Hans Lammers. Bormann was now directly in line for the succession to absolute power, a position he had coveted for years.

Göring's liaison officer was released the day after the arrest. Since art superseded everything else in the now ex-Reichsmarschall's preoccupations, he sent the officer to Unterstein to bring back the railroad cars emptied there, to sort out the collections again, and to put the art inside a completed air-raid shelter originally designed for his personal staff. Eleven cars made the trip back to Berchtesgaden and stood in the tunnel, where S.S. troops began the unloading.

Two cars had been unpacked and the rest were ready for unloading when a French armored division arrived in Berchtesgaden and during the struggle to take the village machine-gunned the tunnel, badly damaging a considerable number of paintings and mutilating statues. The first American division on the scene was the 101st Airborne, whose commanding officer ordered the confiscation of the entire contents of the train and its removal to an inn nearby, even before the arrival of M.F.A. and A. officers. Evidence of looting made such an action imperative.

The inn became a sort of exhibition of Göring art, open to any curious soldiers and eventually to the peasants of the area. The exhibition increased in size as more and more Göring miscellanea turned up, although surprisingly enough, not much was carried off by souvenir hunters. Four or five miniature Dutch pictures, small enough to be slipped into pockets or concealed under shirts or skirts, disappeared. When John Walker, of the National Gallery, inspected the collection, he found it "very uneven" in quality and considerably damaged, although the "most important works of art" from the E.R.R. confiscations were "relatively intact."

The Luftwaffe rescued Göring from the S.S., and he was temporarily free until the day he turned himself over to the U.S. Army. The richest Nazi and the most affable, he carried with him only his collection of medals and his gem-studded Reichsmarschall's baton. Hofer, responsible for the acquisition of so much of the collection, offered his services as a kind of curator to the Allied Military Government in Berchtesgaden. His offer was accepted, and Hofer became what one Monuments man characterized as "our pet prisoner, taken out of jail each morning and put back each night." He worked usefully for several months before complaints of favoritism kept him in prison for a short term. Frau Göring was placed under house arrest at Schloss Mauterndorf on the eve of her departure for unspecified neutral territory. Arresting officers found in her packed suitcases a small but very choice collection of fifteenth-century Flemish masterpieces, one a Madonna from a French Rothschild collection. The Göring family nurse had the Van Meegeren "Vermeer" wrapped around a piece of pipe. Göring had assured her that it would provide for her needs for a long time.

Shortly after May 4, three French Beaux-Arts officers arrived at General de Lattre's First French Army headquarters in Landau. Early in April, Rose Valland, eager to participate in the recovery and restitution of stolen art, had applied for a commission in the French

Army, for she felt that the "possibility of action might be very transitory." The red tape that followed her request was plentiful, and it was not until General de Lattre asked for an immediate assignment of Beaux-Arts officers, either male or female, that she and two Louvre curators received their orders to report. Miss Valland, now a captain, was given a mission of unlimited duration. The three new members, with a fourth man already in Landau, were the French equivalent of the American M.F.A. and A.

Fairly well informed of the very impressive American discoveries, French headquarters had to report only fewer, less spectacular finds of its own. This was not surprising, for the territory occupied by the French was in the Upper Rhine Valley, a location not especially safe or suitable for hiding large quantities of valuable art. They hoped, as a matter of national pride and responsibility, that Captain Valland and the three men would turn up something more sensational. Hence the Beaux-Arts officers sought permission to move freely around Germany outside of French-controlled areas.

SHAEF first limited the French experts to French First Army territory, but a second order, on May 12, allowed the three curators to go "to Füssen, Kempten, and Buxheim to inspect and identify French works of art." Fearful lest SHAEF intervene again, the three left immediately for Füssen, a trip that had seemed an impossible dream to Rose Valland for years. When the French delegation arrived at Füssen, they found all the repositories marked "Off Limits" and their orders of no help in gaining entrance. They hastened to Augsburg, hoping to find James Rorimer, who had been in Füssen the night before, only to discover that he was not in his office. Another M.F.A. and A. officer reassured them as to the condition of the castles and their contents, stressing the number of still-packed cases of art. Considerably encouraged by this news, they gave up the idea of bypassing the Military Government's protective order and did some extra investigating of their own. Captain Valland located Dr. Schiedlausky in Füssen, where they returned, and he confirmed the accuracy of her repository list and told her what had been transferred from aboveground castles to the mine at Alt Aussee during the winter of 1944. Among other items of particular interest, he mentioned the Ghent altarpiece, for which the French felt particularly responsible ever since its kidnapping from the Pau Museum.[6]

[6] As an example of the delicate international situation surrounding the return of art objects and the necessity for a strong central authority, a long, indignant letter writ-

After diligent inquiries in the environs of the Füssen castles and the Buxheim Monastery, the French curators felt that they could send home the good news that a considerable portion of the stolen French collections was intact. The French were now also convinced, quite correctly, that an earlier idea for an inter-Allied restitution committee had been scrapped. They asked to have a C.R.A. representative attached to the U.S. Army. This request went slowly through military channels. In August, however, a French mission of three Beaux-Arts officers was permitted to make an official inspection tour of all the E.R.R. depots in Germany. Rose Valland was one of the group. Finally, in September, General Eisenhower appointed a C.R.A. man to serve with the Americans, and Captain Valland negotiated an agreement with the M.F.A. and A. for the direct evacuation of French art stored in Füssen. She became the C.R.A. representative in Bavaria at that time. On September 25, 1945, an American truck arrived in Paris from Munich. In it were two Monuments officers and a token load of seventy-one paintings from the looted art.

Paris had seen other arrivals earlier that year. During the spring several loads of art were sent at intervals from the châteaux to the Louvre, which reopened its halls of eighteenth- and nineteenth-century French art and held its first public exhibition of paintings since May, 1940. Art may return from imprisonment unscarred, but this is not true of the human being. On a Saturday in mid-April, a day

---

ten to a friend in June, 1945, by the "Advisory Architect for National Restoration and Counsellor to the Beaux-Arts of Belgium" is revealing. The letter mentions Belgian newspaper stories giving publicity to the "discovery" of the Ghent altarpiece by the Belgian director-general of the Beaux-Arts, although the U.S. Army had already announced this discovery a few days before the enterprising director-general set out from Brussels with twenty-five trucks and no official papers or passes. The news items indicated that the Belgian had entered the mine (after mysteriously passing checkpoints and guards), found nineteen panels (there are only seventeen) in nineteen cases ("The Mystic Lamb" had left Pau in ten cases, each marked "*Sint Baafs*"), and had even examined two canvases (the Ghent altarpiece is painted on wood) before being ordered to leave by the Americans. The incorrect information in the newspapers could not fool the officials in Belgium, who knew all about the valuable work of art, but it created much excitement among the general population. In addition, the journey and its purpose—to take the work back to Belgium—were directly counter to the Belgian Government's desire to let the French arrange for the recovery as proof that there was no hard feeling about the unfortunate incident in Pau. One wonders why twenty-five trucks were required to take on ten cases, which could be easily placed inside one truck, what this strange expedition hoped to use the other trucks for, where anybody found so many trucks at this period and the gasoline to run them, and exactly what kind of domestic squabbles were taking place inside the Belgian Ministry of Fine Arts. Fortunately, the expedition was completely unsuccessful. No Belgian was allowed inside Alt Aussee, and it is even doubtful that the trucks arrived at the mine at all. The woods were full of S.S. troops who refused to surrender, and American truck convoys traveled with a military armed escort.

never forgotten by those who saw it, American transport planes brought back eight thousand French prisoners of war. From the landing field they were taken by truck to the Gare d'Orsay in the center of Paris. The emptied planes circled round and round high over the city.[7] On the next day a train pulled into the Gare de Lyon with the first contingent of survivors of the concentration camps, three hundred women from Ravensbrück, a group selected by the camp Kommandant as most suitable (i.e., least likely to shock the French population) for exchange of German women held in France. Eleven survivors died on the train. The others–dazed, skeletal, hollow-eyed, gray of skin, sick, wearing nondescript, faded garments, carrying with them the internal and external scars that would never be healed–were the barely living proof of the atrocities that had gone on for years behind the barbed-wire fences of the Nazi hells. All through that spring, American troops opened prison gates, too late for nearly six million people, and only just in time for the handful of living skeletons still clinging to life. News of the concentration camps horrified the entire civilized world and, like a black, evil-smelling cloud, hung over the peace that came on May 8.

[7] The prisoners returned to a city only slightly better off than it had been during the winter of 1944–1945, the coldest since 1941. It had rained for weeks, the fine Parisian drizzle that freezes the marrow, and then it had snowed. Everybody was cold, indoors as well as out. Coal was in such short supply that only electric trains or those drawn by diesel engines could run. Hence, what coal there was could not be transported. Electricity was turned off at the power plants during the daylight hours with the exception of one hour at noon. The current was so weak that in the strictly rationed number of bulbs (restricted as to wattage also) permitted in any one room, filaments glowed feebly. Buildings were so cold that water was turned off to prevent bursting pipes. Frequently, the only running water allowed flowed between noon and two o'clock. The finest gift any GI could give a French friend was a bar of ordinary American soap that lathered. Frenchwomen tried to feed their families on less food than ever. The black market vanished with the Germans, but a new kind of *maquisard* held up trucks and hijacked trains bringing food from the country. Smoked meats and sausages almost disappeared when a lack of salt put an end to their preparation. During one week in December the food ration for an adult added up to about three ounces of fresh meat, three ounces of butter, and less than two ounces of smoked meat, the *charcuterie* the French love so much. Only babies under three years old could have milk; their older brothers and sisters up to the age of twenty-one might have as many as four eggs a month, at thirty francs apiece, if one could find them. Beet sugar, an invention of the Napoleonic era and the English blockade, could not be processed, for the beet crop stuck in the frozen ground. Newsprint, abundantly available to collaborationist newspapers during the Occupation, became such a scarce commodity that Parisian papers issued half-size sheets, one per day, with highly condensed news. Operating rooms remained dark and unused in hospitals, which also needed drugs to cure pneumonia victims, thermometers with which to take their temperatures, and plaster to set the broken bones of those not too decalcified to break legs and arms on the slippery streets. The average adult Frenchman lost forty pounds during the Occupation years; the first winter after the liberation of Paris put none of those pounds back.

CHAPTER 14

FIFTEEN HUNDRED REPOSITORIES

MONUMENTS, FINE ARTS and Archives played a multiple role in the postwar activities of the Allied Military Government. This small group of men secured the art that they had found and continued to find, removed it to several central collecting points for redistribution to the countries from which it had been stolen in one manner or another, made urgent temporary repairs on art, art objects, and monuments, and instituted a program of reeducation of the German people. Before any of the art could be removed from the mines, castles, cellars, and other hiding places, however, M.F.A. and A. needed a large building to use as a combined storehouse and examining laboratory.

Most of Germany's large cities were shambles, masses of rubble punctuated with skeletons of buildings. Munich was no exception, and its Königsplatz had not been spared. When the Americans first drove in, jeeps could not move across the square, which was piled with chunks of cement and broken bricks, decapitated and limbless statues, shattered glass, and crumpled, torn, and dirty paper. Most of the square's lovely medieval buildings had vanished, but miraculously two constructions of the 1930's were in passably good condition. The ugly neoclassic twins, the Führerbau and the Verwaltungsbau, after bombing by the Allies and sacking by the Germans right after V-E Day, were, if not exactly suitable for use, at least reparable.

M.F.A. and A. chose the Verwaltungsbau, formerly Nazi party headquarters for south Germany, for its principal collecting point and began to search for building materials, window glass, and such elementary necessities as brooms to sweep out the dust and enough labor to handle the repair job. The cleaned-up Bau, as the building was soon called, was divided into large rooms, one for each previously occupied country. The procedure followed was fairly simple and is described in an official report:

> At the Munich collecting point, objects which preliminary inspection reveals to have probably come from a certain country are placed in the collecting room set aside for that country. Here specialists invited to come from the country in question examine the objects and the records more carefully. Approximately 35 percent of the art taken from conquered countries is identifiable at first sight. The rest requires longer study. Where crates have come indisputably from a certain country and do not appear to have been tampered with, they are sometimes sent back to that country unopened. This procedure varies with the particular type of object and other conditions. The recipient country is duty-bound to give over the object to whichever nation is ultimately proved to be the rightful owner, and has been asked to make inventories of the objects as they are received and to send copies to the Office of Military Government.

Since most of the important cultural objects in the western world are cataloged or are known to scholars and dealers, much of the loot could be readily identified and returned without waiting for the formal processing of a claim. Furthermore, the Germans recorded their looting with such thoroughness that it was possible to make good use of their records to turn back the flow of art. Interrogations and reports by the Office of Strategic Services added to the quantity of useful documents.

The O.S.S. used three men, all of them trained art scholars, to conduct the interrogations, calling them the Art Looting Investigations Unit. They worked with the M.F.A. and A., whose one full-time detective was a German-born anti-Nazi who had lived in the United States for years and was a professor of art at the University of California. He was particularly skilled at getting Nazis to talk truthfully by the expedient of telling them that if they did not, they would pay for their lies with their heads. This simple application of Nazi bullying worked very well on former bullies. One of its results was the discovery of the five relics of the Holy Roman Empire, including the real crown of Charlemagne. Despite widespread rumors that an S.S. officer had sunk the relics in the Zell-am-Zee, on the Tyrolean border, somebody else had hidden them eight stories underground in the lowest basement of a Nuremberg apartment house built on a rocky hill. A false wall and a fake flue held the treasures, stored away in the city chosen by Hitler as a center for Nazi demonstrations because of its picturesque buildings, its mighty defensive walls, and its imposing castle high on the rock above the river. The relics and their hiding place were ideologically well suited to fanatical plans for a rebirth of Nazism. The Holy Roman Empire stood second in importance to Prussian glory, as evidenced by the coffin room in the Bernterode mine.

Among the people questioned was Göring, who was taken to the Ninth Army interrogation center near Augsburg when he gave himself up on May 10. The questioning of Göring was deliberately gentle at first, since he was being fed constantly decreasing quantities of his favorite drugs. After admitting that he felt himself "after all . . . a Renaissance type," Göring talked a great deal but said very little and did not tell where most of his art was hidden, even after a drunken evening with a German-speaking French officer. This occasion, arranged by James Rorimer, was disappointing to a degree but did lead to a hundred paintings and a bundle of tapestries in a garage opposite the Berchtesgaden railroad station. A day or so later, the M.F.A. and A. found a two-story cavelike cement structure in a remote wooded area near Berchtesgaden. Very damp and entirely unsuitable for the storage of any kind of art or art objects, this hideout contained so many cases dripping with moisture that forty U.S. Army Engineers were needed to carry them out.

When Walter Hofer offered his services to the Americans, he led Rorimer to twelve more railroad cars on a siding near the Berchtesgaden station. The cars had been well ransacked by Germans and by French and American soldiers, and all sorts of objects were found lying on the floors. One of the cars had contained Göring's art records, and of the original two hundred cases of books and papers, only eleven thousand books and pamphlets were eventually recovered; this number included a selection returned from France, where it had been sent by a French Intelligence officer. From these records and Hofer's memory, it was established that at one time or another the Göring collection of paintings was worth roughly two hundred million dollars. The figure, however, is meaningless, since most of the paintings could not, under any ordinary circumstances, have been purchased.

The small group of Monuments men spread themselves thinly over the vast territory that had to be covered, questioning, detecting, evaluating, and checking security. Among the most active was James Rorimer, who for about a month, beginning shortly before V-E Day, traveled with another M.F.A. and A. man, John Skilton, visiting depositories whose locations or approximate locations were included in Rose Valland's list. Among the first places this team visited was the monastery at Buxheim, a great sprawling building with numerous entrances and a set of German guards who swore that they knew nothing of what had gone on inside. In one room, entered by a side door, they found seventy-two packing cases stamped "D-W," the initials of the French collector David-Weill. The monastery corridors were full of Renaissance and eighteenth-century furniture, some of it still in cases. Twenty-two children were housed in one room. These small refugees were surrounded by the choicest furniture and presented an "appalling sight" to the American art experts. The floor of the chapel was carpeted "eight to ten inches deep" with rugs, tapestries, and bolts of fabric. While Rorimer moved rapidly through the building, noting its contents, his companion remained alone for a moment in a room piled with wooden cases marked "Fragile." One case had been opened, and Skilton absently took from it a gilded bronze medallion of Marie Antoinette. He turned the object over and saw on the back the owner's red catalog number and immediately above this in black letters: "E.R.R." The medallion and the cases were from the David-Weill collection; the date was May 3, 1945.

Buxheim Monastery had two rooms set aside as a studio, the principal restoration center for the E.R.R. A German couple had worked there on the finest art that Rosenberg's task force collected. Rorimer ordered them to stop work immediately, not because they were incapable as restorers but because it was much too easy to hide a valuable painting beneath a hastily created daub and equally simple to turn a mediocre work into something signed by a great master.

A few days after visiting Buxheim, Rorimer and Skilton arrived at Neuschwanstein Castle, an elaborately pinnacled and turreted structure built by Ludwig II, the Prussian king who died insane. The castle follows the contours of the mountain upon which it rests like a fairy-tale building. Steep stairs inside and out lead to countless rooms, and the agility of a mountain goat is demanded of its visitors. With the exception of the throne room and a few other state apartment-chambers, all the rooms held crates, hundreds of them, numbered, lettered, and marked "E.R.R." Thirty baggage cars from France had been emptied into the castle in April, 1941, and twenty-three others disgorged their contents a few months later, so that by October, 1941, Neuschwanstein was crammed with paintings, books, and art objects. As they toiled up and down the stairs, Rorimer and Skilton hoped that the Germans had kept records of the art in the crates and were astounded to discover in one room a steel door behind which were two large chests containing Rothschild jewels and a thousand pieces of the David-Weill silver collection.

Off one of the castle courtyards is a two-story building, the Kemenate. One of its rooms held the E.R.R. filing cabinets, containing the collectors' own catalogs, and some photographic equipment. In another room were two coal stoves that disclosed the remains of two hastily burned Nazi uniforms, several charred documents, and a set of rubber stamps, incompletely burned so that names of other repositories could be deciphered. To make certain that the files remained intact, Rorimer and Skilton nailed down a trapdoor in the floor, for it led to a secret escape ladder, and covered the trap with a heavy steel trunk. Rorimer then locked the doors and romantically sealed them with a cord and wax, marking the wax with an antique Rothschild seal bearing the words "*Semper Fidelis*." He gave the door key to the sergeant of the guard and retained the seal.

The two Americans then paid a visit to the clinic in nearby Füssen, where they found Bruno Lohse, who was ill, as well as Günther Schiedlausky and several other E.R.R. people. Lohse had left the Luftwaffe unit in Paris to go to a Berlin hospital for an operation for kidney stones. When the heavy bombardments caused the evacuation of the hospitals, Lohse was sent to Füssen. The operation had not taken place and was actually postponed until Lohse was in Dachau prison. On May 2, two days before Rorimer's arrival, Lohse and Schiedlausky had turned over Neuschwanstein to the 44th Infantry Division of the American Seventh Army. Both men still recall that the officer handling the details was a lieutenant colonel whose grandmother lived in Heidelberg. The two art historians reported to American headquarters in Füssen, where Lohse reported the presence in the castle of valuable art treasures for which the Americans were now responsible and added that he and Schiedlausky had also very important documents concerning French art in their possession. They were told to go back to Neuschwanstein to await the arrival of the M.F.A. and A.

The events of May 2 were the climax of an action that had begun early in April, when Robert Scholz, then at Kogl in Austria, received an order from Bormann, transmitted by Dr. von Hümmel, to destroy all the art objects placed in security in the shelters. Both Alt Aussee and Neuschwanstein were under Scholz's jurisdiction, and his first reaction was to call in Lohse, who immediately declared his willingness to do anything at all to prevent such destruction. Lohse also felt that it was imperative to save the E.R.R. files, then kept in Kogl, for the honor of Germany and for the world of art. Although Gauleiter Eigruber had forbidden all travel and any kind of evacuation in his district under pain of death, Lohse undertook to transfer the files from Kogl to Füssen himself. He took an army car and made three trips, bringing back all the files and the photographs, which he placed in Neuschwanstein and separated from the documents, which were too valuable to be left under S.S. guard and which he and Schiedlausky kept with them. Schiedlausky turned the papers over to Rorimer when he arrived, explaining how they had been saved.

These thirty-one documents, which Rorimer called "worth my work in Germany," included a report with summaries of all Rosenberg activities in France and elsewhere in Western Europe through July, 1944, and orders from Hitler, Göring, Rosenberg, and Wilhelm Keitel referring to the confiscated art. The papers were so important that their contents were immediately radioed to Washington and fifty pages of mimeographed translation were promptly sent to fifty high-ranking American and Allied officers. Nevertheless, although he had no authority to do so, Rorimer thought it "a good idea to arrest Lohse at once, as the head of the E.R.R.," a piece of misinformation he undoubtedly believed at the time. Ironically, Scholz and his Berlin staff had gone into hiding, and Scholz had suggested such a course to Lohse, who had refused, since he felt that he could "justify his position." He could, to the Americans, who tried to have him released on American-occupied territory, were unable to do so, and saw him taken off by the French. He then spent five years in Paris prisons despite the efforts of M.F.A. and A. men who had intensively questioned him and saw no reason for this protracted incarceration. Lohse finally came to trial in Paris in August, 1950, and was acquitted when the charges against him were proved false. Even more ironically, while he remained in prison, other Germans, actually guilty, enjoyed freedom before they were sentenced to long unserved terms in absentia.

Once the files were placed in Neuschwanstein, Lohse and Schiedlausky set their minds to saving the castle from destruction under Bormann's "scorched earth" order. One day late in April the S.S. Gruppenführer in charge of the sector, Jürgen Stroob, asked another S.S. man, Georges Erbrecht, to accompany him to the castle to make arrangements in case of enemy occupation. Erbrecht, an artist in civilian life, feared that Stroob intended to blow up the castle and went with him to try to save the art works. When they arrived, the two S.S. men found the two art historians. Stroob made a brief inspection and ordered the art works removed to Alpine huts, adding that any that could not be removed would be blown up with the building itself. Lohse and Schiedlausky made it clear that Neuschwanstein was a national monument and that destroying it would be not only completely irresponsible but also a disgrace to Germany. They added that damp mountain huts were unsuitable as storage places for art, that an extraordinary art file was stored in the castle, and that preservation of the file was required for the honor of the German nation.

Stroob, quite unmoved, showed a Himmler order: a formal command to blow up the castle. The art historians protested even more vigorously, to no avail. Finally Erbrecht had a flash of inspiration and suggested to Stroob that since as Gruppenführer he was so very busy carrying out other orders, it might be a good idea to let a subordinate handle this one. Stroob agreed to this, and when he left, Erbrecht promised the art historians that the order to blow up the castle would never be executed and the building and its contents would be preserved for the historians to hand over to the "enemy" (i.e., American) art staff. Erbrecht's court deposition on this incident noted that without the vigorous support of Lohse and Schiedlausky he would never have been able to override Stroob's stubborn determination to destroy the castle. Neuschwanstein was thus saved without the intervention of any "enemy" (French or American) action, for the two German art historians simply waited for the arrival of the first American troops to hand it over intact.

The discovery of only one painting or of small parcels was frequent. Paintings were found wrapped around pipes, covered with any kind of camouflage, or even used as doors to bomb-wrecked hovels.

One of the most famous finds of the last kind was that of a huge Titian that kept the lodging of a Berlin prostitute more or less decent. Exposed to extremes of heat and cold, wind, rain, and snow, the painting was almost unrecognizable when it was finally found. The four-century-old canvas and the pure pigments used on it were so weather-worthy, however, that the painting was restored to a very close approximation of its original splendor. Small cloth bags or valises filled with jewelry were found buried in piles of manure or under haystacks. Sometimes the finds were valuable; sometimes they were not. One Monuments man recalls giving up a portion of his leave to go and look at some "valuable old silver"; it turned out to be cheap silver-plate. Another man was called to a bank in Augsburg to inspect a few parcels found in a sewer. When he examined these, he found several sacks full of gold wedding rings, cigarette cases, and dental fillings. Mixed in were some filthy American bank notes and many tarnished coins. When the coins were cleaned, they turned out to be twenty-dollar gold pieces–thirty thousand dollars' worth. This loot was believed to have come from a concentration camp in the area. Larger collections were quite often discovered in abandoned railroad cars that might contain thousands of French lipsticks in wartime gunmetal cases or cases of champagne. One siding near Munich yielded twenty carloads of art objects. Not all of this art, of course, was from France, for the Third Reich stole with as much zeal from every occupied country, from Russia, and from its one-time ally, Italy. It had also been clear as early as 1942 that Allied bombing raids would spare no part of industrialized Germany, so the country's own treasures had been carefully hidden or crated and put on trains in desperate last-minute attempts to reach safety.

Official Nazi propaganda art also had to be hidden, and one of the largest caches was discovered in a particularly strange setting in Bavaria. The trail led to a woodcutter's hut in the forest, and the American officer who followed it had an old man and a young boy with a knapsack with him as guides. When they arrived at the hut, the officer was astonished to find it surrounded with a "set of S.S. uniforms with corpses inside them." The sight was gruesome enough, but it was explained as protection against curious visitors. The small group entered the hut and found another set of uniformed corpses, this time of the Luftwaffe. The two groups, one inside and one outside, had killed each other off, each thinking the other American. Nothing could be seen of the art. The boy, however, knew where it was and led the way to a space between the ceiling and the floor of a kind of attic. He took from his knapsack a small hammer, tapped at a few boards, found the right one, and pulled. Several thousand pieces of art intended for the decoration of Nazi military barracks and clubs were neatly packed away. Some of them had been pierced by bullets, and field mice had nibbled the edges of many others.

Field trips made as rapidly as possible immediately after the end of the war prevented further loss by looting or damage in unsuitable storage places. On May 18 a visit to the Laufen mine in Bad Ischl disclosed a theft by German officers just before V-E Day. Two truckloads of art from Viennese collections had been spirited away to "prevent their being lost to the Russians." The trail led from the mine to a Tyrolean mountain inn and from there to the cellar of a house next door. The cellar had two rooms, both of them damp and one actually water-soaked. In the rooms were thirty-two uncrated paintings (including eight by Brueghel, five by Rembrandt, seven by Velázquez, and eight by Titian), forty-nine sacks of tapestries, and nine wooden packing cases. The paintings had become spotted with mold during their two-week stay in the cellar and needed immediate attention.

Another little trip led to the hideaway of Gustav Rochlitz and his wife, a farmhouse not far from Hohenschwangau Castle. The sullen, thickset, fiftyish Rochlitz expected the Americans to believe he was the unwilling victim of Göring's power, had had no knowledge of the origins of the paintings he accepted in exchanges, and was, in fact, innocence personified. Rochlitz had with him twenty-two French contemporary paintings, all masterworks, removed from their stretchers and rolled around an ordinary cardboard mailing tube. He was quite concerned over the bulk of his stock, stored near Baden-Baden in the French zone, and asked the Americans whether they thought he would get it back. The Monuments men made an ambiguous statement about being sure justice would be done, placed the couple under house arrest for further questioning, and took the French art.

Such a delivery of art to the Munich collecting point was a simple one. Emptying the chambers of the mine at Alt Aussee took weeks. Sieber acted as general supervisor and assistant, but two Monuments men did the most difficult part of the work, going down into the chambers to select the works of art in order of importance. The mine was cold, 40 degrees, and very damp—so damp that after a brief time inside, a salt crust formed on garments like frosting on a cake. The

Austrian miners who helped wore thick woolen jackets over heavy sweaters, and the GI guards on duty huddled in sheepskin coats specially tailored for German use on the Russian front. The same type of garment came in handy for packing unframed, uncrated paintings, also liable to wear the white encrustation from the wet, salty air. The Monuments men went along on the "dogs" to their destination, the track lit by sketchy electrical installations–bulbs strung on wires. Once off the main tunnel, if a man turned a corner suddenly, he found himself in cavernous blackness. M.F.A. and A. began in the large Springerwerke chamber, which contained the most fantastic collection of paintings.[1] The first ones selected were those marked "E.R.R.," as these, reasonably enough, were sure to be superior works. Using flashlights, the men selected a couple of hundred paintings in a few hours, handed their selections over to the American soldiers and Austrian miners providing the labor, and saw the art carefully placed on the "dogs" for the brief rail trip to the minehead. There, when they examined the paintings again, almost invariably what had seemed good in the bowels of the earth became superlative in the daylight.

After the fifty-foot-long, thirty-foot-wide Springerwerke, the men turned to the Kammergraffen, an even more difficult chamber to work in, and so gradually worked their way through the mine, finding strange treasure in strange hideaways. The Kapelle–with its salt-crystal statue of the slain Austrian chancellor, Engelbert Dollfuss, erected as a tribute by the miners–held a cardboard box on an upper shelf. In the box was a set of eighteenth-century libidinous watercolors by the French master Boucher. The straitlaced Führer, who disapproved of social dancing, was extremely fond of salacious art of all kinds, and his personal library contained a great many eighteenth-century pornographic books. The box was intended for Linz. Behind some large Renaissance bronzes in the Kammergraffen the men found two unimportant-looking cartons. Inside these were forty small white cardboard boxes containing Rothschild jewels, so valuable that the M.F.A. and A. took them to Munich in a jeep rather than entrust them to the ordinary truck convoy that shuttled between Munich and the mine each day.

The Americans and their helpers worked twelve hours a day, alter-

[1] The tunnel ceilings were too low to accommodate very large paintings. M.F.A. found a cache about one mile from the mine in the salt-processing plant in Bad Aussee. The paintings were literally buried in piles of salt.

nately examining, sorting, and packing. Each convoy consisted of six trucks, which left the mine with a jeep escort that was relieved at Bad Aussee by two armored cars, one at the front and one at the rear of the convoy. The trip, over twisting, narrow mountain roads, was doubly dangerous because of small bands of stubbornly resistant S.S. men interested principally in destructive action and unwilling to surrender. Both armored cars carried two-way radios to call for help in the event of an ambush, and the trucks were not completely filled so that if one was disabled, its contents could be quickly repacked into the other trucks and the convoy could speed away.

Packing fine art is a highly specialized trade, requiring skilled packers, padded trucks, specially built crates, and all kinds of special packing materials; none of these were available. Everything had to be improvised in a hurry. To replace the usual waterproof papers for lining art cases, the M.F.A. and A. found a clothlike green paper that the Germans had developed for protection against gas attacks. With this they lined the trucks, leaving enough paper hanging over the sides to flap over the tops of the cargoes. A strip of felt was laid around the edge of the truck floor, and then two rows of "sausages" were laid along the floor from front to back. Ordinarily "sausages" are tubes of lightweight brown paper stuffed with excelsior. These were made of a cheap machine-made cotton-lace found in large quantities inside the mine, cut into yard lengths, and wrapped around anything soft that was handy. The miners worked at making these constantly, sitting at long benches as if at some kind of country sewing bee.

After the pictures for any given truckloads had been selected, sorted for size, and wrapped in pads made of Nazi overcoats and blankets, they were stacked from the sideboards of the trucks to the center. The top flap of paper was pulled down and tied firmly in place. A few art objects were always carefully placed in nooks and crannies to hold everything steady, for a badly balanced or slipping load would have been disastrous on hairpin turns. On clear days the men packed two trucks at a time; when it rained, they could pack only one truck under the one sheltered doorway.

After the paintings had all left, it was the turn of the Ghent altarpiece and of the Michelangelo Madonna, which had arrived at the mine in September, 1944, casually lying on a mattress on the bottom of a Red Cross truck. It had been unceremoniously placed there by a group of German officers who removed the statue and several valuable paintings from their hiding place in the crypt of a church in Bruges by simply holding the dean of the church at gunpoint. The truck with its priceless cargo had passed along a series of roads constantly shelled by Allied bombers. When it left the mine, the Madonna was heavily wrapped, handled gingerly by twelve miners, and placed on a truck that had been overhauled to make sure of its satisfactory condition. The huge heavy bundle was wedged between heavy cases that were further swathed in blankets to prevent their bumping against the statues. Between the statue and the tailgate was a stone sarcophagus in a crate firmly fixed to the floor.

A second truck received the ten cases of the Ghent altarpiece, standing upright and fastened securely in place, with other cases wedged between them so that no slippage was possible. When the trucks left, the men at the mine relaxed somewhat but did not really breathe freely until they knew that the trucks had reached Munich safely. "The Mystic Lamb" had already caused enough international uproar.

After the paintings and the most precious sculpture, the mine still had to be emptied of every piece of furniture, every object, and every book that had been stored in it. This meant more weeks of backbreaking labor, more records made of each article or crate placed on the trucks, and more trips down precipitous roads. The Alt Aussee's convoys had no accidents worth noting, and the other mines were emptied and their contents transported with equal efficiency.

The Munich Bau was the principal collecting point for painting and sculpture from all the occupied countries. An unbombed factory in Offenbach received E.R.R. confiscations of Jewish libraries from synagogues and private documentary collections. A German government building in Marburg sheltered German-owned art from the Rhineland, and the Landesmuseum in Wiesbaden received collections belonging to Berlin museums. Seventy-five rooms in the museum were piled with cases of paintings, drawings, and prints bearing the greatest names in the history of art from Cimabue to the French Impressionists. In the Treasure Room, behind heavily guarded locked doors and stoutly barred windows, were the gold, silver, and jeweled possessions collected for centuries by the nobility of church and state, an unbelievably splendid exhibition of the wealth owned by the German state.

CHAPTER 15

RESTORATION AND RESTITUTION

MONUMENTS, FINE ARTS and Archives was also responsible for the Military Government's specific cultural objectives in the reeducation of the German nation. The isolation imposed by National Socialism's bellicose program of race hatred had to be replaced with the integration of German people into the "world community of nations." The long cultural past of the Germans and the regional folk traditions had to be resuscitated. The Germans were urged to participate in the work of cultural reconstruction, and their initiatives were encouraged so that international cultural relations might be reestablished.

Hence, the M.F.A. and A. helped German authorities to protect and preserve cultural institutions—religious, charitable, educational, scientific, and artistic—aided in the reorganizing of museums, libraries, and schools; and worked to salvage historical monuments, archives, and collections of art. One notable exception to this rule, which applied to all public and private property, was the perpetuation of institutions and monuments dedicated to the principles of National Socialism or to the glorification of German militaristic traditions. Such institutions were neither protected, preserved, nor respected.

The reestablishment of international cultural relations, which were needed for the reorientation of the German people, was to be accomplished by travel into and out of Germany of persons useful for this program (subject, naturally, to availability of facilities) and by the free flow of cultural materials to and from Germany. Exchanges of art historians, museum directors, librarians, archivists, and contemporary artists in the fields of painting, graphics, sculpture, and decorative arts were arranged between Germany and the United States or other countries.

M.F.A. and A. also advised and aided in the reconstruction of German museums, libraries, and archives while it encouraged democratic principles in these institutions and their use as media for popular education. For this they set up training courses for administrative personnel. Another important task was assistance in the rebuilding of historic monuments not completely destroyed during the war. Monuments men scurried about trying to find cement, logs to shore up shaking walls, cables to throw around bulging buildings, roofing materials, and window glass. Some of the men particularly interested in the historic buildings destroyed in what had been occupied Europe engaged themselves personally after their discharge from the army in the search for American funds to help in reconstruction. They also worked in close liaison with men holding similar positions in the British and French zones, with UNESCO, and with other nations on all matters pertaining to monuments, fine arts, archives, and libraries.

It was because of the overall cultural objectives of the American Military Government that the collection of Nazi official art was permanently removed from Germany and placed in cold storage in the United States. M.F.A. and A. also organized exhibitions of art by German contemporary artists, some of whom had died in concentration camps and whose survivors, children or widows, were deeply grateful to the American officers who collected the artists' works and arranged the showings. The Landesmuseum in Wiesbaden was the setting for two M.F.A. and A.–sponsored art exhibitions: one of fifteenth-century paintings by Flemish, French, Italian, and German artists and one of engravings. Both shows printed catalogs in both English and German, an indication that occupying troops and civilians could enjoy the same international art. The French Government sent a traveling collection of contemporary art of the type that Hitler had labeled "degenerate," and it was shown with the respect due such artists as Van Gogh and Chirico.

The Landesmuseum was also the source for a collection of 202 paintings (owned by German museums) that crossed the ocean to the National Gallery in December, 1945. Monuments men selected the works, carefully packed them, and sent them on what they called the Westward-Ho Plan, of which they almost unanimously disapproved. The idea was contrary to Monuments' basic belief that conquering nations should leave conquered art where it belonged. Twenty-four of the thirty-two Monuments men signed a letter, the "Wiesbaden Manifesto," protesting this action and the use of such a term as "protective custody," which seemed to them a phrase borrowed from the Nazis, who had "protected" everything they stole. The powers and the reasons behind this transfer of eighty million dollars' worth of art were somewhat obscure, although eventually the office of the Secretary of State, James F. Byrnes, issued a statement to the effect that "General [Lucius] Clay [the administrator of American-occupied Germany] . . . did not have adequate facilities and personnel to safeguard German art treasures and . . . could not take the responsibilities for their proper care." The outcry against this transport was clear. *The New York Times* and two important, widely read art journals reprinted the "Wiesbaden Manifesto" in its entirety. Museum officials, art historians, and the American press disapproved vociferously.

Early in 1948 General Clay asked for the return of the paintings to Germany as an indication of good faith. In March the National Gallery showed the entire collection, and nearly a million people came to see it. During this brief exhibition other public opinion demanded the showing of the paintings elsewhere so that more Americans might view them. Among those suggesting this were several art critics and museum heads, and, more officially, Senator J. William Fulbright, who encouraged the showing of the works in twelve important museums.[1] Cataloged as "The Berlin Masterpieces," 150 of the paintings went on tour accompanied by United States Army guards and a representative group of German museum curators. Fifty-two of the paintings, too fragile to travel, went back to Germany immediately after the Washington showing. This action and the agreement that entry fees were to be used to aid children in the American zone in Germany were an integral part of the arrangements. Paints, canvases, and other materials purchased with part of the proceeds of the sale of

[1] In New York, Philadelphia, Chicago, Detroit, Cleveland, Minneapolis, San Francisco, Los Angeles, St. Louis, Pittsburgh, Toledo, and Boston.

catalogs were to be given to artists in Germany. When the tour ended,[2] the paintings returned to Germany, where their arrival received wide publicity.

The principal efforts of the M.F.A. and A. in addition to their interrogations and field trips in preparation for the Nuremberg trials, their compilation of a stack of German documents, and their efforts to save as many partly destroyed historic buildings as possible, while also assisting in the reeducation of the German people, were devoted to the speediest possible return of confiscated art belonging to the once-occupied nations and of German art stored to prevent destruction in the battles fought on German territory. The hopefully optimistic first estimate of a six-month period for the return of art, a serious burden to the Military Government because of its value, had to be extended and has, in fact, never been officially concluded. In September, 1948, a report on the number of art works returned to non-German countries indicated 480,000 works worth an estimated five hundred million dollars. This number does not include 1,500,000 books, worth fifty million dollars. Between May, 1945, and September, 1948, the M.F.A. and A. received and processed 1,900 claims for works of art and 1,500,000 claims for books. To this number must be added 1,300 dropped claims for works of art and 900,000 dropped claims for books. In addition, 3,200,000 works of art were returned to German owners. The value of these works was estimated as a billion and a half dollars. Books returned to German owners were worth thirty million dollars; there were 1,100,000 of them. The fifteen hundred repositories had held 10,724,000 objects worth five billion dollars.

The figures are staggering, as was the task of a relatively tiny group of men through whose hands the books and works of art passed. Fortunately, objects in distinctly marked cases and recorded in found documents could be directly returned to the countries of origin without going through the collecting points. Thus in October, 1945, the contents of Neuschwanstein Castle, after careful inventory, were carried down the endless staircases by a group of twenty young Germans, former naval cadets. Under the supervision of two M.F.A. and A. officers the cases were loaded on trucks driven by Frenchmen,

[2] Other museums besides the original twelve were scheduled to receive the exhibit, but the tour was cut short, according to some authorities, because of more public disapproval.

and the long convoy moved to a railroad station whence, on October 24, nineteen freight cars filled with treasure moved on to Paris.[3]

Inside the collecting points painting racks and examining tables were set up, and the M.F.A. and A. men with their assistants—German curators, librarians, art experts, and rare-book dealers—examined each painting, sculpture, art object, and book that came in. Only absolutely essential first-aid repairs were done by German restorers under the direct supervision of American experts. Mold had to be removed immediately, and flaking or blistered paint held down with tissue paper. Armor had to be examined for signs of rust; sculpture for cracks and broken fingers, toes, or other appendages; porcelain and glass for cracks; gold and silver objects for dents or small missing parts; tapestries for holes or hanging threads. The next step was identification, quite readily accomplished in the case of important works of art, always cataloged and readily recognized by experts. Less-important works had to be matched to the claims on hand. The last operation was packing, done by German packers, again under expert American supervision.

Books were most often identifiable by bookplates or special family or institutional bindings. Rare books were usually found cataloged, marked with dates of purchase and provenance, or could be so identified by their owners if no marks were found on them. Other methods of identification invented by owners prior to confiscation were also acceptable, and some of them were most ingenious. A group of German nuns, for example, marked every book in their convent library with a pinprick through a certain letter of the alphabet the first time that letter appeared on a specific page. The return of the millions of books was so well handled that when the job was finished, only about seven hundred books remained—worthless items that nobody bothered to claim.

Among the bulkiest and heaviest items to be returned were church bells, for only Paris had saved all its bells. The huge bronze cast-metal

[3] In May, 1946, the French National Museums organized an exhibition entitled "Masterpieces from French Collections Found in Germany by the Commission for Recovery" and hung the works in the Orangerie. Included were fourteen paintings especially chosen by Hitler for himself, works of art and masterpieces by goldsmiths and silversmiths chosen for Linz, and paintings from Göring's personal collection. For six months thousands of French men, women, and children filed past one of the most extraordinary exhibitions ever seen in a museum world-famous for the splendor of its collections.

objects belonged to cities and towns all over Europe, and each bell had to be returned to its original home. This was not simply a matter of returning any suitably sized bell to a given steeple, for people are very attached to the sounds of particular bells they have heard all their lives. Bells are identifiable by cast and foundry marks, by decorations, and if necessary by metallurgical tests for composition. They were difficult to handle because of weight, and once, some of the bulky bells from one barge-load fell into a river. They were finally fished out, but some of them cracked in the accident.

The amount of stolen property returned to each country depended on pure chance. About 80 percent of what was taken from France, officially and unofficially, was recovered. Individualized looting by German officers and soldiers, who did not care if their victims were Jews, Catholics, or Protestants, amounted finally to a startling figure. In December, 1947, the French Government published an official account of what had been stolen between 1939 and 1945. The second volume of this list was devoted to haphazard stealing and added up to 8,470 paintings, 423 tapestries, 634 marble sculptures, and 1,096 bronzes. Works of art that left France inside German suitcases and knapsacks arrived in German homes that were later totally destroyed by Allied bombing raids. Other works were prudently buried in hiding places from which they have not yet been disinterred. Others surely left the country with Nazi officials who scattered all over the world under assumed identities.

A considerable part of Göring's collection was either damaged, destroyed, or dispersed to some hiding places still not uncovered—if, indeed, they exist. Göring and Hitler exchanges also sent French-owned paintings all over the world into art dealers' reserves and into private collections ordinarily unexposed to public view and to the type of recognition by knowing amateurs that led to the tracing of works from the Paul Rosenberg collection from Fischer of Lucerne to the private collection of Burle d'Orlikon in Zurich. In 1950 the Detroit Museum of Art innocently purchased a work from an equally innocent New York dealer only to discover that the painting had been stolen and should never have been put up for sale. This matter was quietly settled, for both museum and dealer had acted in good faith.[4]

[4] To prevent just such incidents, Jacques Seligmann, of the French art firm, who was in New York during the war, proposed to Francis Henry Taylor, of the Metropolitan Museum, a kind of moratorium on the sale of art. He suggested that all art "identifiable as looted property or as having been sold by force, or suspected of such actions because no satisfactory provenance could be furnished, be neutralized for a

Early in 1969 a small news item announced the finding of three paintings stolen during the war—two of them in German museums and one in the private collection of Baron von Thyssen in Switzerland. Since the Thyssen art is open for viewing by the public, nobody doubts that his acquisition, like those of the German museums, was quite accidental. Unfortunately, many private collectors keep their art completely for themselves, and some show a curious passion for works that they can never show because of their provenance. Only time, mortality, and the need for money disclose such acquisitions. It is therefore not surprising that paintings from French collections have been found in other European countries or that Italian-owned works turned up quite suddenly in California, offered for sale by owners with no real idea of the value of what they wished to sell.

The search for stolen art treasures has never stopped, and strange stories often lead to curious places. In August, 1969, the London *Sunday Times* published an article entitled "Art Trail Leads to Brewery"[5] about the "Amber Room," so named for its carved amber paneling, removed intact by the Nazis in 1941 from the summer palace of the former czars near Leningrad. The room, worth fifty million dollars and "packed in long, narrow cases," may be, according to this article, in the air-raid bunker near the old church in Ponarth on the Baltic Sea, in an old castle near Königsberg, or in the unused vaults of a brewery. Presumably, this investigation continues, for the room has not been found. In the context of any discussion of lost stolen art, such a story indicates that the last word on any lost masterworks cannot and may never be written. The story also explains why a skeleton M.F.A. and A. staff is still attached to the American Embassy in Bonn and why a West German citizen sent a written question to the Bundestag on February 12, 1969, on the subject of the use made of German-owned art that once belonged to the Third Reich. In reply to this question, the German Minister of the Treasury prepared a four-page public report.

---

twenty-five-year period. A list of such works would have been circulated to museums and dealers." Taylor thought the idea a good one. Seligmann tried to interest two Rothschilds living modestly in New York during the war years. Both the Rothschilds approved, but neither one wished to draw public attention to himself or to the entire Rothschild family. The Baron Robert, in addition, was much less interested in the fate of his art collections than he was worried over the possible fate of his two sons, French prisoners of the Germans. Seligmann's idea, excellent though it was, unfortunately never went beyond the talking stage.

[5] Reprinted in the Washington *Post*, August 28, 1969.

In January, 1963, the Treuhandverwaltung von Kulturgut (or roughly, the Trustees of Cultural Goods) of Munich gathered up about 20,000 pieces of art left over from the restitution action of the American collecting points in 1945. The list includes 2,708 paintings and frescoes, 1,398 graphic works, 161 statues, 321 pieces of folk art, 3 paintings on glass, 1 mosaic, 1 sketchbook, 2 manuscripts, 51 Gobelins tapestries, 49 rugs, 206 pieces of furniture, 73 reproductions (printed copies of works of art such as paintings and drawings), 100 photographic prints, 1 violin, 6,000 coins, 9,000 books, and 8 unclassifiable art objects. Most of these had been intended either for the projected museum in Linz or for Göring's more imaginary museum at Karinhall. About 700 paintings had been taken from the House of German Art in Munich. Many less-valuable paintings and graphics had been purchased for minor Nazi installations. An examination of these works by experts divided them into three categories. The first included about 2,200 pieces, among them 857 paintings, suitable for museums; the second included about 1,100 pieces suitable for decorative use in government buildings at home and abroad; the third category was of no interest to the government at all.

After a meeting and inspection tour by German museum directors late in 1965, 1,985 works of art (including 660 paintings) were divided up between 111 German museums. At current market prices this art is worth about six million dollars. Other art in this prime category needed considerable, expensive restoration. Its value has been estimated at about ten million dollars. German government offices received 838 art objects, landscapes, portraits, and still lifes, some graphics, several rugs, and one Gobelins tapestry, worth slightly less than a million dollars in all. Works in the third category were sold at auction. The sale, not much of a success, brought two hundred thousand dollars. Unsold works joined the official Nazi art purchased for the House of German Art in Munich between 1939 and 1944 in storage. Before any of this can be sold, a careful evaluation of its artistic value must be made, and this has not been undertaken.

The gift to 111 German museums brings the story of Hitler's attack on art collections to a rather lopsided conclusion. The current market value of the works destroyed in Germany before 1939 can be conservatively estimated as at least sixty million dollars. To this must be added two hundred million dollars' worth of art owned by other European countries and not returned because it has not been found. The cost in lost cultural heritage is inestimable.

The Hitlerian attack on art, inside and outside of Germany, was only one facet of totalitarianism. Hitler did not invent the looting of art, nor Göring the Medici syndrome, and the control of art or the acquisition of it to glorify a political system are specific aspects of dictatorship. Hitler's reign added a word to the languages of the world: Nazism. Its connotations–hypocrisy, hero worship, race hatred, religious persecution, the suppression of criticism and of freedom of expression, brutality, violence, destruction, terrorism, nationalism, militarism, and the desire for world domination–were not new ideas in 1933 and did not die with the Führer in 1945. Symptomatic of an illness endemic to mankind and recorded constantly from the earliest written histories to today's newspapers, these savage compulsions corrupt and destroy. With massive illogic, men struggle to preserve the past and to revere its best manifestations even while they imitate its worst evils, to which succeeding generations add the refinements of advancing knowledge to imperil or preclude the future.

BIBLIOGRAPHY

UNPUBLISHED DOCUMENTS

National Archives, Washington, D.C.

AMG-107. *Art Looting Investigation: Bunjes.*

SHAEF-G-2. Consolidated Interrogation Report #1: *Rosenberg Activities in France.*

Consolidated Interrogation Report #2: *Index to Rosenberg Activities.*

Consolidated Interrogation Report #3: *The Göring Collection.*

Consolidated Interrogation Report #4: *Linz.*

SHAEF-G-5. Document 2220: *The Looting of Art in Occupied France* (Record Group #331).

Washington National Records Center, Suitland, Maryland

OMGUS, MFA & A. Record Group #260: *Göring Exchanges; The Ahnenerbe; Ribbentrop Collection; Restitution Procedures; Ardelia Ripley Hall Collection; French Repositories.*

Deutscher Bundestag, Bonn, Germany

Drucksache V/4537. *Verwendung von Kunstgegenständen aus ehemaligem Reichsbesitz.*

Miscellaneous documents: American, French, German, Austrian, and Swiss court records, affidavits, letters, diaries, bills, military orders, memorandums, etc.

PUBLISHED DOCUMENTS

Trial of the Major War Criminals before the International Tribunal, Nuremberg. Nuremberg, Germany, 1949.

BOOKS

English

Collins, Larry, and Lapierre, Dominique. *Is Paris Burning?* New York: Simon and Schuster, Inc., 1965.

Flanner, Janet. *Paris Journal, 1944–1965*. New York: Atheneum Publishers, 1965.

Gilot, Françoise, and Lake, Carlton. *Life with Picasso*. New York: McGraw-Hill, Inc., 1964.

Gimpel, René. *Diary of an Art Dealer*. Translated by John Rosenberg. New York: Farrar, Straus & Giroux, Inc., 1966.

Hitler, Adolf. *Mein Kampf*. Translated by Ralph Manheim. Boston: Houghton Mifflin Company, 1943.

Howe, Thomas Carr, Jr. *Salt Mines and Castles*. New York: The Bobbs-Merrill Company, Inc., 1946.

Novick, Peter. *The Resistance versus Vichy*. New York: Columbia University Press, 1968.

Penrose, Roland. *Picasso, His Life and Work*. New York: Schocken Books, 1962.

Rorimer, James J., and Rabin, Gilbert. *Survival*. New York: Abelard Press, 1950.

Roxan, David, and Wanstall, Ken. *The Jackdaw of Linz*. London: Cassell and Company, 1964.

Seligmann, Germain. *Merchants of Art*. New York: Appleton-Century-Crofts, 1961.

Shirer, William L. *The Rise and Fall of the Third Reich*. New York: Simon and Schuster, Inc., 1959.

Speer, Albert. *Inside the Third Reich: Memoirs*. Translated by Richard and Clara Winston. New York: The Macmillan Company, 1970.

Wright, Gordon. *The Ordeal of Total War*. New York: Harper Torchbooks, 1968.

French

Amouroux, Henri. *La Vie des Français sous l'occupation*. Paris: Librairie Arthème Fayard, 1965.

Bizardel, Yvon. *Sous l'Occupation, souvenirs d'un conservateur de musée*. Paris: Calmann-Levy, 1964.

Cassou, Jean. *Le Pillage par les Allemands des oeuvres d'art et des bibliothèques*. Paris: Editions du Centre, 1947.

Cotta, Michel. *La Collaboration*, 1940–44. Paris: Armand Colin, 1964.

Fouchet, Max-Pol. *Un Jour je m'en souviens*. Paris: Mercure de France, 1968.

Mazauric, Lucie. *Ma Vie de châteaux*. Paris: Perrin, 1967.

Michel, Henri. *Vichy, année 40*. Paris: Laffont, 1966.

Morize, André. *France, été 1940*. New York: Editions de la Maison Française, 1941.

Papazoff, Georges. *Derain, mon copain*. Paris: Valmont, 1960.

Saint-Paulien. *Histoire de la collaboration*. Paris: Esprit Nouveau, 1964.

Skilton, John D., Jr. *Défense de l'art européen.* Translated by Jacqueline de Gromard. Paris: Les Editions Internationales, 1948.

Valland, Rose. *Le Front de l'art.* Paris: Plon, 1961.

German

Brenner, Hildegard. *Die Kunstpolitik des Nationalsozialismus.* Reinbek bei Hamburg: Rohwohlt Taschenbuch Verlag, 1963.

Roh, Dr. Franz. *"Entartete" Kunst: Kunst Barbarei im Dritten Reich.* Hanover: Facketrager-Verlag, Schmidt-Kuster, 1962.

PERIODICALS

Flanner, Janet. "Annals of Crime," *The New Yorker*, February 22, March 1, and March 8, 1947.

Giraud, R. C. "Le Rôle des marchands de tableaux dans la première moitié du XXième siècle," *Jardin des Arts*, April, 1960.

O'Connell, James P. "The Devil's Architect," *The New York Times Magazine*, October 26, 1969.

Scholz, Robert, and Borchers, Walter. "Bildersturm in Frankreich," *Das Schönste*, No. 12, December, 1962.

Walker, John. "Europe's Looted Art," *National Geographic*, January, 1946.

Anonymous. *L'Art français.* Clandestine newspaper. 1941–1944.

INDEX

Despiau, Charles, 98, 99